D0699254

OBJECTS
OF
DESIRE

OBJECTS
OF
DESIRE

The Lives of
Antiques and Those
Who Pursue Them

Thatcher Freund

PANTHEON BOOKS

NEW YORK

Library of Congress Cataloging-in-Publication Data

Freund. Thatcher, 1955–
Objects of desire / Thatcher Freund.
p. cm.
ISBN 0-679-42157-2
1. Furniture—United States—History—18th century.   2. Furniture—
Collectors and collecting—United States.   I. Title.
NK2406.F74   1994
749.214'09'033075—dc20   93-24202
CIP

Book design by Jo Anne Metsch
Manufactured in the United States of America
First Edition
9   8   7   6   5   4   3   2   1

For Laura

OBJECTS
OF
DESIRE

One

ON OPENING NIGHT OF THE NEW YORK WINTER ANTIQUES SHOW,
Mario Buatta greeted his guests at the entrance to the 7th
Regiment Armory on Park Avenue. To flourish, pretty people and pretty things need to be seen. Buatta, a rotund
society decorator, had come to understand this truth through
his long tenure as chairman of the most prestigious antiques
show in the country. On this Friday evening in January
1991, as guests such as Ralph Lauren and Mary Tyler Moore
walked through the door, Buatta shook their hands and
whispered a brief personal greeting to each one. Most of his
guests came from New York society. They had such names
as Carroll Petrie and Robert Metzger, wore sequined shifts
or dark suits, and at the door paused for the photographers.
Some had been in the Bahamas the day before and were
leaving for Paris in the morning. The cavernous armory
swallowed them. In every corner, arrangements of flowers
stood in Chinese vases. Mahogany chests, gilded eagles, and
polished silver sauce boats glimmered from a succession of

exquisite booths. Seventy dealers had set their wares out in the room. These objects were among the most beautiful to be had anywhere in the world, and they made the people who stood beside them seem more beautiful still. In return, the people lent the antiques a charming sophistication. They came together in the armory, the pretty people and the pretty things, each giving something to the other and each gaining something in return.

The people did not come to look at the antiques. They came to look at one another. They came because Brooke Astor would probably be there or because they liked to see their pictures in the newspaper. Beautiful surroundings, though nice, were not necessary to their happiness. Carroll Petrie pointed this out at the show one year when she recognized her friends from the Concorde Lounge at Kennedy International. "This," she said as she glanced around the armory, "is as social as the airport."

A charity called the East Side Settlement House runs the Winter Antiques Show for a week each January. The best dealers exhibit there and wealthy collectors—people who do care about antiques—plan their winter vacations around it. In the days that follow the opening, they come from places such as Cleveland, St. Louis, and Atlanta. Some buy antiques from France or England, but most want only things made in America. These Americana collectors arrive in such numbers that the auction houses of Sotheby's and Christie's schedule their largest sales of American furniture for this week. Dealers in American furniture have come to call the last week in January "Americana Week."

On this opening night, few of the guests knew much about Americana Week. When they stopped to notice an antique, it was usually a piece of the rich English mahogany furniture that was so fashionable in 1991. The most expensive item on the floor that evening, a George II library desk, belonged to an English dealer named Carlton Hobbs and was offered for $2.8 million. Despite this price, not many visitors bothered even to look at it. They preferred to nibble on the fried wontons filled with shrimps or turkey, the little ham sandwiches, the salmon mousse. They strolled about the room in search of friends and seemed pleased when strangers recognized them. Even though a large number of guests moved in and out, the armory felt peculiarly still that evening. Conversations disappeared into the lovely filigreed arches high overhead. Somewhere far away a banjo played "Don't Get Around Much Anymore."

In one corner of the room, two dealers named Fred and Kathryn Giampietro stood beside their small booth. They smiled politely as wealthy New Yorkers swirled through the aisles. A booth at the Winter Antiques Show can sometimes mean sales that will account for half of a dealer's yearly profits, and ambitious men and women spend years trying to secure an invitation. This was the Giampietros' first year at the show. Fred had spent considerable energy trying to get noticed by the show's exhibition committee, but now that he found himself here, he did not appear entirely comfortable in these surroundings.

For years, Kathy Giampietro had kept the books, and told Fred what she liked, and done a great job of selling things when her husband was away. Kathy likes antiques, but she is not obsessed with them the way Fred is, so the business of buying and selling falls to him most often. Fred is a large, friendly man who stands six feet tall and weighs more than two hundred pounds. He is going bald at the front of his head and he is going gray at the back, but he does not seem the least concerned with this evidence of age.

In its own way, his booth was a work of art. Against the white walls, Giampietro had placed such objects as a Goddess of Liberty weathervane, circa 1865, which he had priced at $95,000. A large wooden Indian in a painted headdress stood in one corner. A Pennsylvania chest, a Navajo blanket, and a portrait by an itinerant artist named George Hartwell also awaited prospective new owners. Track lights shone on each thing. Arrangements of stargazer lilies, snapdragons, spider chrysanthemums, and eucalyptus bloomed from a pair of cast-iron urns. Giampietro's mother ran a florist shop, which was lucky for him since it saved a considerable expense. Although Giampietro had earned a reputation as one of the leading folk art dealers in the country, he was by no means one of the wealthier dealers on the floor. Giampietro reckoned the total value of the items in his booth at $1.2 million, a sum that probably placed it in the show's bottom third.

At the center of his exhibit, in a position to attract the most attention, Giampietro had placed a piece of furniture known in the trade as a blanket chest-and-drawers. A casual observer could not have told it from an ordinary chest of drawers. It was painted blue and it looked nice against the stark white walls. This chest had been made for a simple Connecticut farmer in about 1750, and had endured more abuse over the ensuing two and a half centuries than most of the objects in the room. Compared with the heavy and fashionable English furniture, it looked rather humble. Some of the antiques had sat in palatial country homes, where their owners rarely so much as touched them, but generations of people had used the blue blanket chest every day of their lives. They had set cups on its top and banged brooms against its sides. Unlike many of the things for sale around it, the chest had never had a finer moment than this.

While connoisseurs of folk art prized such things as Giampietro's weathervanes and his country furniture, many people disdained them. To Carlton Hobbs—the man with the $2.8 million library desk—an object like the blue blanket chest more properly belonged in someone's garage. But Fred Giampietro cherished the blue chest more than anything else in his possession. He had priced it accordingly. On that night, anyone who liked this object could have it for $245,000.

The chest stood nearly four and a half feet tall and was painted in the same coat of paint—a thin, robin's egg blue—that a craftsman had applied more than two centuries earlier. One couldn't tell that the first three of its five drawers were false, or that its top opened on leather hinges for the storage of blankets. The chest sat on a frame with a scalloped base and short, beautifully curved Queen Anne legs. No hardware cluttered it. A craftsman had constructed the chest in the spare aesthetic of the Queen Anne period, without knobs or hand-pulls on its drawers. It was possible to open the two bottom drawers only by digging one's fingers under the lip on each side. Over the past couple of centuries, many fingernails had chewed at the edges of the working drawers and the chest underneath them.

Giampietro had first seen the chest fifteen years ago, quite early in his career, when he ran across a copy of *American Painted Furniture,* a seminal book on folk art written by a scholar named Dean Fales. Besides studying the material inside, Giampietro observed on the book's back cover a painted blanket chest-on-frame described as having been made in his own hometown of Cheshire, Connecticut. He couldn't get the blanket chest out of his mind.

The more Giampietro thought about that chest, the more he liked it. Its original paint astonished him. He didn't often see pieces of eighteenth-century furniture that had never been repainted. The chest had never been varnished, refinished, restored, or repaired in any way. Though its leather hinges had torn, no one had replaced them. Giampietro wondered why one of the chest's many owners hadn't gotten tired of having to dig his or her fingers under the two working drawers to open them. He was thankful they hadn't. He'd seen many beautiful chests ruined by hardware that someone stuck on in the 1920s. Fred viewed such people as halfwits. He thought the blue blanket chest so rare and so beautiful that he considered it a work of sculpture. He wasn't alone. Every folk art dealer in the country had seen the back cover of the Fales book. A dealer ran across such an object perhaps once in a lifetime, and every dealer who thought himself important wanted that chest. From the first moment that Fred Giampietro gazed on the photograph of the blue blanket chest, he dreamed of owning it.

Over the course of the next fifteen years, Giampietro grew in stature as a dealer. His inventory came to include items of antique furniture and folk art priced in the hundreds of thousands of dollars each. One day, a man called to ask if he wanted to buy the blue blanket chest. He certainly did, Giampietro told the man. He drove out to a house in suburban New Jersey to inspect the chest, and there it sat, an icon of American folk art, waiting for him to liberate it. By this time, he had learned a lot about the history of the chest. A number of interesting people had owned it over the past several years. It had led a somewhat peculiar—even mysterious—life. Dealers usually disdain objects that have passed through so many hands. They prefer goods fresh to the marketplace, goods none of their clients has ever seen. Even though he knew it might be difficult to sell, Giampietro did not hesitate. He bought the chest in the spring of 1990 for $150,000.

Dealers like Fred Giampietro fill much of their lives with the struggle to find what others consider to be the finest examples of a form. Dealers in Chippendale furniture need to find rare highboys, dealers in silver need to find rare teapots, and dealers like Giampietro need to find rare country chests. They need to find such things, but they do not need to keep them. Giampietro had bought the blue blanket chest because he felt, in a strange way, that his destiny demanded it. Now that he had the chest, he would try to sell it.

Giampietro carried the blue chest home, placed it in his bedroom, and filled it full of clothes. He thought a lot about what he wanted to get for the piece. Had hardware been added, the chest might have been worth only about $100,000. But Giampietro believed the blue blanket chest, in its original condition, more properly belonged in a museum than in someone's house. He thought it ought to fetch nearly a quarter of a million dollars. He understood that the market for such an object is extremely small. When Fred came down to it, he could think of only about five individuals—most of them his own clients—who had a taste for rough country furniture and who might spend a quarter of a million dollars on a piece of folk art.

All summer long, Fred worked at selling the chest. He showed it to his best clients. None was interested. Its severe aesthetic was at once its appeal and its curse, but Giampietro nevertheless maintained the optimism that all dealers must possess to survive. Having failed to sell the chest, he decided it might help him get an invitation to the Winter Antiques Show. He carried it to the Fall Antiques Show in New York City. Even though he knew that the chest cost too much for the crowds that regularly attended this show, he hoped someone from the East Side exhibition committee would notice him there.

Fred could see that the blue blanket chest seduced many who saw it. Time and again, he watched couples spot the chest and hurry over, as if to get there before anybody else snapped it up. These people thought they knew the prices of great folk art. They hoped to find something to place in a position of prominence in their living rooms, and they had decided that if they really loved a piece, they might spend $20,000 to possess it. The blanket chest was just this sort of object. Giampietro watched as innocent couples walked up to the chest, watched when they noticed its price, and then saw the shock arrive on their faces. These men and women nearly always shook their heads and walked away. "A quarter of a million dollars for a chest of drawers," Fred could almost hear them saying.

Most dealers believed that to sell the chest, Giampietro would have to make it disappear for a while. In the antiques business, things pass through the hands of dealers, onto and off of advertising pages, moving for a while and then stopping for a while. Sometimes, though, they can't find a home. They pass from dealer to dealer and soon everybody has seen them and nobody wants them. Then it is time to put such things in storage for months or even years. Some dealers believed that for Giampietro to sell the chest at the price he wanted, it might have to disappear for as long as ten years. Unfortunately, Fred Giampietro didn't have that long.

In December of 1990, the exhibition committee of the Winter Antiques Show asked Giampietro to participate in its 1991 fair. He greeted this news with great joy even though he found himself unprepared for such a venture. Dealers generally require a year to stockpile a booth full of objects worthy of the Winter Show. As soon as one show closes, most dealers begin to prepare for the next. During the course of the year, they find objects they might sell quickly but that would fit perfectly in their booths. And so they carefully refrain from selling these things.

Giampietro needed to create a booth in two months. He knew that he must take the blue blanket chest with him. For all its exposure to the market, the chest carried the aura of a magnificent antique. In a way, it seemed as if all its life the chest had struggled, and that somehow it deserved to be seen at so elegant a venue as the Park Avenue armory. It almost seemed destined to go there.

What was more, the chest even had a chance of selling there. The Winter Antiques Show attracted people who did not normally inhabit Giampietro's world and who had never seen his beautiful chest. It was not unknown for the Park Avenue armory, filled with the splendors of the Winter Antiques Show, to turn those who had never spent a hundred dollars on an antique into avid collectors. At such a place as this, a man might sell something even with the exposure the blue blanket chest had previously received.

Opening night went well for Fred Giampietro. Senator John Heinz of Pennsylvania bought a pair of weathervanes from him. Other dealers in the hall seemed to have done just as well. Quite a few people managed to spend substantial sums of money between bites of thumbnail fruit tarts and sips of champagne. Watching closely, one could see that underneath the social whirl real collectors parted with real money. One could see the quick, happy transfer of personal checks from client to dealer. A Massachusetts dealer named Wayne Pratt sold a Newport kneehole desk for a sum that was later reported to have been more than $1 million.

Many people stopped to ask about the blue blanket chest. Couples would scrutinize it, leave for a while, and come back to scrutinize some more. They would pull out its drawers and sniff inside it and examine the construction of its dovetailed joints. They'd stand back from it and fold their arms and squint at it. Fred Giampietro eyed these couples carefully. Maybe one of them would bite, he thought.

Two

IN ABOUT 1750, PERHAPS IN CHESHIRE, CONNECTICUT, SOMEONE asked a man who called himself a shop joiner to make a blanket chest and drawers. Historians don't know much about the man who made the blue blanket chest. They don't even know his name. He probably lived with his wife and family in a small clapboard house in town, and worked six days a week from sunrise to sunset. He probably owned a patch of land that he farmed in the cool, humid New England summers. In the winter, he made furniture. He gave the blanket chest its clean lines and its good proportions and its faithful interpretation of Queen Anne design—qualities one normally associates more with fine Boston highboys than with painted country furniture. He made the chest from white pine, and its construction showed a careful attention to the sorts of details that would make it last. The chest survived because the joiner gave it advantages necessary for a long life. Like people, things thrive on good beginnings.

Cheshire stood in the valley of the Mill River, on the edge of the Connecticut frontier. It had only one church, the Congregational, and one pastor, the Reverend Samuel Hall. A traveler passing through Cheshire in the summer of 1750 might have come upon a scene like that which the farmer and writer Hector St. John de Crèvecoeur discovered a few years later. Crèvecoeur remarked on the well-fenced fields and ample barns, the tolerable roads, the sturdy bridges. "Everywhere you saw the people busy either at home or on their farms," he wrote. "Everywhere they seemed contented and happy."

In the winter of 1750, the Mill River flowed past a tannery owned by a cobbler named Ephraim Cook. It passed the grist mill to which farmers made the ten-mile trip from Waterbury, on their two-horse wagons, with loads of wheat and corn and rye. Finally the river poured through the giant waterwheel of the sawmill, where carpenters and joiners bought their rough boards of white pine and cherry and tulip and oak. Watching the river, farmers thought of ice floes breaking up in spring, and of their impatience to plant again. The joiners, who farmed from necessity rather than a feeling of reward, looked forward to a snowbound winter in their shops.

Some of the men and women who settled Cheshire were still alive in 1750. These people had crossed the Blue Hills in 1696, and they told stories of how they cleared the forest with their hands and how they built their houses of rough-hewn planks, with thatched roofs. Stephen Hotchkiss remembered dressing up in a thick canvas coat, quilted with cotton wadding to shield him from arrows, and marching out with other men to fight the Indians. People still did

things the old way in Cheshire. They employed home rem-
edies such as peppermint and syrup of buckthorn. They
caught the pigeons that flew overhead in such numbers,
Crèvecoeur observed, that they "obscured the sun in their
flight." Cheshire families spun their own cloth, sewed their
own clothes, brewed their own beer, and made their sugar
from maple sap. After the harvest, a farmer gathered some
provisions, picked up his musket and compass, and set off
for a week to hunt deer and bears in the woods. Strangers
trusted one another. In the winter, people left the doors to
their houses unlocked, and went to bed, expecting that trav-
elers would let themselves in, light a pipe, and spend the
night by their fires. Change came slowly to a place like
Cheshire. "In this vast monotony of days," as the art historian Henri Focillon once observed in an essay on folk art,
"one does much, but nothing ever *happens.*"

In many ways, Cheshire resembled a small medieval
village. People lived together, worked together, and slept
together in the same small beds. The citizens of Cheshire
did not own many things. They had only begun to think of
the few possessions they did have as belonging especially to
any one of them. Furniture was scarce. Half the families in
Cheshire did not own a chest of drawers, principally because
they had nothing much to put in one.

Though one could sail in six months from England to
Connecticut, ideas took much longer to arrive. As many as
thirty years stood between towns at the edges of the New
England birch forests and the latest concerns of London. If
someone had plucked a Cheshire farmer from out of his
pastures and deposited him in the Strand, this man would
probably have felt that he had traveled in time. London in

1750 was the most modern city in the world. What particularly astonished visitors was not the size of this metropolis, or its huge public buildings, but the quantity of merchandise for sale in its shops. Middle-class matrons streamed back and forth along the city's muddy streets, crowding the silk shops and fan shops and the shops run by silversmiths. Other London stores sold furniture, pottery, mirrors, hats, and pets. For the first time in history, ordinary people now owned *things*. Having some, they wanted more. One manufacturer described this newfound appetite for goods as an "epidemical madness."

No such madness had yet infected Cheshire. The impulse to want things came first to Boston and Philadelphia and Charleston, then passed on to smaller towns before it reached towns at the end of the road. New objects did arrive in Cheshire, but they arrived thirty years late. They came in wagons that horses pulled across the hills. They came back from trips that farmers took to such bustling Connecticut River ports as Middletown. Merchants in Middletown had grown rich from trade with the West Indies. They had built great houses and filled them not only with china and maps and brass telescopes imported from England, but also with cherrywood bookcases and maple side chairs and mahogany clocks made by local craftsmen. Rich Cheshire farmers saw things they had never thought of wanting, and began to wish for what they hadn't needed. "As the self-consciousness of medieval people was spare, the interiors of their houses were bare," wrote the historian John Lukacs. "The interior furniture of houses appeared together with the interior furniture of the minds."

A Cheshire farmer probably ordered the blue blanket

chest. Perhaps a friend had recently acquired a chest of drawers himself, or perhaps the farmer's season had been especially fruitful, or perhaps he had listened to the urgings of his wife. This was most likely a simple man who struggled between a love for the familiar and an interest in the new. This man's parents never owned more than a few pieces of furniture of the simplest kind. His mother put only her best tablecloths away, inside a low chest with no drawers. The farmer viewed drawers in the same way some people considered early videocassette recorders—as something that might well be a passing fancy, a luxury best left to rich people.

The blue blanket chest was made by someone like Timothy Loomis, who lived not far from Cheshire in the small town of Windsor. In 1750, Loomis was twenty-six years old and had been married for seven years. In the summer he farmed and in the off-season he worked at his craft. Loomis spent much of his time building, remodeling, and repairing his neighbors' houses and barns. He made coffins, bookcases, cupboards, and staircases. He constructed stills to make hard Yankee liquor, repaired people's mills, laid floors, and erected hogpens and fences. In 1748 he had even helped to build a sloop for a group of speculators.

Loomis stayed busy, but he was not getting rich. In Windsor, everyone but the minister and the blacksmith farmed to support their families. Life was much the same in Cheshire. A joiner like Loomis could expect to receive three shillings a day for his services—and even then, only when his clients had cash. Few ever did. Instead, Loomis made furniture for the minister in lieu of paying his church taxes. He traded services with dry goods merchants, physicians, blacksmiths, tanners, weavers, and clockmakers. He also traded the turnips, tobacco, potatoes, and corn that he grew on his small plot of land. Loomis came as close to a professional tradesman as any rural joiner of the time, and yet he managed to remain in debt. As the chronicler of his life, the historian William Hosley, has written, he owed money to a "bewildering array of cousins, in-laws, and neighbors."

Loomis never quite escaped his debts. In spite of this, he led a comfortable life. He ran a woodworking shop at the center of town, where men gathered to smoke their pipes and talk of recent rains. Like many joiners of the day, he operated a side business in nails, paint, lumber, and panes of glass. In large towns, the joiners often lived transient lives, staying long enough to earn a stake to buy some land out West. Journeymen cabinetmakers came and went as they pleased, and some earned the reputation of drunkards and drifters. Small towns such as Cheshire fostered a greater sense of community, and often kept their craftsmen around for years. The joiners in Cheshire occasionally worked together on houses and barns, the way Tim Loomis was working in Windsor with another joiner, his friend Zebulon Hoskins. Such joiners did carpentry with friends, but they didn't share many clients for their furniture.

The man who made the blue blanket chest probably owned a small two-story house with a shop added to the ground floor. Large windows lit his benches, and fine planes, saws, and gouges hung on his walls. These tools had cost him a great deal because, like all decent ones, they came from England. One joiner, having lost his tools, placed an advertisement in a local newspaper that read, "The Turning Tools were made in this country, and are very clumsy, and may be known by that." A lathe that an apprentice turned by hand might have stood in one corner of the Cheshire cabinet shop. Unfinished chests and chairs lay about the room. Stacks of sawn panels and turned rails leaned against them. Hammers and clamps hung from sawhorses. Bottles of stains and varnishes lined the shelves in neat rows, each covered with a piece of leather tied to its top with string. The room smelled of boards stacked in the rafters, of sawdust and curly shavings that littered the floor, of glue from animal skins, of paint and varnish and woodsmoke.

The joiner and his client probably discussed how it might be possible to have a chest of drawers and a blanket chest at the same time—to have both the new and the old. They talked about how large to make this chest. Most people wanted their pine furniture painted and could choose among several primary colors. People often painted such chests red, green, black, or yellow, but these men agreed on blue. The joiner probably sketched this object on a piece of scrap lumber until he satisfied his client. He agreed to construct the piece from white pine, the cheapest material available in southern Connecticut. Many rural New Englanders, having their roots in the Puritan church, distrusted showy things. For this reason the joiner would make the chest plain, unadorned with hardware. In concession to the conservative tastes of the country, the joiner and his client must have agreed that the chest's legs would remain small and discreet.

The joiner designed the blanket chest in a style that would one day be called Queen Anne, for the English monarch under whose reign it was first conceived. Queen Anne furniture was popular in England during the first three decades of the eighteenth century. It is characterized by its simplicity and its graceful lines, and by the elegant S-curve of its cabriole legs. The style was a product of Enlightenment principles, which held that human beings could discover a rational order to the universe. For a culture emerging from the Middle Ages, Queen Anne furniture represented a change as novel as the new Georgian architecture it complemented. Suddenly things had a meaning apart from God. Rooms flowed together. The curving lines in chairs echoed lines in the architecture of rooms. People suddenly took notice. Chairs, tables, and beds must almost have seemed to sit up and begun to speak.

Though Queen Anne objects had decorated London interiors for more than thirty years, by 1750 the Queen Anne style had passed out of fashion. In Cheshire it was just arriving. New things came to such places like pieces in a puzzle. A new chair might appear in town one day, but how was a country joiner to understand that the curves in the chair were meant to relate to the scalloped apron of a high chest? A traveler from London might spend all day describing the grand Georgian houses, the elegant rooms, and the spirit of the Enlightenment that suffused the city, and still the people of Cheshire would not understand the context in which new styles were made.

A country joiner tried to duplicate the things he saw. He studied engravings and the occasional examples that came his way. But most country joiners were unschooled carpenters whom farmers such as Crèvecoeur thought to be "sometimes great bunglers." Such men tended to stick parts of the new style onto old and familiar forms. Even those joiners who understood Queen Anne design might fail to convince their clients. Simple farmers preferred the familiar. It is very difficult to produce a thing that fully comprehends a new style while satisfying those who value what is over what will be.

The joiner who made the blue blanket chest probably worked with an apprentice or two. It took a day for a boy to plane the rough pine boards by hand. Then the joiner started from the bottom of the chest and worked his way up. Standing at a lathe, he turned the four slipper feet out of cherrywood blocks, since craftsmen found pine too soft for carving. He finished each leg by cutting out the S-curve of the cabriole leg with his carving tools. He cut the wood for the little skirts, or aprons. He drew the pattern of the scalloped base and cut this out with a small frame saw. He pegged and glued the aprons to the legs. With his molding planes, he made the decorative strips that run around the chest's top and base. Then he built a carcass of three boards, finished the drawers, and completed the top. Considering the balance and spontaneity of the blanket chest, one imagines that he might well have started and finished this project within a day. When he was through, the joiner made his blue paint from pigments that he mixed with animal glue or resin. Since the pigments had cost him dearly, he applied only one coat.

When the paint had dried and the joiner had tacked on the leather hinges that joined the chest's top to its frame, his work must have pleased him. Many chests made in the country looked squat, but this one had the well-proportioned verticality of things made in the city. The drawer-fronts graduated nicely from large ones at the bottom to smaller ones on top. Though only five inches high, the Queen Anne legs gave the piece an elegance rarely seen on such painted pine furniture. By avoiding the ornamentation from an earlier period of design, the chest showed a great understanding of the Queen Anne system. It also revealed the gifts of an artist. It revealed, as Henri Focillon once remarked, "that magic we call talent, which all our efforts cannot reduce to formulas." The joiner made a thing that his client would never really understand but would always love.

This farmer no doubt admired his chest because it was new. Now that he had a place to put things, he could acquire the things to put. The blue blanket chest may have helped give its first owner a sense of who he was. He must have cherished it. Perhaps he passed the chest on to his favorite daughter, and she passed it to hers, and in this way it made its way through the years, from one generation to the next. Things lead lives like people do, and they prosper, like people, on the strength of their character.

Three

SOTHEBY'S THREW A COCKTAIL PARTY ON MONDAY EVENING TO inaugurate the largest auction of the year in the world of American antiques. Many of the same guests who had attended the opening of the Winter Antiques Show on Friday night also received invitations to this gathering. Such parties had become annual events during Americana Week, and the only people missing from this scene were dealers such as Fred Giampietro, who stood guarding his booth, just ten blocks away, at the Park Avenue armory. Those guests who had attended the opening of the Winter Antiques Show had all seen Giampietro's blue blanket chest and Carlton Hobbs's George II library desk. Now they wanted to look at other things. A wide array of antiques competed for the attention of the partygoers that evening.

The most prominent of these objects was a card table, which stood on a platform in Sotheby's main exhibition room. The top of this table had been folded over so it could fit snugly against a wall, and a note that rested on the dark, smooth, shiny surface read, "Please Do Not Handle." This table, though very different from the blue blanket chest, was no less extraordinary. Lush vines dripped down its legs, and the claws of its feet clung tightly to wooden balls. If you stared at it for a while, the table almost sprang to life. Sotheby's had placed a guard beside the table to clarify any ambiguity in the note, which might fail to deter those guests for whom it was possible to touch a thing without handling it. At an auction to be held on Saturday, experts at Sotheby's estimated the card table would bring more than $1 million.

All great antiques are known for someone who once owned them. The card table happened to be known for the man who commissioned it, a Philadelphia merchant named Thomas Willing. So far as anyone could tell, somebody had made the table in the middle of the eighteenth century, around the same time the country joiner made the blue blanket chest, but in a very different style. From the choice of woods and the quality of the carving, it was clear that this table began its life as a rare and fine object. A craftsman made the Willing card table of solid mahogany and adorned it with the finest brasses then available from Birmingham, England. This man shaped its two front corners like the turrets of a castle, a method of construction that vexed any carver who wanted his vines to flow effortlessly around them. Such turret-top card tables were as difficult to make as the finest highboys and, when new, they cost about as much. Few survived to the twentieth century. Those that have almost never come to market.

The individual most responsible for bringing this table to Sotheby's was William W. Stahl, Jr. Rare objects are his stock in trade. Stahl is a handsome man of forty whose face makes him look younger than his years but whose hair has turned prematurely gray. Through a combination of hard work and good luck, Stahl was named head of Sotheby's American furniture department when he was only twenty-two. Within a few years he occupied a seat on the board of Sotheby's North America. Like many people who achieve great authority at an early age, Stahl carries an attitude that some might mistake for self-importance.

Stahl attended his first major auction on January 29, 1971, at an American furniture sale held by Parke-Bernet, Sotheby's corporate predecessor in New York. Though only nineteen, Stahl thought he knew a lot about antiques. His mother dealt in what he called a "general line"—Oriental rugs, glass, American and English furniture—and he often helped her in the business. This life had taught Stahl a great deal about cupboards, chests, and Windsor chairs, but it failed to prepare him for the glamor of the sale room at Parke-Bernet. The country's most important dealers and collectors filled the room that day. The auctioneer carried himself like a celebrity. What Stahl remembered most, however, was that soon after the auction began, a dealer from Philadelphia suffered a heart attack and died on the spot. "The individual was taken away and the sale went right on," Stahl recalled many years later. "And I said to myself, 'This is for me.' "

Objects have preoccupied Stahl for so long that when asked to explain just *how* long, he can only think to say, "I have always loved things." As a freshman at Trinity College in Hartford, he decorated his room with a good Chinese

rug, an eighteenth-century oxbow-front desk, and some antique prints of sporting scenes. After he became an auctioneer, Stahl saw it as a benefit that his job would require him
to examine a couple hundred thousand objects each year.
When he left town to spend the weekend at his country
home in Millbrook, New York, Stahl relaxed most easily
underneath the tents of country auctions.

As an auctioneer, Stahl spends about ten days each year
actually selling goods from the podium in Sotheby's main
saleroom. He fills most of his time talking on the telephone
about objects or traveling to see them. Objects pull him to
the spreading lawns of Connecticut, New Jersey, and Long
Island, and to places even farther afield—to California and
Georgia and Florida. He keeps running lists in his head:
lists of objects that he has seen someplace and might get to
sell one day, and lists of objects that he has only heard about.
The business of remembering where things are, or where he
has heard they are, is occasionally referred to at Sotheby's as
"keeping track of the bodies."

One day in 1982, a dealer from Philadelphia approached Stahl to tell him about a fabulous Chippendale
table, which, the dealer believed, would eventually reach the
marketplace. That was the first Stahl had heard of the Willing card table. If the table lived up to the dealer's description, such an object would highlight a major sale, and for
this reason the card table became one of the more important
bodies that Stahl kept track of. Through a lucky coinci-
dence, a colleague of Stahl's happened to be a friend of the
family that owned the table. Whenever she returned from
Philadelphia, after a visit to the family's house, the colleague

told him, "It's still there." It remained there until one day in the summer of 1990, when Stahl was able to pick it up in his Chevrolet Blazer and drive it to New York City.

Now on the evening of Sotheby's cocktail party, from where he stood amid the crowd, Stahl could see the card table bathed in yellow beams from the spotlights overhead. Beyond the table spread a vast array of other shiny things. Furniture stood on the carpeted floors, paintings and quilts hung together on the carpeted walls, porcelain plates and silver teapots rested on shelves inside lighted glass cases. Employees had dusted, cleaned, and polished each item, and each one waited patiently for its moment on the stage. Because of its enormous value, the card table occupied one place in Stahl's mind, and everything else occupied another.

Stahl had mailed invitations to his most reliable customers, who were couples, mostly, in their forties or fifties. The men wore blazers and ties like those that Brooks Brothers marks down after Christmas, while the women wore dresses whose lengths were not currently in, but would probably return to, fashion. Many of these couples lived in large stone houses, sent their children to boarding schools, and fit into a category of antiques buyer known to Stahl as "the $25,000 range." This figure represents the amount such people can afford to spend on a single object. It is a sum which would allow them to choose among most of the goods for sale that week but which nevertheless left them in a category Stahl refers to as "low-end buyers." Stahl, of course, has nothing personal against these people. As a client of other auction houses, he considers himself a low-end buyer. Many of the guests at Sotheby's that night were his good friends.

He invited them because he liked them and because they made up the bulk of his market, and also because all the high-end buyers in the country would not have made much of a cocktail party.

The people who milled about the room that evening did not occupy the same place in the world of American antiques as the couples who longed for Fred Giampietro's blue blanket chest. The people at Sotheby's knew a lot about antiques. They understood when someone said, "I have always loved things." These gatherings ordinarily thrilled them. On that evening, however, their attention seemed to drift uncharacteristically, from the subject of walnut lowboys to the subject of the war then taking place in the Persian Gulf. They talked about the videos being sent back by smart bombs and of how, or when, or whether the United States should follow these bombs with troops. Although Stahl could not himself refrain from discussing smart bombs, he found the topic of war incompatible with what he considered the proper climate for a good sale.

Waiters in white coats carried trays of canapés through the crowd, and bartenders poured white wine spritzers. Even so, the chatter that evening drifted in what, to Stahl, were other unpleasant directions. The clients in the Brooks Brothers jackets and the Lord & Taylor dresses talked also about the effects of war on the economy, a conversation that led inevitably to the effects of the economy on the art market, which led, in turn, to a discussion of the last Americana sale in October. Stahl did not find this subject any more compatible than the others.

In Stahl's language, successful Americana sales "happened" and unsuccessful ones "did not happen," and the way he described the October sale was that it "didn't happen." Sotheby's figures its successes by calculating its failures—the estimated value of the goods that go unsold at each of its auctions. The lower the percentage of unsold merchandise, the better the sale. In normal times—in the eighties, anyhow—an Americana sale went badly when Stahl could not sell 12 percent of his merchandise. Last October he had failed to sell nearly 40 percent. Stahl remembered the October sale as the worst in the history of the department.

In times such as these, Stahl recalled a maxim of the antiques business which suggested that great things always sell and that cheap things always sell but that goods in the vast middle ground suffer most during economic slumps and Middle Eastern wars. This maxim did not come to an auctioneer's mind if he happened to be selling very great things (such as the Willing card table), or if he happened to be selling very cheap things (Stahl rarely did), but in every other situation it was one of those truths by which he lived. Most of the things Stahl hoped to sell that week fell into just this middling category. The American silver rowing trophies, the Currier and Ives lithographs, and the Imari plates that packed the exhibition rooms appealed to people in the $25,000 range. Such objects were in a category of antiques known in the trade as "stuff." Despite the large amount of stuff he had to sell, and in spite of the difficult times, Stahl tried hard to turn the skeptics into buyers.

When Stahl thought about the Willing card table, he began to doubt the maxim that great things always sell. People feel skittish about paying $1 million for a piece of furniture in the middle of a recession. Though many coveted the Willing table, the actual number who might spend $1 million on a single piece of furniture was about ten: the Dallas billionaire Robert Bass, who had once paid $12.1 million for a Newport secretary-bookcase; Eddy Nicholson, the former chairman of Congoleum Corporation; and Bill Cosby. The other collectors in this group had accumulated less fame, perhaps, but no less wealth.

The world of American antiques is small, and news gets around. It was commonly known in this world that each one of these ten collectors had a reason not to spend a million dollars on a card table. One collector had stopped buying altogether. Another already owned a turret-top card table. A third was rumored to be getting a divorce.

"I won't say I was lying awake at night worrying about it," Stahl remembered later. "I'm happiest when I'm out at the end of a limb, as long as somebody friendly is holding the saw. But we didn't know exactly where the competition was going to come from."

Competition over objects is essential in the antiques business. An understanding of this principle led Stahl to contact Alan Miller, an acquaintance who runs a small furniture restoration business out of a shop in rural Pennsylvania. Miller often wears flannel shirts, aviator glasses, and heavy work boots, and thinks of New York City as someone's idea of a bad joke. He travels to Manhattan as infrequently as possible.

To call Miller's business "small" is unfair in every sense but the physical one. His shop occupies a dusty, tumbledown stucco building in a town whose chief feature is its view of bright, green, rolling pastures. But Miller's workshop inhabits a very special place in the world of American furniture. Collectors of American antiques care more about construction and authenticity than other collectors do. They place a high value on good restorers. Since Miller specializes in some of the most expensive antiques to be had anywhere, and because of his skill as a great craftsman, it might be fair to say that Alan Miller is the most important furniture restorer in the world.

As soon as Stahl acquired his new card table in the summer of 1990, he gave Miller a call. He wanted the woodworker to make some minor repairs on one of the table's legs. It happened, though, that Stahl had failed to notice a much greater problem with the table. It had a flaw. A carved shell that had once been attached to the table's front had broken off some years earlier and disappeared. A new owner decided to replace the broken shell and carried the table to a local restorer. Perhaps this man had refinished the table—Stahl could see the evidence that someone had. The man was not bad at what he did, but he was not as good as Alan Miller. Carving a shell presents great difficulties, and to replace what is lost, a restorer must have an intimate understanding of the style in which the table was designed. He must also understand the man who made the table in order to duplicate the idiosyncrasies of his leaves and vines. The restorer understood neither of these things. Where the shell should have been convex, he made it concave. What was supposed to have been concave, he made convex. To an ordinary eye, the shell that decorated the front of the Willing card table looked just fine. Bill Stahl could see that the shell had been replaced, but even he could not tell that the restoration was a mistake. Alan Miller excelled at solving just this sort of problem.

The most important reason Stahl called that summer had nothing to do with repairs of any kind. In addition to being a knowledgeable craftsman, Miller is one of the country's leading scholars of Philadelphia Chippendale furniture. No one spends $1 million on a table without first getting an expert to look at it. When Stahl's mind took him to the list of million-dollar collectors, he knew that at least one—and probably three or four others as well—would not have considered buying the table until Alan Miller examined it. He believed that the table would probably not sell without Miller's blessing.

Alan Miller makes it no less his business than Bill Stahl to keep track of bodies. For some time rumors of the card table had drifted into his cluttered shop. Having heard about the table, Miller hoped one day to see it. He considered such tables not only among the most beautiful of American furniture forms but also the most difficult to make. When Stahl told him of the recent acquisition, Miller grew excited. Few things in life could give Alan Miller so much pleasure as examining a recently discovered Philadelphia card table. In fact, he made immediate plans to see it in New York.

Miller is not by nature an especially effusive man. As Stahl remembers it, when Miller saw the card table across a room at Sotheby's, he casually said, "That's the Garvan carver." Stahl found this information to be particularly interesting, since he knew that scholars of American furniture consider the man known as the Garvan carver among the best craftsmen ever to work in this country. Miller knelt in front of the table to study it, in the attitude of an altar boy at the benediction of a pope. Stahl and his colleagues asked Miller some questions about the repair on the leg, but he seemed lost in thought.

Alan Miller became interested in restoration through his background in woodworking. Once he started fixing up colonial furniture, he found that he needed to work in many different styles. He gathered an impressive collection of carving tools to imitate the different carvers he encountered. Then he found that some pieces required further knowledge of the Philadelphia carvers and their techniques, a discovery that led him to research libraries throughout the Northeast. Through careful study, Miller amassed a knowledge of American furniture that few others possess. He has contributed essential scholarship on the work of Philadelphia carvers with names such as Hercules Courtney, James Reynolds, and Nicholas Bernard.

One day a few years ago, Miller paid a visit to Mount Pleasant, the finest Chippendale-era home still standing in Philadelphia. As he toured the house, Miller stumbled across the work of a particularly skillful carver on a highboy that stood in the corner of an upstairs room. From the nature of the work and the design of the piece, Miller could tell it was made in Philadelphia during the 1760s. He thought the carving on this highboy particularly exquisite, and he wanted to know the man who had made it. Then other pieces—pieces made by the same carver's hand—started appearing in Miller's workshop. He ran across a lowboy that used the same lexicon of shapes he had seen at Mount Pleasant. One day, after studying a clock carved by this same man, Miller suddenly realized that all the things he had seen by the carver resembled a set of furniture in the famous Garvan furniture collection at Yale University—so named for the couple who donated it. Others had made the same discovery, but Miller advertised it. Because the carver did not have a name, Miller began to refer to him as "the Garvan carver." Miller believed that this man was the greatest American-born carver ever to work in this country.

Learning to know the Garvan carver felt to Miller like learning a beautiful new language. This man intrigued Miller because each of the leaves and vines and flowers carved out of the mahogany appeared to be in a state of motion. Every carved image seemed to turn. Every leaf and every flower petal appeared as if beginning to flip back on itself. The images came to life. Miller found that the vocabulary of shapes did not exactly correspond to the natural world but that "they are completely lucid and understandable as carved. His leaves are his leaves. His vines are his vines."

Miller then began to identify work by the Garvan carver on pieces made in the early 1750s. Since these objects showed the hand of a young man learning his craft, Miller concluded that he must have been in his early twenties. Miller also discovered a highboy constructed in the middle 1760s that he believed to be the last the carver ever made. Miller could see the parts the Garvan carver made, like a shell-carved drawer, and those that somebody else had finished. No objects made by the Garvan carver exist after that highboy. The Garvan carver—a man in his middle thirties—must have died.

This man's work on card tables particularly intrigued Miller. Through his research, Miller discovered a pair of such tables in a museum at Colonial Williamsburg. They are known as the Vaux tables—for a family who once owned them—and they are very famous. What Miller thought most important about the Vaux tables was that the carver had made them early in his career. In a museum in Houston, Texas, Miller soon discovered another card table, made very late in the carver's life. The evolution of this man's talents never ceased to amaze Miller. By the middle 1760s, the Garvan carver had found the full command of his style. The curves of his vines had grown longer and the look of his ball-and-claw feet had matured. Though exquisite, the table in Houston did not possess a little skirt that the most expensive card tables usually employed and that Miller had hoped to find. Such skirts are known as rails, and they required some of the most difficult carving that a man could attempt. Miller had seen such carved rails on tables like the Vaux, made early in the carver's career, but he longed to see a rail made during the carver's finest period. He wanted to see the carver when, in Miller's words, "he got more head of steam up."

On his visit to Sotheby's, Miller found the table he'd been waiting for. He saw immediately that it did indeed possess carved rails. "When I walked in, to me it was like something I've been waiting to see for years," Miller remembers. "And then suddenly I see it. It just put me in a state of aesthetic shock. Every good Philadelphia table from the fifties has this essential design, but this one is the apotheosis. There are certain pieces that not only sum up the potentials that seem inherent in that form but that seem to surpass them. The really great stuff seems to be more than the sum of the parts. That's what this table was."

Four

THOMAS WILLING, THE MAN WHO GAVE HIS NAME TO THE WILL-
ing card table, enjoyed beautiful things. He adored new silk
suits and wigs made by men recently arrived from France.
He lived in a Georgian-style mansion that he regarded not
so much as a dwelling but as a box to fill with treasures.
Because of his passion, the grand stores on Chestnut Street,
in Philadelphia's most fashionable shopping district, often
seduced him. He liked to linger over ruby solitaires at The-
odorus Carbin's jewelry store and to gaze into the imported
looking glasses at John Elliot's. Shopping expeditions turned
into military campaigns for Willing. He frequented the
enormous emporium of Wikoff's to stroke its rich imported
fabrics and to finger the Oriental bibelots. When he departed, a column of packages carried by his servants trailed
behind him down the sidewalks of Third Street. He took
great pleasure in the "amusement," as Henry James once
wrote, "in seeking." He browsed to dream, and he bought to
take a piece of his dream home. He hung velvet curtains for

a season and then discarded them. He banished old mahogany side chairs to the counting rooms of his merchant trading firm. Sometimes it seemed that Willing discarded things as happily as he kept them, a habit that endeared him to the merchants of Chestnut Street. The shopkeepers of this neighborhood treated him with the humility and respect they accorded anyone whose taste for expensive objects was equaled only by his capacity to pay for them.

From portraits of Willing, one can see that he was an attractive gentleman with dark eyes, bushy brows, and a thin, ironic smile. Strangers remembered him as "sociable." His friends called him Tommy. Few men in Philadelphia were more popular than Willing, perhaps in part because few men in North America were richer. Besides his vast mercantile empire, Willing owned a partnership in the largest insurance company on the continent; a three-thousand-acre indigo plantation in western Florida and another, half that size, along the Mississippi River; and houses and other properties both in and around Philadelphia. Willing had inherited a great deal of money at age twenty-four, when his father, Charles, the mayor of the city and captain of the militia, died suddenly of yellow fever. He made a lot more on his own. "The proper object of a reasonable man," he once wrote a friend, "is the pursuit of riches."

The center of Willing's large domestic operations stood a dozen yards behind his house on Third Street. Inside these rooms, among the obsequious clerks, the banished chairs, and the smells of musty ledger books, Willing practiced the art of making money. He liked to plot strategies with his best friend and business partner, Robert Morris, with whom he shared the natural self-confidence of youth, but without the usual recklessness. Willing started with a legacy of £6,000 and the interests in three ships, to which he added a knowledge of the law gained from study in London. Morris, who started with no legacy of any kind, possessed the unique ability to spend other people's money as if it were his own—and make two people rich. Morris unstintingly applied Willing's fortune to the construction of ships with names such as the *Carrington* and the *London*. He opened new markets for Pennsylvania grain in Spain and Portugal. Willing, meanwhile, negotiated their huge vessels through the narrow loopholes of British trade laws. They employed a network of agents around the world. Within four years of Charles Willing's death, the two young men had built the firm of Willing & Morris into one of the largest mercantile operations on the continent.

Twenty thousand people lived in Philadelphia in 1759. It was the second most populous city in the British Empire after London, and the most affluent and sophisticated city in the American colonies. In the hot, wet summer of that year, mown grass and cocks of hay dotted the hillsides outside of town, and fields of wheat spread as far as one could see. Merchant trading vessels such as the *London* tugged at ropes that held them to the wharves along Front Street. Immigrants, delirious from the crossing, waited to be sold into indentured servitude. Gulls cried and men shouted and ragged urchins darted among the overloaded wagons. Pigs wandered untethered through the city streets. That fall, convoys of a hundred wagons were not uncommon on the road from Lancaster. The markets filled with German farmers, Irish servants, African slaves, and squawking geese. Hammers pounded on the rooftops of houses that carpenters were erecting at the rate of one hundred each year.

Commerce and the smell of money filled the air in Philadelphia that fall. No one had a better nose for this than Willing. The holds of the *London* slowly filled with Philadelphia's famous brass buttons and its famous leather breeches, its pots, pans, chairs, candles, rum, and whale oil. Wagons of wheat and corn rolled up to Willing's wharves, where strong men wrestled with Willing's bales of furs, his stacks of Pennsylvania timber, and his barrels full of apples. The *London* carried sixteen six-pound cannons and a crew of fifty men and was bound for Jamaica in November. After it sailed, Willing would worry for a year or two while his ship sailed through Atlantic storms and engagements with French privateers on its way to Africa and the Mediterranean. His habit of worrying was well established in Philadelphia. Morris had made the same passage to Jamaica two years earlier, and while he was gone Willing had mailed off a daily stream of anxious letters. When the *London* landed in Kingston, it would take a couple of months for Willing to hear the good news. He would receive reports from the African Gold Coast, from Portugal, and from England. In a year or two, with any luck, the *London* would sail back up the Delaware with a cargo of sugar, wine, slaves, lemons, Irish linens, Liverpool china, and Bristol beer. And its wealthy owner would be richer still.

The art of making money, through the certain principles of trade, appears to have run in Willing's blood. His grandfather was a rich London merchant and a director of the Royal African Company. Willing's father, Charles, had expanded the family business to Pennsylvania. During his youth at school in England, Thomas spent the holidays at his grandparents' country home near Bristol. While there, he learned other things besides an appetite for riches. He acquired a love for music, art, and hunting foxes, for fancy balls, lavish banquets, and the fine manners to go with them. When Thomas played around the Bristol mansion, he did not so much study fine things as sit on them. He apparently concluded from the evidence at hand that if the point of living was to make money, then the point of making money was to spend it. This attitude formed the simple philosophy of his life.

After he moved back to Philadelphia, Willing maintained the bearing of a prince. He drove about town in one of only eight coaches to be found there, complete with a coachman in full livery. He owned a magnificent house which was built on a model of his grandfather's country home and which he had filled with his own exquisite objects from around the world. His dining table seated fourteen. It stood in a room where crimson drapes framed the windows and seven bronze busts were mounted to the walls, a room that was further furnished with a marble-top side table, a gilt-framed looking glass with matching sconces, and two large mahogany tea tables. Having learned his taste, Willing now discovered its value. He loved his things not only for their beauty, but for their silent testimony to the beauty of his soul. Willing had inherited what the sociologist Pierre Bourdieu has called "a fund of cultural capital"—a fund from which he earned "a profit in distinction." Few things give a man his place in life more than his tastes.

In the fall of 1759, Willing entered a cabinet shop on Chestnut Street, where he met the carver who would make his card table. This man came from a very different world than Willing's. He probably wore a leather cap, leather breeches, and a leather apron. Like Willing, he was about thirty. He would have seemed at home among the smells of glue and varnish. Sawdust covered the floors of this shop, and the carcasses of unfinished furniture cluttered its aisles. These objects would soon become some of the finest highboys, the best lowboys, and the most elegant piecrust tea tables that the city had yet produced, but now each was in a state of humble beginning. Their rough appearance must have seemed at odds with the beauty Willing expected of such things. Without the vision of an artist, it is difficult to imagine what can be.

From the opulence of the Willing card table, one can speculate that the man who commissioned it knew exactly what he wanted. The table he ordered was known as a "card table with rounded corners," and what he had in mind was something as fancy as anything Philadelphia had ever produced. As an Anglican, Willing took a more liberal attitude toward the display of riches than the city's Quaker founders did. He apparently believed in a literal interpretation of Lord Chesterfield's famous remark, in 1750, that "if you are not in fashion, you are nobody."

Such tastes led Willing to what Alan Miller believes to have been the largest cabinet shop in Philadelphia. The man who owned this shop employed four or five men, including the carver, to keep up with orders from the city's merchants. Apprentices labored from dawn until dusk, sawing boards, turning lathes, and running errands to other shops along the dusty streets. Two or three journeymen spent their hours joining cabinets and chairs. Only one carver worked there. He was probably acknowledged to be the best in the city, the only carver suited to fulfilling Willing's desires.

The commission for this card table could hardly have failed to delight the shop's owner. Of all the furniture made in the city, only high chests produced larger profits. Philadelphians of all sorts wanted card tables. Inventories of houses there show that most middle-class families owned at least one. Of those objects a prosperous tradesman might covet, only tea tables came higher on his list. Eighteenth-century households viewed their furniture not as stationary objects with fixed locations but as pieces of a stage set to be moved according to need. Rooms had many uses. When the women of the house used a parlor to sew, things like card tables stood against the walls. The tops usually folded up so that when not in use these tables remained out of the way. When a foursome wished to play, servants carried the table to the center of the room, unfolded its top, and swung one of its legs around for support.

Ladies and gentlemen like Willing often played whist, a game that had become one of the most celebrated recreations in England. The man who helped to make this possible was Edmond Hoyle, who in 1742 had published a book called *A Short Treatise on the Game of Whist*. This little volume proved so popular that by 1759 it was in its eleventh edition. A copy no doubt stood on a bookshelf in Willing's library. He liked to play whist, to drink madeira, and to win serious sums of money from his friends. Occasionally they remained at his house until after ten o'clock.

Willing found a great advantage in a card table with turreted corners. After his servants opened it up, the table's top revealed four niches at the corners—each the size of a nice coaster—where the players could place their candlesticks. This luxury did not come cheaply. Such tables were available only in mahogany and only with ball-and-claw feet. Their cost started at the staggering sum of £5 and went up from there. A man like Willing who wanted a pink baize playing surface paid another £1.5. If he wanted carved knees, as Willing did, he committed £1.5 more. The largest expense was incurred by those who wanted carved rails to run on all sides except the backs of their card tables. To a casual observer, the rails looked like little skirts that seemed a part of the box that formed the body of the table. Though they extended only an inch or two below this original box, they cost another £2. The expense for such a table—in all, it came to £10—owed to the multitude of curves that added dimension to the table and gave it its lovely seamlessness. The turrets curved one way—in a horizontal direction around the table's two front corners—while the legs that sat below them curved down in a vertical direction. The rails of these fancy card tables did not hang straight down, but canted slightly out from the table's edge. Across this difficult terrain, a carver had to make his vines seem to twine just as those in nature did. Of all the furniture that a cabinet shop produced, no object was more difficult to carve.

Willing had himself decided what sort of card table he wanted. Since most gentlemen of his generation oversaw the decoration of their houses, Willing undoubtedly pursued this task no less energetically than he followed the latest scientific thought. He got his ideas about fashion from designers in London. He approved of the Georgian style of architecture, whose principles incorporated the English fondness for buildings of the Roman Empire. Other influences seeped into England through small cracks in the embargo against France. The English adopted the French fashion in clothes and furniture, and then subdued it to accommodate a more conservative taste. This fashion was known in 1759 as the "style moderne." A century later it would be called rococo after the *rocaille* rockwork with which the wife of King Henry II, Catherine de Medici, had once adorned her grottoes in the Tuileries.

The London furnituremaker Thomas Chippendale had recently published a book that assisted Willing in his role as decorator. This book contained 160 engravings for the design of chairs, chests, cabinets, beds, and mirrors. Chippendale had illustrated styles that included what he called "Gothic, Chinese and Modern Taste," so that a man such as Willing could make his own decisions about the interior of his house. To convey the essential nature of this involvement, Chippendale titled his book *The Gentlemen and Cabinetmaker's Director*.

Chippendale was the son and grandson of simple carpenters. His wife could not read. His cabinet shop on St. Martin's Lane stood across the street from Old Slaughter's Coffee House, where London's rococo designers often congregated. Chippendale employed sixty men at the occupations of joinery, carving, gilding, glassmaking, and metalwork. Other furnituremakers ran larger shops—George

Seddon employed four hundred men—but no one ran a shrewder operation.

When Chippendale's *Director* appeared, anyone in the trade could see that he had stolen his ideas from the engravers who gathered at Slaughter's. Like P. T. Barnum's genius, Chippendale's talent lay not so much in what he had to sell as in how he made the offer. No one had ever thought to publish a book like the *Director*. No one had advertised like Chippendale. Before printing a single copy of his new book, Chippendale lined up such subscribers as the Duke of Portland; the Earl of Morton; the Hon. Francis Chartres of Ampsfield and his wife, Lady Catharine; the Duke and Duchess of Norfolk; and even Lord Chesterfield himself. Three hundred others also subscribed to his new book—not only gentlemen, but also other cabinetmakers and upholsterers, joiners, carvers, booksellers, enamelers, and plasterers. Even one organ maker ordered a copy. Chippendale dedicated his book to the Duke of Northumberland, the most enthusiastic patron of them all. Before long he had a thriving business, not only as a furnituremaker but also as a decorator to the stars. He sold china, wallpaper, and bedhangings. He filled orders for carpets and feather pillows, window curtains, blinds, and tassels. Upon its publication, in May of 1754, the *Director* achieved a quick success in London. By August a copy had probably landed in Philadelphia.

Philadelphia's cabinetmakers could produce anything described in the pages of Chippendale's book. Its craftsmen were making some of the finest tables, chairs, and desks in the world. Just as the English achieved a quiet interpretation of French design, so these men developed a style that suited the city's even more conservative taste. In some ways, Philadelphia stood as far away from London as Cheshire, Connecticut. Philadelphians maintained a love affair with ball-and-claw feet, a rococo form that had passed from fashion in England twenty years earlier. Though the English by 1759 preferred chests whose drawers ran to the floor, Philadelphians were so taken with the long curving legs of their Queen Anne highboys that cabinetmakers there developed a furniture form—the rococo representation of this object—that never existed in England. Despite these odd provincial tastes, Lord Chesterfield would nevertheless have approved the lavish carving that most things made in Philadelphia displayed. These objects confirmed the city as one of the most sophisticated in the world—they helped to make Philadelphia the sort of place it wished to be. Things can create a place as much as a place creates its things.

The card table began to take its form in sketches that the carver made to scale. It was a graceful and well-proportioned design. If you knew where to look, you could see its great promise. A casual observer might have been struck, however, not by how nice the table was, but how ordinary. Its feet looked like the ball-and-claw feet on other tables of the day. The tops of the curving legs—what cabinetmakers call the "knees"—looked like the knees on other tables. In fact, much of the object's promise lay not in its design, but in subtleties that the plans did not reveal and that most people would never understand. Its beauty would lay in how its twisting vines would come to life, and also, oddly, in the empty spaces that would gape between the vines. Like all designs, this one was as interesting for its mysteries as for its revelations.

The plan for this card table was the most ambitious of the carver's life. Its execution required every skill that he had learned since he began his career, perhaps at age fourteen, as an apprentice. As a boy in his first employer's shop, he unloaded logs, sawed wood, and swept floors, and at lunch he fetched pails of beer for the older men who worked there. Somewhere along the way, he began to learn the art of carving from a master. One can tell from a carver's work whether he was born in England or America. When the labor of a carver trained in England first appears on a piece of Philadelphia furniture, it shows the evidence of someone who is already highly skilled—a man, as Alan Miller puts it, "who's got his running shoes on." The Garvan carver's work first appears on objects made in about 1750, and it reveals a young hand learning its craft.

Carvers in eighteenth-century Philadelphia generally worked as subcontractors. They took blocks of wood and the plans of others, and turned out only those portions of furniture that required their skills. The Garvan carver worked for a great many shops during the 1750s. As his technique improved, the number of his commissions rose. Perhaps he lived in a narrow house on Second Street, or perhaps in one of the tenements then springing up on the outskirts of town at the rate of one a week. Some craftsmen had as many as fourteen children. Some lived in one small house together with a second large family. Working as he must have at a small bench, amid the din of screaming children, the Garvan carver turned out some of the most exquisite furniture produced in Philadelphia. Increasingly, he devoted his efforts to the operation on Chestnut Street. Alan Miller believes that the man who owned this shop—

whose name we don't know—finally hired the Garvan carver permanently in about 1758.

The card table began its life as a wooden box that a joiner fit together without a top or bottom. The wood for Willing's table came from a single mahogany tree, which might have measured twelve feet across and which had stood for at least one hundred years in Jamaica or Cuba or Santo Domingo. To a consumer, mahogany had the advantages of a deep, rich color, the ability to keep a shine, and the expectation of long life. The carver liked this wood for other reasons. Mahogany didn't dent when a tool banged against it by accident. Mahogany was strong, held a sharp line, and its grain didn't tear away as the grains of other woods sometimes did. It gave a carver the great control necessary to reveal his beautiful forms. Most furniture was available in other, less expensive woods, but some pieces were so difficult to make, and required such perfect control, that they came only in mahogany. A turret-top card table with carved rails was one of these.

After someone drew the plans, a joiner made the box of dovetailed joints from which the rest of the table would grow. Then a boy in a leather apron sawed blocks for the legs, and blocks for the turrets, and blocks for the rails that would run like little skirts around the table's front and sides. In the hands of most people, these blocks were nothing. But if you had seen the carver's work before, it was possible to imagine that lovely images—claws and leaves and vines— waited inside the wood for him to release them; and that art, as the engraver Albrecht Dürer once observed, "lies hidden in nature."

To an eighteenth-century carver, the art that most often lay hidden in nature was, generally speaking, nature itself. The images with which he had to be familiar included not only claws, leaves, and vines, but also shells, flowers, fruit, birds, lions, and dragons. Even people were not exempt from the carver's knife: Busts of John Locke and John Milton sometimes decorated the tops of secretary-bookcases. Such images from the natural world—what would later come to epitomize rococo carving—had first appeared on Philadelphia furniture in about 1750. These images did not disturb the shapes of Queen Anne chairs or chests very much. These shapes merely got fancier.

To make a living at carving, a man needed a trick. As Alan Miller explains, "Since he has to move fast in order to make money, as any pieceworker does, he needs a way of attacking these things." All carvers evolve a vocabulary of images that belong to no one else. The images are like voices so distinctive that one carver may know another man's work from across a crowded room—just as Miller recognized the Garvan carver when he entered the office at Sotheby's. As the Garvan carver improved his skills, his vines soon began to look like no one else's. His claws became his own. "His way of doing things is constantly refined toward a particular form language—an idea of what the carving can look like," Miller says. "And his idea is a little different than everybody else's." It was like making up a world. In this carver's world, every leaf looked as if it had grown fat from summer rains and was turning to face the sun. His flowers seemed to have only just then bloomed. His shells had a kind of tension— what one observer has called "taut membranous surfaces"— that made them look astonishingly real. He also learned to carve ruffles and C-scrolls and things that resembled little jewels. Even these forms appeared to have grown from the earth. His C-scrolls looked as wet and heavy as his leaves. When one examined these images closely, each seemed to have a purpose. His world made sense.

Ten or fifteen carvers inhabited the small world of Philadelphia cabinetmaking in the late 1750s. Some of these men worked at shops on Second Street and some worked at home. Presumably they knew each other well. As the Garvan carver's skills improved, rivals began to imitate his twisting leaves and vines. Miller discovered copies of the carver's technique on things made in other shops. He even found exact reproductions of the carver's designs on work done inside his own shop. The copy "doesn't make sense," as Miller explains it. "It is not coherent. His outline is meant to have a leaf flipping one way and then starting to flip back on itself in a certain way. If a carver doesn't understand that, it occupies the same space, probably took as long to do, but it doesn't make any sense when you look at it."

The carver must have stared for some time at four small blocks of mahogany that an apprentice stacked on his workbench. Despite their seeming insignificance, these blocks held the keys to his most ambitious design. They measured an inch across and about two inches high, and they fit between the tops of the table's legs—its knees—and its carved rails. Their purpose was to help an observer make the transition between these knees, which stuck out underneath the two turreted corners, and the flatter surface of the rails. The knees must somehow join to the rails, and cabinetmakers had long since discovered that the shape that best made this transition was an S turned on its side. When the carver finished, these pieces would be called ogees for this

S-curved shape. Among the parts of a turret-top card table
to which a carver must apply his skills, no pieces are more
difficult than the ogees. Small things often have large jobs,
and it is the job of such an ogee to move in three directions
at once. An ogee must curve up and down—in what
amounts to the two directions of the S—to make the smooth
downhill transition between the knees and the rails. Because
the rails cant slightly from the table's edge, the ogee also has
to move out from the table in a third direction. If all this
were not difficult enough, vines must blow carelessly across
these little hills and dales, as if carried on a breeze.

A carver achieves his shapes by removing what he
doesn't want. In Alan Miller's world, the flat areas between
the shapes are known as the "ground." In Miller's words,
"This smooth area doesn't come easy. You've got to carve it
out and make it look like nothing's happened." It is so
difficult to achieve a smooth, flat ground that many craftsmen cover these areas with a cross-hatching. The Vaux
tables, which the Garvan carver made earlier in his career,
exhibit a liberal application of this cross-hatching—and still
they are considered so magnificent that one sits in a museum. The Vaux tables are masterful works of art. But they
are not as accomplished as Thomas Willing's table.

It took a couple of weeks for everyone involved to put
this table together. When the carver finished, he had
achieved his most ambitious design. At a distance, the table
flowed gracefully from its turrets and its knees, across the
little ogees, to the carved rail that ran along the front. Its
leaves and flowers popped out. No cross-hatching lay between them to distract from their beauty. When the table

was finished, it was probably the finest piece of furniture that had ever been made in Philadelphia.

Perhaps the table arrived at Thomas Willing's house in the autumn of 1759. In those cool evenings, ladies drifted through his parlors. Friends such as the McCalls and the Cadwaladers came frequently to savor banquets of venison, duck, and turtle. Willing's parties were so remarkable, in fact, that John Adams remembered one of them long after he left the city. On such nights as these, the light of a hundred burning candles was reflected by Willing's silver services, by his china teacups, and by the other perfect surfaces that no one seemed to notice, but whose effect, somehow, everyone admired. Now the candlelight was reflected by a beautiful new card table as well.

Willing entertained, like all good hosts, to help others forget. His home shut out the muddy and distasteful world of Philadelphia commerce. Each party shone as an exquisite moment for his guests to savor. Each soiree created a perfect world where his friends might feel suspended in time, if only for an evening, as if they had entered a stage set. Most of the things that created this world were of the latest fashion, but none was so fashionable as the mahogany card table. With his large fund of cultural capital, Willing must have understood the power that can lie in what is new. "A sense of good investment," Pierre Bourdieu wrote, "dictates a withdrawal from the outmoded."

There is something seductive about new things, which capture the spirit of the moment. New things connect us to our time. The card table held the vigor of Philadelphia in its exotic claws and vines, and helped to give its owner a sense of his place in the world. What was more, this table possessed the possibility of immortality. The art historian George Kubler once observed that "objects are portions of arrested happening." They are pieces of human energy and industry and genius frozen in time. Long after the merchant had turned to dust, and the Philadelphia he knew had faded to a distant memory, the echoes of their world would survive. These echoes lived inside the flowers and the twisting vines that came to life on Thomas Willing's card table.

Five

AT SOTHEBY'S ON MONDAY EVENING, WHILE THE COCKTAIL party swirled around Thomas Willing's card table, Bill Stahl paid his respects to a dealer named Harold Sack. Collectors stood aside when Sack entered the room, and waiters with their silver trays steered clear, but some of the bolder guests found themselves drawn in Sack's direction. To most of those at Sotheby's that evening—to anyone who knew anything about American furniture—Harold Sack was a legend. He was nearly eighty years old but he had not slowed down. His reputation, in fact, had grown over the past several years. Of the six lots of American furniture that had then sold for more than $1 million, Sack's firm had bought half of them.

There is something about Harold Sack that a cataloging of his power and his money cannot quite explain. He is tall and good-looking in a rough-edged way. He has a head full of hair that is not yet entirely gray; a gentle smile; and deep, penetrating eyes. As the result of an inner-ear ailment, he walks slowly, with a shuffle. Bill Stahl spoke warmly to him on the evening of January 28, 1991, because the two men had become good friends since Stahl's arrival at Sotheby's, and perhaps also because he considered Sack one of his most important potential customers for the Willing card table.

The firm of Israel Sack, Inc., which Harold runs with his two brothers, stands on East Fifty-seventh Street in New York City. It holds two floors of Chippendale highboys, Queen Anne tea tables, and Sheraton side chairs. People in the business tend to refer to the firm as "Sack's," and even more simply sometimes as "Sack." Though no one knows for certain the value of the firm's inventory, many people have speculated about it. More than one dealer believed the value of these goods, together with inventory warehoused in Long Island City, to be as much as $10 million. No firm is more highly regarded for its taste, scholarship, and integrity.

The antiques business is filled with fake furniture and with the charlatans who sell it. It is also full of those who deal in what are sometimes called "gray areas." These are antiques whose provenances—or histories of ownership—are likely but uncertain, or whose countries of origin are difficult to tell, and which are therefore identified with the place that will command the highest price. The Sacks do not deal in gray areas. When they sell a piece, it is always described as what they believe that thing to be, and since nobody knows better than the Sacks what a thing is, their clients have included the world's most important collectors of American furniture. The Sacks paid $12.1 million in 1989 to buy a Newport secretary-bookcase for the reclusive Fort

Worth billionaire Robert Bass. This was then a record price for any object anywhere in the world. Sacks' commission on this deal might have been as much as $1 million. As in most family businesses, the three Sack brothers have employed a division of labor, which, though not hard and fast, has served them well. Albert Sack, whose eye for lovely objects is no less highly regarded than Harold's, does much of the buying. Harold spends more of his time with the customers. The third brother, Robert, takes care of bookkeeping and administration. This division is so well known that the brothers have come to be described in an epigram: "Albert buys, Harold sells, and Robert delivers."

Bill Stahl and Harold Sack share many interests in common, among them a prestigious clientele. Harold and Albert Sack's blessing is, and always has been, essential to the sale of any masterpiece American antique at Sotheby's. Stahl had immediately telephoned them when he arrived in New York with the Willing card table in the back of his Chevy Blazer. After the brothers examined the table and stroked it and peered underneath its carved rail, Harold had concluded, much to Stahl's satisfaction, that the Willing card table was a "very, very choice example."

At the cocktail party, a pocket of empty air formed around the card table, as it will around anything worth that much money. Dealers remained at a respectful distance, drank their gins and tonic, and spoke unflatteringly about other objects that they themselves hoped to acquire. Stahl liked such ritualistic gatherings. He enjoyed the little lies. Everyone in the room that evening understood such small dissemblings, and took them as signs less of venality than of great affection for antiques. These people knew what it meant to love a thing so much you might hide your desire to get it.

As Stahl watched the crowd, he thought about a great many other objects as well. Exactly 1,213 other things intruded on his peace. Stahl wanted to sell a solid silver dressing table, with a companion mirror and upholstered stool, for $450,000. He hoped that a sword once owned by Admiral Richard Byrd might bring as much as $35,000. Chinese export armorial large plates, folk art paintings of little girls, gold-mounted inkwells, silver spoons, and mahogany bookcases all vied for his attention. History filled each object. Each one seemed to speak to Stahl. Each had its special market, its own peculiar customers. All the chattering objects at Sotheby's that evening had their own unique destinies, and Stahl, for the moment, was master of their fates.

Among the objects whose destinies lay in Stahl's hands was a group of things from the home of a well-known Americana collector. These objects stood in a partitioned alcove around the corner from the card table. Stahl had arranged them to resemble the living room in Belmont, Massachusetts, where they had sat for the past few years. They included a particularly fine Massachusetts Queen Anne highboy, which Stahl hoped might bring from $200,000 to $300,000; a rare Federal-era American mirror; and a chair that once belonged to George and Martha Washington.

The owner of these things, an engineer named Richard Rosen, milled about the cocktail party with a sense of purpose one found rare that evening. Rosen had traveled to New York to take in the action of Americana Week. He attended the opening of the Winter Antiques Show on Friday night, where he strolled more than once past Fred and

Kathy Giampietro's blue blanket chest. Painted country furniture did not appeal to him. Rosen admired the sorts of antiques that Tom Wolfe once called "all this flashy mahogany." Dealers and collectors often referred to such merchandise as "brown furniture," to distinguish it from just such colorful objects as the blanket chest. Rosen had not stopped looking at antiques after opening night. He stood in the saleroom at Christie's during its auction on Saturday morning, returned to the armory on Sunday, and went back again on Monday. Rosen was passionately—one might even say obsessively—consumed with an interest in American antiques. Nothing could make him happier than to find himself standing in the middle of a crowd, among his own fine possessions, at a cocktail party thrown by Sotheby's.

If it was possible for a human being to offer greater distraction than the thousand objects that chattered around Stahl, Rosen did it. Auctioneers generally do not encourage consignors to attend sales of their own merchandise. Sellers tend to distract buyers, who prefer to examine goods without the help of those who have become attached to their things, or who might be calculating their riches in the nuance of each critical judgment. Buyers do not normally care to see the personification of profit. The dealers at Sotheby's that Monday evening had an unwritten code about the sort of standard retail markup they found acceptable in other people's merchandise—a rule that, it is true, they didn't always follow themselves. Since they believed the estimates placed on Rosen's things to be unusually high, he irritated them. As the evening wore on, Rosen pointed out rare or significant features of the things he had to sell to the buyers who had gathered there. Stahl believed, as he later said, that Rosen "would have been better off sitting in Belmont, Massachusetts, and not hovering as much as he did."

Richard Rosen is an enormous, frank man of fifty. He weighs well over three hundred pounds. He holds doctorates in physics and applied engineering, and at the time of his sale he owned a company that was building a medical waste incinerator in Concord, New Hampshire. He likes his secretary to call him "Dr. Rosen." His self-confidence sometimes takes one's breath away. When Rosen travels to New York, he frequently stays at the Harvard Club, and often dines at a sushi bar down the street. He likes to lecture the staff—in Japanese—on such subjects as yellowfin tuna, a habit that has led to such inquiries as whether he ever fought as a sumo wrestler.

Rosen took an engineer's approach to the study and acquisition of American antiques. During the early 1970s he was involved in a number of long-term projects that produced few short-term results. His wife, Marguerite, could see that such projects frustrated him, and suggested he find a hobby that combined his love for art with his love for engineering. Rosen decided on American furniture. He began to read about antiques. He drove to local auctions. He examined objects. Before buying his first piece, Rosen spent seven years studying antiques. After he did start buying, each purchase involved hours of research. He placed every new object carefully in his home and talked about it with great enthusiasm to anyone who would listen.

A sign outside Rosen's redbrick house in Belmont tells those who visit something of its history. A farmer named Jonathan Stone erected the house in 1775. Beautiful American chests, tables, and chairs, which Rosen had collected over the course of a decade, filled the house in the fall of 1990. Richard and Marguerite arranged each room around a different period of American furniture design. Nothing rigid or orthodox characterized these arrangements. The Rosens showed an eye for good taste and a preference for comfort, and they did not hesitate to place a Chippendale chair next to a Queen Anne table so long as the two things looked good together. An exquisite blue French wallpaper covered the walls of one parlor, which Rosen referred to as the "music room." Craftsmen silkscreened this paper in about 1820. Its images included a collection of peacocks, parrots, and cranes set among exotic Japanese flora and gazing cerebrally upon a lake. A Persian carpet covered the floor of this room. A wing chair, upholstered in salmon damask, stood in one corner. The feet of a small gaming table looked like the heads of dragons.

One heard an almost tender regard when Rosen talked about the life of the man who once lived here. He'd say, "Jonathan Stone built this house in 1775, after he returned from the Battle of Lexington." He'd recall that Stone was "a Minuteman, an apple farmer, and a very important guy." Rosen knew when the Stones had erected each addition. The house inspired him to imagine their habits. He extolled the virtues of the fireplace, which he called "very large," and the architectural detail, which he called "excellent, exquisite." Rosen imagined a life lived happily. "I rather think that these people did entertain a lot," he said. Sitting in this house, among the ghosts of the past, Rosen described one of his own antiques as "the finest Federal work table built," and another as "a particularly important Chippendale mirror." Rosen's house and the things that filled it allowed him to imagine the lives of his predecessors. Thinking of the past, his face filled with emotion. In that way, he could express his feelings.

To those who do not collect—to those who have not, like Bill Stahl, "always loved things"—these passions can seem somewhat fanatic. Craftsmen in America made their furniture to last, and devotees carry a regard for such qualities as construction and authenticity to nearly bizarre lengths. Replaced parts diminish the value of American antiques to an extent that they would not begin to affect, for example, the value of French furniture. Collectors of French furniture do not care as much whether the leg of a Louis XIV chair has been replaced, in part because such chairs break easily and few have survived in their original condition. But a single replaced leg on the Thomas Willing card table would have made the difference of hundreds of thousands of dollars in its estimated selling price. For these reasons, collectors of American furniture kneel before objects with large-wattage floodlights and high-powered flashlights to examine the merchandise they intend to buy. People with expertise in other areas think Americana collectors a little odd. John Marion, who is Sotheby's chief auctioneer, once described them as "termites."

All collectors place themselves into the things they buy. Just as Thomas Willing's card table reflected his tastes, so do collections reflect the tastes of their collectors. These tastes have value. When a collection comes to market, dealers ponder its strengths and flaws. Richard Rosen's collection was thought by most dealers to reflect his engineer's background. He cared a great deal about construction. He had a fondness beyond the average Americana collector for what was rare. Dealers do not always agree about matters of beauty. Some did not like Rosen's collection, believing it "lacked soul," while others admired it. Harold Sack once said, "Rosen had very good taste."

Among the 115 objects in Richard Rosen's sale, customers in the $25,000 range could afford all but 13. These clients came frequently to auctions, and Stahl had gotten to know many of them well. The years when such people reach their forties and fifties are the years when they have what Bill Stahl refers to as "the money and the empty house." Stahl has watched dozens of collectors enter this window of collecting, spend their time in passionate search, and then pass out of it. A couple might buy actively for twenty years, showing up for auctions and attending parties and inviting Stahl to their house. And then one of them stops working, or they both stop working, and Stahl no longer sees them, and they fade from memory. This phenomenon makes it difficult for Stahl to remember where some objects are. Having bought their things, these people now want to enjoy them.

Most collectors will do anything to keep their things, but a few view their furniture the same way dealers do—less as objects in permanent residence than as capital. Some buy their things with a view to making a profit, and have no trouble selling should they need to. This was the case with Richard Rosen.

In fact, Bill Stahl had never encountered so many people who needed cash quickly. He came into the business at a time when people like Richard Rosen were busy buying, and not at a time when, as Stahl put it later, "consignors

needed the money either to pay us or other creditors." When
Stahl thought about the terrible sale in October, the Persian
Gulf War, and the consignors trying to raise cash, he remembered the months preceding this cocktail party as "a
particularly nerve-racking time." Rosen had decided to sell
his collection in the fall of 1990. Stahl had a rule, which he
found useful in normal times, against accepting merchandise
this close to a sale. But these were not normal times. "We
had to sell him," Stahl said later.

As head of the Americana Department at Sotheby's,
Bill Stahl oversees sales of all the American decorative arts.
Another man, named Leslie Keno, carries the title Director
of American Furniture, and was just as important as Stahl
to the sales coming up that week. Keno was then thirty-four
years old. He has high cheekbones and blue eyes and blond
hair, and is so striking that the editors of men's fashion
magazines sometimes ask him to model clothes. Keno grew
up in the small town of Mohawk, New York, and had spent
the days of his youth digging up shards of old pottery. By
the time he came to Sotheby's in the fall of 1979, as a student
in its training program, Keno had spent most of his young
life around antiques. Within a few short years, Keno made
himself indispensable. Like Stahl, he spent a few days each
year helping with the auctions and the rest of his time in
search of objects.

Stahl and Keno drove to Rosen's house for Thanks-
giving weekend. Right there on the Persian carpets, bent
underneath Rosen's eighteenth-century chandeliers, the two
auctioneers examined each object for consignment, read descriptions into a tape recorder, and gave directions to the
photographer they'd brought along. Collectors of Rosen's

stature require experts to drop in from time to time to appraise their things at current market values. Keno had stood on the same carpets two years earlier, examining the same objects, speaking into the same tape recorder. He recognized many of the antiques that filled the house.

Months later, Keno could remember verbatim descriptions and precise locations of two dozen things. He remembered the fine Massachusetts Queen Anne highboy that had once belonged to a family named Kittredge. He remembered an American mirror. One object he knew best was a drop-leaf sofa table that had been made in Massachusetts in about 1800. Keno knew the table so well that he referred to it as "an old friend."

A cabinetmaker had designed this table in what is known as the Federal period, to sit before a sofa in the parlor of a grand house, possibly in Salem, Massachusetts. Like the card table, it was made of mahogany, but instead of carved decoration it employed the bright satinwood inlays that characterized other objects of its day. Its legs looked like four sabers pointing to its front and back. Two drawers opened on its front, and two mock drawers decorated its back. The drawers were made of wood selected from the crotch where a tree's limb met its trunk—a material known in the trade as "flamed satinwood" that is particularly prized by some collectors.

Rosen didn't own many objects from the Federal period. He preferred things from the Queen Anne and Chippendale eras, which had preceded it. But occasionally Rosen came across something that struck him so much by its form or its uniqueness that he could not resist. The sofa table sat in the largest room of Rosen's house, an addition that

Jonathan Stone had completed in about 1790. The Federal objects that Rosen did possess fit most comfortably here. Red drapes in the Federal style framed the windows of this room, Federal china decorated the bookshelves of a mahogany secretary, and a Federal-era sofa sat against one wall. Rosen had placed arrangements of home-grown azaleas—he once won a prize for the best suburban garden in America—into two exquisite Chinese bowls. Other objects from other periods, such as the Chippendale secretary, mixed easily with the Federal things in this room. One day shortly before the sofa table was scheduled to leave his house, Rosen had reflected for a moment on what it meant to him. "I basically do not collect Federal period objects," he said. "But this object is so rare and important that we decided to buy it." Most of the things that surrounded Rosen were leaving for new and separate destinies. As he looked upon these things, he seemed a little sad at the thought of living without them. His gaze rested for a moment on the sofa table. "It is truly a wonderful object," he said.

At the cocktail party on Monday evening, the sofa table stood with the other things from Rosen's collection in an alcove around the corner from the Willing card table. Sotheby's had prepared a special catalog just for Rosen's things, and a photograph of the sofa table occupied three quarters of a page above its description. "A Very Fine and Rare Federal Satinwood Inlaid Mahogany Sofa Table," read the text. This description also included a caveat that read, "Repairs to legs and uprights."

Stahl had arranged Rosen's things together behind two

high, carpeted partition walls, as if to suggest a setting much like the one they had left. Now, however, the chairs carried little signs asking people not to sit on them. The backs of the upholstered furniture had been ripped open, in order that connoisseurs might inspect their construction. Everything possessed a little round tag that read "Sotheby's, Founded 1744" and that carried the lot number under which the item would be sold. The things from Richard Rosen's house were numbers now. The number of the sofa table was 811.

No one at the party paid much attention to lot 811, not in the way they stooped to admire the Willing card table. Although it was permissible to do so, no one stroked the sofa table's smooth top or tried to open one of its drawers. It was not, like the card table, a masterpiece. The sofa table fell into the category of things that some dealers refer to as "quality home furnishings." Collectors do not prize its period of construction so highly as the Queen Anne or Chippendale. But because of its rarity, Stahl estimated that the sofa table would bring as much as $100,000. The market for such a table consisted of other collectors like Rosen, who possess a nearly obsessive passion for things that others do not have.

At the party that evening, Rosen extolled his things to anyone who would listen. He stood among the objects that he had spent years acquiring and that until a few days earlier had been a part of his life. He explained again and again that these objects belonged to his children's trust, whose terms required him to do what he otherwise would not have dreamed of doing. Just as he might at home, he spoke of his things in glowing terms. He called a Newport table "one of the most important tables of that period." One mirror was "a really extraordinarily important object."

Harold Sack heard a great many of these descriptions himself. As soon as Sack entered the room, Rosen took him by the elbow and followed him to a table. Rosen praised a chair once owned by the Marquand family of Boston and spoke highly of the Queen Anne highboy. Harold Sack sipped from a can of Coca-Cola, nodded politely now and then, and watched the party around him. Sack had seen millions of objects in his life and heard descriptions of millions more. He had literally helped to determine what makes one piece of American furniture more beautiful than the next. Sack didn't need to hear that the sofa table with the flamed satinwood drawers was "the best American sofa table." He had owned it once himself.

Richard Rosen told him anyway. He lavished praise on the table, on the Marquand chair, on many of his things. His words came straight from the catalogs that once featured his antiques for sale. These descriptions, flat and unimaginative, gave Rosen an air of not caring much for his things—an air that seemed odd, since one knew that he loved them. Watching Rosen now, selling what had so recently been vital to his life, one felt a little sad. One wondered if there was anyone in the world to whom he could say, "I will miss them."

Six

THE MAN WHO KNOWS MORE THAN ANYONE ABOUT THE CON-
struction of Federal sofa tables is a cabinetmaker named
Allan Breed. Although his business card reads "Cabinet &
Chair Maker," the furniture that emerges from Breed's shop
in York, Maine, falls more into the category of unique historical reproductions than of kitchen cabinets. Breed has
applied his considerable skills to all periods of American
furnituremaking. He once copied the Nicholas Brown secretary, which sold at Christie's for $12.1 million (Breed
priced his version at $35,000). He has made sets of twelve
Philadelphia Chippendale chairs at $1,000 apiece. He has
produced Pilgrim-Century chests and William and Mary
tables. But Breed also specializes, particularly in what he
describes as "fancy inlaid Federal pieces" like the sofa table.

Breed is thirty-eight years old. He is a trim, fit man
with blond hair that sticks up from his head at odd angles,
like straw. He wears freshly laundered jeans splattered with
specks of paint. Breed and his partner, Art Swanson, have

built a nearly perfect cabinet shop, which affords a wide view of a rural Maine landscape. Understanding the importance of natural light, they bought six gigantic windows from a naval shipyard and designed the building around them.

While jumbled stacks of antiques in various states of restoration characterize Alan Miller's shop in Pennsylvania, new objects give Breed's shop its flavor. Amid the enormous bandsaws, drill presses, and boxes filled with sawdust stand large secretaries and chairs in the startlingly pale state of unfinished mahogany. Nobody understands better than Allan Breed the constraints that time and money placed on eighteenth-century cabinetmakers who built such things as Federal inlaid sofa tables. He has to make a living the same way those men did.

As a boy, Breed liked to remove the drawers from his grandmother's Queen Anne lowboy and to ponder the fact that they were "held by a guy when the freakin' Indians were running around." In the summers during his college years at the University of New Hampshire, he volunteered his services to the restoration department of the Boston Museum of Fine Arts. He worked with the museum's restorer, a man named Vincent Cerbone, who had trained in Italy in the early part of the twentieth century. "He knew a lot of stuff," Breed says. "I worked with him, and after the first year they hired me. I wasn't even out of college. I was *really* interested in furniture. Interested in history. They thought I was kind of a nut case."

For a while after college, Breed worked for an antiques dealer in Portsmouth, New Hampshire. He then started what his partner Art Swanson refers to as "an uncooperative co-op" of woodworkers who shared tools and space, but who had little else in common. Breed built his business by word of mouth. At first, he made only chairs. He estimates that over the years he has made more than fifty of those country chairs with the spindle backs that are commonly known as Windsors. "I got out of that business," he explains. "Everybody was doing Windsors. Pretty much anybody can make a decent Windsor. So I started doing more high-style stuff."

To earn a living making reproductions, Breed has to compete against such giants of the reproduction industry as Ethan Allen. Breed doesn't like these mass-produced copies, with their bright shiny finishes, each one exactly like the other. He harbors a special disdain for one company at the high end of this market, the firm of Kindel, Inc., of Grand Rapids, Michigan. Breed believes that by producing copies by hand, he has developed a better understanding of eighteenth-century construction methods, and that this understanding has given him a better feel for the proportions of the furniture and their weights. "That's the difference between my stuff and something you get from Kindel," Breed says. "With my chairs, all the crests won't match perfectly. They'll wobble a little. You can feel the tool marks. They're all handmade. They come out uneven. The Kindel ones are all clones. People want things not too slick."

The clients who come to Breed—those who like their things not too slick—tend to be collectors who want to fill gaps in a set of chairs, or those who desire a particularly rare form that they either cannot find or cannot afford. Breed has discovered most of the collectors with whom he deals to be exceptionally knowledgeable about such American cabinetmakers as Eliphilat Chapin, whose furniture stands alongside the work of the Garvan carver at Yale University. These collectors will ask Breed, "Can you do me a Chapin chair like the one in the Garvan collection?," a question to which Breed invariably replies in the affirmative. "They know I know," Breed says. "We're into the same thing. I'd be a collector if I could afford it."

Working under the same conditions as eighteenth-century cabinetmakers has taught Breed a lot. He has learned, for example, that carving requires window light to produce the proper shadows; not even floodlights produce shadows exact enough for his work. He once borrowed an X-ray machine from a doctor friend to examine the tenons that joined the crest rails of chairs to the side rails. Breed discovered to his surprise that even on the most beautiful Chippendale chairs, such tenons were, as he puts it, "hacked out." He had no trouble understanding why. "These guys worked fast. The stuff that didn't show could be really rough."

Breed discovered why the old cabinetmakers worked fast in the course of earning a living the same way. Examples of the learning process stand all around his shop. Observing a set of twelve Chippendale chairs, each with two ball-and-claw feet, Breed says, "The challenge with furniture is to make it so you don't go nuts. Like these feet. I did 'em as fast as I could. You don't keep a stopwatch on them, but you're looking at the clock. The first foot took an hour and a half. The second, an hour and twenty minutes. By the end, I was doing some of them in an hour. If you don't go fast, you're just completely gonna lose your shirt, which I've done plenty of times. Once you get into the groove of doing it, you learn tricks about going fast."

The construction of Federal-style furniture requires techniques very different from those necessary to make Chippendale furniture. Federal pieces employ inlays and veneering for their decoration. Breed learned about Federal-era cabinetmaking while working for Vincent Cerbone at the Boston Museum of Fine Arts. He learned how to inlay with animal glue, how to know which side of an inlay goes down and which side up, and how to soak his veneers in solution.

Breed grew so adept at the construction of Federal-style Massachusetts furniture that in 1989, the Essex Institute in Salem asked him to make more than twenty pieces of furniture for one of its historic houses. A wealthy merchant named John Gardner built this house in 1804. The institute has reproduced its interior furnishings—the curtains, the wallpaper, the furniture—to look as they might have looked when Gardner occupied the house. Breed's objects sit among legitimate antiques and are so accomplished that a casual observer who enters these rooms feels instantly transported to the most prosperous moment in Salem's history.

Salem had by 1800 grown into one of the richest cities in the world. Its natural harbor made it an international shipping center, and its captains had opened routes to Calcutta, Canton, and Sumatra. They traded American lumber for Indian cotton prints, wheat and rum for Chinese silk and opium.

They picked up ivory in Africa and bird's nests in the Philippines. People on the far side of the world thought of Salem not as a city but as a country. Rare treasures filled the shops along Essex Street and added to the mystery of a place that had once burned witches at the stake. Old black men hawked strange spices, rare shells, and satin dresses from China. At tea in Salem, one ate kumquats and Malaga grapes and Eastern preserves. Even families of modest means fed their guests on damask tablecloths and services of Canton china. "In the summer, you might meet the merchant princes of Salem dressed in Nankeen from India," wrote Caroline Howard King of her childhood there. She remembered the faded palanquin at the East India Museum and the "stately Orientals" who came and went. She remembered also "the queer spicy indescribable Eastern smell that floated out from those huge warehouses."

Riches from trade paid for huge new Salem mansions constructed in a style that had eclipsed the Georgian. The Scottish architect Robert Adam first conceived this style in England during the 1760s and 1770s. After a trip to Italy to study Roman buildings, Adam believed that designers such as Thomas Chippendale had misinterpreted the classical style. He thought that the rococo designers had evolved their lavish forms from studying architects such as Andrea Palladio who had focused on Roman exteriors. Adam concentrated instead on the interiors, leading him to evolve a more delicate style. The houses Adam designed, and the furniture he conceived in complement, emphasized lightness over structural soundness. His chairs carried such symbols of classical antiquity as urns. The backs of these chairs were of a delicate construction, often in a shield design. Adam didn't seem to care that his furniture broke easily. He cared what the objects looked like. To Adam's mind, the idea of the chair was more important than the chair itself.

Americans adopted this neoclassical style after the Revolution. Longing for symbols to dignify their new country, they appropriated the new designs with great zest, and even gave the style a name—the Federal—that seemed appropriate. Much as Thomas Willing's things had helped to create his sense of identity, so the new Federal things themselves helped to give America a sense of itself. Architects such as Samuel McIntire began to erect Federal houses in Salem in the mid-1790s. Furnituremakers there adapted the patterns of George Hepplewhite and Thomas Sheraton and other English designers to fill them. Sixty cabinetmakers lived in Salem in 1800. They shipped furniture to the southern states and the Madeiras, to the East and West Indies, and to South America. So much furniture left Salem that its chests and chairs continue to turn up in places such as Capetown, South Africa. All this activity did not make Salem's cabinetmakers rich. Shops stayed busy, but profits remained small. Just as Timothy Loomis had done in rural Connecticut a half century earlier, cabinetmakers in Salem took work as carpenters. At one time or another, every one of them made coffins. The estates of Salem cabinetmakers show most of them to have been in debt when they died. Largely, they owed each other.

Elijah and Jacob Sanderson were the city's most successful cabinetmakers. After the Revolution, the Sanderson brothers started a cooperative with the town's other cabinetmakers and its carvers, gilders, turners, and upholsterers. Their clients included virtually every wealthy merchant in town. The Sandersons made clock cases, desks, bureaus, beds, card tables, breakfast tables, and backgammon boards. Once when the brothers shipped nineteen cases of furniture to the East Indies, they listed among the items on the manifest six sofas valued at $100 each. Presumably the Sandersons made an occasional sofa table as well.

The Sandersons owned a large shop on the town's busiest street. English saws and planes and gouges hung from the shop's walls. Smells of sawdust and glue filled its rooms. Only the shapes of the unfinished furniture distinguished this shop from the sort where the Garvan carver had worked a generation earlier. Now, instead of heavy rococo forms, most of the objects there had no carving on them at all. The legs of secretaries and bookcases tapered into narrow points. Thin strands of wood shaped the backs of unfinished chairs. According to Mabel Swan and Margaret Clunie, who have each written about the Federal furniture of Salem, the Sandersons and their employees kept six workbenches busy full-time. As many as twenty dozen bureau fronts might have leaned against the walls of the shop. Eleven hundred feet of mahogany and five thousand feet of other woods lay in a shed out back. In a cabinet shop such as this, someone made Richard Rosen's inlaid sofa table.

Thomas Sheraton explained that these tables are "used before a sofa" and that "the ladies chiefly occupy them to draw, write, or read upon." They stood as high as a dinner table. Designers had not yet created the more useful form of the coffee table. Sofa tables were extremely rare in the United States. Of the few that have survived, many were made in New York City. At the turn of the nineteenth century, New York was already replacing Philadelphia as the most cosmopolitan city in the country. Not many people owned sofa tables because not many people owned sofas. Though Chippendale had included sofa designs in his *Director,* even fifty years later hardly anyone in America could afford sofas. Only about two in ten of the wealthiest families in Boston owned even one.

"A client looking for someone to make a sofa table in Salem in 1800 would go to the cabinetmaker who'd have a design book by Sheraton or Hepplewhite," Allan Breed says. "The cabinetmaker would show you examples of things. You'd say, 'I have a particular space and I want an eighty-two-inch sofa.' These houses had big rooms with sliding doors for a ballroom. They had pairs of tables between windows at either end of the long room. Maybe a prominent family brought back something from England and a local person copied it."

The satinwood drawers of the sofa table—both the real ones in the front and the mock drawers in the back—had to match perfectly, and for this reason cabinetmakers such as the Sandersons bought their woods in huge quantities. "The stuff came in green and you had to dry it," Breed says. "The log is hauled off the boat. The sawyer cuts it up into green boards. Then you stack them and dry them, with one-by-one sticks between them so the air can circulate. They're lying in a shed out back, maybe a year, two years, with a couple of crummy boards on top."

A good cabinetmaker admired satinwood because of its flaming pattern that appeared where a tree limb met its trunk. He cut it into thin veneers so he could reproduce this natural design identically on all four drawer-fronts. "He's making the patterns," Breed says. "He's figuring out how to put them together. He's doing the designs. He's talking to the customers. He's doing the PR and the design, the skill, the fun stuff. Nowadays the first thing a cabinetmaker would do is a full-scale blueprint. But paper was expensive then, and a lot of stuff was laid out right on the wood. You can see the scribe marks and compass marks. You take a piece of pine and do a rough sketch on it in pencil. The depth. The size of the drawers. Block out the panels. This would be a fairly good-sized shop. He gets a kid to start planing down a piece of mahogany. You'd need a big plank of thick stuff for the legs."

The cabinetmaker would create the top of each sofa table out of four boards that came from the same mahogany tree. He used one board for each of the leaves and two more for the main section. In Breed's words, "They were just cut up and rearranged. That way you get a good color match. These guys had good control of their wood." He made the legs of this table from the same stock of wood. After an apprentice had sawed the curving saber legs, and a man had used a lathe to turn the stretcher that ran between them, the cabinetmaker put the table together. He finished the top by using rule-joint planes to form the joints of the drop leaves.

Cutting out the grooves for the inlays and applying the satinwood presented Salem cabinetmakers with their most difficult challenges. The craftsman inscribed a band around the edge of the table's top and cut out the mahogany. He took a scraper blade to scrape thin grooves for the inlay he would apply to the legs. "He glues this stuff down with hot glue, made from hooves and hides," Breed says. "It's an all-natural Jell-O, nice and warm. If it's summer, it's okay. If it's winter, you stand it next to a stove or use an iron. If the surface is cold the glue will congeal and it won't bond. Once you get it warm, you have time to wiggle everything down in and clamp it down. Then you scrape it down with a steel scraper to the level of the tabletop." After he made the dovetailed box for the drawers to slide into, and constructed his drawers of pine, the cabinetmaker applied the flamed satinwood drawer fronts. These came in a veneer that a subcontractor had cut, as Breed puts it, "like a loaf of bread into a length called a flitch. If you open the veneer flitch like a book you get mostly grain, and when you glue it down you get mirror images on the two adjoining drawers." A cabinetmaker was then ready to sand the table with a piece of sharkskin or sandpaper, or to burnish it with a piece of pumice, and then to rub it down with wax or varnish.

The satinwood bands around the edges of the tabletops, and the strings of inlaid holly wood that ran down each leg, contrasted nicely with the dark mahogany. Only the turned stretcher that ran between the legs gave this table a slightly provincial look—a look one does not associate with more elegant sofa tables from New York. The table was beautiful, but, like most Federal furniture, it was not strong. The four saber legs, which curved to the front and back of the table, rested on brass casters that looked like lion paws. Casters of this sort had first appeared on neoclassical furniture and allowed the tables to roll easily about a room. The legs and the casters on their feet gave one a slightly uneasy feeling. "That's the weak point of any of these pieces," Breed says. "It's the only iffy construction on them. If you lean on the table, especially with the casters, you'll split the legs apart." Owing to the flaw in Robert Adam's designs, to the delicate construction, and to Adam's notion that the idea of the thing was more important than the thing itself, such tables usually did not endure the abuses of time. After two hundred years, one saw a great many Federal objects at flea markets around the country, with legs gone and pieces of wooden shields missing from their backs. Tables with saber legs fared no better. As Allen Breed says, "Sooner or later— ka-powie."

The merchant John Gardner ordered a sofa table like Rosen's. Gardner wore his hair to his shoulders and with bangs. He owned a dozen ships in partnership with his brother, Richard. One of these, the *Hazard,* then among the fastest ships in the world, had made several spectacularly profitable voyages to India. John Gardner had grown so rich by 1804, when he was thirty-three, that he decided to raze his house on Essex Street—one of Salem's major thoroughfares—and to erect another on the site. When it was finished, this dwelling was one of the grandest mansions in the country.

The furniture carver and architect Samuel McIntire designed Gardner's house. It was made of brick and stood three stories high, with a wooden railing that ran like a widow's walk around the flat top of its roof. A semicircular portico, complete with carved Corinthian columns and ironwork in gold leaf, decorated the front door of this palace. Having completed his grand new house, Gardner now needed the Federal furniture to fill it. His riches paid for chests, chairs, dining tables, beds, rugs, and looking glasses. He also bought beautiful new sofas. He would have needed tables to go with them.

Gardner's new sofa table—perhaps one of a pair—

occupied a place in his grand front parlor. This parlor ran forty feet long and sixteen feet across. Its ceilings reached fifteen feet in the air. Visitors must have stared open-mouthed at the elegance of this room. Gardner ordered its wooden wainscoting painted the color of sandstone and the walls above them a straw yellow. Brussels carpets covered the floors. One can imagine the beautiful mahogany lolling chairs with their striped covers and the wing chairs uphol-stered in the same fabric, the shield-back side chairs of which Thomas Sheraton was so fond, and the little sewing tables with their baskets hanging underneath. Now, per-haps, one could see a sofa sitting against the wall, and before it a lovely inlaid table.

Rosen's sofa table stood in a place of much distinction. It carried the approval of high fashion until that time when such things passed out of fashion, or until its owner suffered setbacks of the sort that occasion liquidation sales. Given Salem's history in the first quarter of the nineteenth century, one possibility seems as likely as the other.

After reaching the peak of its success—a success marked especially by its fine furniture—Salem began a long and steady decline. In 1807, President Jefferson imposed a trade embargo to protest British harassment of American shipping. The embargo devastated merchants like Gardner. A great many of these powerful men found their empires in ruins after the War of 1812. Salem's harbor proved too shallow for the huge ships made after the war. A good deal of moving in and out of houses occurred in Salem as great fortunes collapsed. Times changed and fashions changed, and by 1820 Federal-style furniture, which had once seemed so modern, fell from grace. Other styles replaced it, and people like Gardner put their belongings in attics or sold them at auction or simply gave them to devoted servants or to penniless cousins.

Salem's great moment remained alive in the memories of the captains who told stories in the East India Museum amid the smells of frankincense and myrrh. Those years stayed alive in the literature of Nathaniel Hawthorne, who served as the local customs agent in the late 1840s. Hawthorne knew the glories of Salem only through the stories of the mariners and in the tattered remnants of the past. By then, the prosperous Salem of 1800 had faded into a legend. In the same way that Philadelphia lived inside the vines of Thomas Willing's card table, Salem lived in the lovely inlays of the things conceived by Robert Adam—in the urns fashioned into the backs of chairs, in the flamed satinwood veneers, and also in the cracks and the repairs of a flawed concept.

No one knows what happened to the sofa table after its creation in Salem. No one can say what history it endured. This table disappeared, as many things do, into the months and years and decades. No one thought such a thing distinguished any longer. The table moved from one family to another, staying for a while and giving use, and moving on when death or dissatisfaction drove it away. It did not make its way through history without blemishes—Robert Adam had seen to that. But it survived. Though people no longer found it lovely, this object was rare. Its rarity made it special, and its special nature saved it from destruction.

Seven

IN LATE 1959 OR EARLY 1960, AN ELEVATOR CARRIED THE SOFA table to the third floor of the New York antiques firm of Israel Sack, Inc., on Fifty-seventh Street. Though Israel Sack himself had died the year before, his three sons carried on his business of selling only the finest old American furniture. An atmosphere of patience, evoked by hundreds of objects indifferent to time, filled Sack's rooms. It seemed as though some great power had denied dust entrance there. Richly glowing mahogany chairs beckoned one to sit, mirrors reflected the light from chandeliers, and fresh flowers sprung from Chinese vases. Baltimore sideboards, New York tall clocks, and Boston chairs spread throughout the cozy rooms, each thing waiting to find a new home. The wood glowed from recent polishings, and the glass gleamed from recent cleanings. No object could have found more auspicious quarters from which to launch a new career: The firm of Israel Sack remained unchallenged, as it had for nearly fifty years, at the pinnacle of American furniture dealers.

The sofa table arrived on Fifty-seventh Street without a history. The firm of Israel Sack gave it a new life. By their ownership, the Sacks bestowed dignity on it and gave it status in the marketplace. Henceforth this sofa table would carry the Sack name on its provenance. It mattered to the people who bought the table that it had passed through Sack's hands, and those who sold it would never fail to add an extra dollar to its price from the mere fact of this history.

The sofa table arrived from an unknown past only because Harold Sack could not remember where he got it. History often exists for us only when it's recorded, and though his firm generally keeps accurate records of its purchases and sales, sometimes this information gets lost. Years later, Harold could not remember much about the sofa table. "I believe it came from a dealer in Boston, probably around 1959 or early 1960," he recalled. "It would be the kind of thing we'd find in some dealer's place in Boston, or some picker would find. They'd bring it here, or they'd call us and tell us it was there and we'd go up."

Though the Sacks deal in antiques from all regions of preindustrial America, they prefer things made in New England. This preference has given them more contacts there than other firms have had, and led the pickers and the small-time dealers to their doors. By the time the sofa table came into their hands, the Sacks had accumulated a vast inventory of clients, so that whenever one died, Harold could put his hands on a collection of fresh new merchandise. Perhaps the preference for New England things owed to Harold's belief, as he once said, that "New England furniture excels in proportion," and perhaps it owed also to the fact that his father, Israel, began his career in Boston.

Israel Sack was born in 1883 to a middle-class Jewish family in the small town of Kovno, Lithuania. Kovno was then a center of fine cabinetmaking, but it happened also to be a place where Czar Nicholas II liked to round up Jewish boys to fight in the Russian army. When Sack as a teenager thought about career choices, soldiering did not come first to mind. He could imagine studying the Talmud, or perhaps conducting business with his merchant father, but he apparently concluded that neither of these occupations lay before him so long as he remained in Lithuania. Harold Sack told the story of his father's life in a book called *American Treasure Hunt*, which he wrote in 1986. The book is partly a memoir and partly the story of American furniture collecting. According to Harold, Israel Sack decided in his youth to emigrate from Lithuania. Figuring that he would benefit from having a skill, he apprenticed himself at age seventeen to a Kovno cabinetmaker. This plan met with opposition from his parents, who felt such an occupation beneath their son. But he persisted. Within two years, Sack had embarked on an odyssey to England that included a narrow escape from the czar's troops. He worked for a year with a cabinetmaker in Liverpool, dovetailing little wooden shaving mugs, and in 1903, at age twenty, he left for America.

Fortune brought Sack to the Boston cabinet shop of a Mr. Stephenson, a man who had made it his business to repair the ancient furniture of Boston Brahmins. Though the old American furniture immediately appealed to Sack, he soon discovered that his new employer's talent lay not so much in repairing antiques as in creating them. The secret to Stephenson's operation rested largely inside a room filled with ammonia fumes, in which the dealer placed new chairs and tables and desks to age them. Sack quickly learned the intricacies of making up antiques. Stephenson usually called such objects "imitations," but Sack discovered that another word sometimes used to describe the efforts of his labors was "fakes." "We'd make up such monstrosities," he remembered later. "After a while, I became his right-hand man. I was his greatest concocter. You always had to use your intelligence in that sort of work. You had to meet the questions you knew would be asked by people who'd examine your concocted furniture later."

After a few years, Sack worked out a plan to set up his own cabinet shop and have Stephenson subcontract business to him. He rented a place on Charles Street—the center of Boston's antiques trade—and began to repair the old furniture of Boston collectors. Within a short time, fixing broken legs became a sideline to a large business of dealing antiques. He preferred selling what was genuine to creating fakes, and earned the nickname "Crazy Sack" for the huge prices he paid to pickers.

By 1920, Sack owned the largest antiques shop on Charles Street. Dealers and collectors came there in such numbers, he remembered, that "it got so my place was like a beehive." Sack acquired his education in antiques from the things themselves. Most furniture is made to be taken apart and put back together again, and knowledgeable antiques dealers frequently take apart fascinating objects to learn more about them. Sack acquired an intimate knowledge of eighteenth-century construction methods. He learned to spot a replaced leg from across the room.

The more Sack studied the pieces that passed through

his hands, the more he felt that some were better than others. He knew that the price of an object depended on its rarity, for example, or on its provenance. It didn't require genius to value a chair once owned by the seventeenth-century pioneer Peregrine White more highly than an identical piece of unknown origin. But Sack began to appreciate the beauty of American objects. He believed that some things possessed stronger designs than others. When he saw a great piece, he would say, "It speaks to me."

Sack had discovered in old American furniture a connection to his new home. Objects from the past connected him to the present. "As I worked on the fine American pieces which came into the shop for repair, I became very attached to them," he once wrote. "From a cabinetmaker's standpoint they appealed to me as having stately lines and a quality for which I soon developed a sincere and deep attachment." Sack's passions began to seep out of the store on Charles Street and to spread across the country. Important collectors such as Eugene Bolles began coming to him. His passion for the material was so great, and his knowledge so vast, that the market listened to him.

Sack bought what he responded to—a "quality" inside a thing that one could spend years trying to comprehend. When he talked about "stately lines," it was difficult to know exactly what he meant. He could show a customer what he thought was a bad cabriole leg, and what was a good one, and his visitor either understood the difference and responded, or he or she did not. Some of the ways in which Sack extolled furniture fell into a category of enthusiasm that the historian Jay Cantor has described as "dealer mumbo jumbo." In Cantor's opinion, the old dealers believed the more elaborate a piece the better, or, in Cantor's words, that "carving a foot out of a solid block of wood is somehow more desirable than making the carving out of several pieces of wood." Dealers generally preferred those things made in the largest cabinet shops, out of the most expensive materials, and by the most highly trained craftsmen. It's difficult to know exactly where ideas about quality begin, or how they do, but it is not hard to know why. These ideas make one thing more expensive than the next. They create a structure for the market.

Sack sold great chests for more money than those he thought merely good. Some of the country's greatest collectors bought these things from him and kept them. Sack's taste soon became ingrained in the antiques culture. Everyone could tell the good leg from the bad one because great collectors owned only those things with great legs. Sack had shown these men and women what was right and what was wrong. The next time they saw a leg that looked like the one Sack thought great, they bought it.

Israel Sack invented the code of beauty for American furniture. His sons Harold and Albert soon began to learn it. As a boy in his father's shop, Harold Sack listened to the dealers who haggled over prices. They spoke in what he remembers as an "unintelligible private language," filled with code words, shorthand descriptions, and Yiddish. Israel Sack was a brilliant salesman. The Boston Brahmins who entered his shop to acquire his knowledge sometimes endured a sales pitch that featured his descent from a long line of rabbis—as if a thorough knowledge of Sack's heritage would build a greater trust. Harold stood on the edges of the room, listened, and learned. He poked around the furniture that filled the upstairs floors. He got to know the other dealers along Charles Street—Mr. Grossman, who amused Harold because he never moved from a chair at the front of his store; Mr. Finnerty, who handled primitive country furniture; and Mr. Stainforth, who sold antique ship models. The boy watched fistfights between a dealer named Ben Flayderman and a wholesaler named Red Jacobs, over who had the right to a particularly fine antique.

In the late 1920s, Israel Sack realized that the center of the antiques trade, like the centers of many other businesses, had moved to New York City. He opened up a store on Madison Avenue, but he could not stay inside it. Finding rare antiques thrilled him more than selling them, and kept him on the road throughout New England. He spent so much time looking for antiques that people used to say of him, "Sack has slept in more houses than Washington." In the apparent belief that prices of antiques could only go up, Sack bought and bought. He might have become rich had it not been for the stock market crash of 1929. The subsequent Depression nearly bankrupted him. In 1932, Sack liquidated "one hundred important pieces" at the American Art Galleries in New York. Few people thought that his firm would stay in business very long.

In the antiques trade, as in most businesses, buying and selling require very different talents. To buy, one must have a passion for what antiques dealers sometimes call "the material." It is difficult enough to become expert in one field—American furniture, say. Antiques dealers who sell a general line must understand not only furniture but also silver, ceramics, paintings, textiles, and glass. Experts often have the temperaments of scholars. They must spend hours researching the history, use, and methods of construction for each new object they encounter. They must love to spend hours on the road, to enjoy the endless conversations that ensue from those who might part with their things, and to cajole. They must love to buy.

Selling antiques, on the other hand, requires a head for business. One must spend one's time inside the shop and on the telephone. One must bring a dispassion to the loss of favored objects. Because of the very different natures of these two lines of work, many dealers work in partnership and enjoy the benefits of divisions of labor. As Israel Sack floundered in the early thirties, a rival New York firm named Ginsburg & Levy thrived. Its owners had been in business as long as Sack. Ginsburg and Levy ran a large shop at Sixty-eighth Street and Madison Avenue. Its elevator took customers not up, but down, through three subterranean floors filled with antiques. While Israel Sack dealt only in American objects, Ginsburg & Levy sold things from England as well.

Isaac Levy immigrated to New York in the 1870s at age four, went to work at age seven, and by the turn of the century was the foreman of a china factory. His sister's husband, John Ginsburg, had not succeeded quite so well in his own chosen line of work. Ginsburg operated a junk shop on Grand Street, among the fruit stands, the cheap butchers, and the bustle of immigrants. Ginsburg loved to buy things. But, like Israel Sack, he didn't like to sell the things he bought. Goods filled the store on Grand Street, but they never left. One day, Ginsburg ran out of money and the sheriff came to close him down. In a panic, his wife asked her brother Isaac Levy to help them out. Levy gave his brother-in-law some money. "Couple of months later, she came to see him again," Levy's son Bernard remembered years later. "The sheriff was back." Levy figured he had better unravel the mystery of the losses. He took a leave of absence from the china factory and went to see, in Bernard Levy's words, "what the hell was going on." Isaac Levy soon ran a partnership which became one of the country's most successful antiques businesses. "John would not stay in the shop—all he wanted to do was buy," Bernard Levy recalled. "My father was a businessman. He did not have the same feeling or knowledge for the material that John had. So it was a good combination."

Ginsburg and Levy paid $25 a month for rent, and within a few months of his arrival at the firm, Isaac Levy decided that they could not afford to stay there. In 1904 or 1905, Levy went to find a shop with affordable rent.

"John, I've rented a space," he told his new partner on his return. Levy explained that the new shop occupied a storefront on Fourth Avenue and Twenty-seventh Street. He also mentioned that its rent was $75 a month.

"But we can't afford $25," Ginsburg said.

Levy figured that Ginsburg's things had cost too much for the crowds on Grand Street. He gambled that the uptown crowds would buy them. "We have enough money to last three months," Levy told his partner. "We have nothing to lose."

After moving their wares, Ginsburg and Levy discovered an interesting phenomenon: People uptown wanted even nicer things than those the Grand Street immigrants could not afford. To accommodate their new clientele, the two partners began buying better goods. While the dealers on Grand Street continued selling junk, Ginsburg and Levy had to acquire a knowledge of better things and what to pay for them. "They began to learn about what they were handling," Bernard Levy remembered. "They had an interest in the material. There was something within them."

In 1916, Ginsburg and Levy left once again, for a fancier location at Forty-seventh Street and Madison Avenue. Ten years later they moved up Madison Avenue yet again, to Sixty-eighth Street. Other dealers thought them crazy because the location was far from the center of the antiques trade. Isaac Levy had observed that although the store on Forty-seventh Street might draw in thirty people on a good day, he'd make only one sale. He thought that one reason might lie in his not having enough time for any of his customers. He was right. At Sixty-eighth Street, only seven people might wander in, but Levy could sometimes make three sales. His firm became one of the leading antiques dealers in the country. Ginsburg & Levy sold English furniture, ceramics, textiles, and silver. But the firm also sold the sort of fine American antiques that Americana collectors were looking for.

While Isaac Levy plucked price tags off the Sheraton sideboards and Queen Anne tea tables that his clients had just bought, John Ginsburg roamed the countryside in search of things on which to put the tags. Traveling to small towns throughout the Northeast, Ginsburg frequently ran into Israel Sack. Fierce battles over merchandise ensued. They often met in Connecticut at the shops that lined Route 7 in Fairfield County and Litchfield County. So many antiques shops sprang up along that route that it came to be known as "Antique Alley."

Ginsburg and Sack also encountered each other in the little town of Ansonia, which lay on Route 8, not far from Antique Alley. On one side of the street there, two brothers named George and Benny Arons ran a shop out of a building with eight garage doors. On any given day their stock might include ten highboys, fifteen desks, and twenty-five sideboards, all of the sort that would each bring tens of thousands of dollars today. The Arons got $500 or $600 apiece for most of their things. Across the street from George and Benny's shop stood one owned by their Uncle Harry Arons. His merchandise cost even more than theirs.

The New York dealers spent much of their time on the telephone to Ansonia. They wanted to know what the Aronses had just bought from the house of some unsuspecting widow. If they heard of something that sounded choice, they drove up that night. Generally, they waited for Saturday. Ansonia came first on the weekend tour that took the dealers up Route 7. Sack and Ginsburg often showed up as early as eight o'clock on Saturday morning. They started with George and Benny Arons, whose prices undercut their Uncle Harry's. They hoped that Harry hadn't wandered across the street already, because if he found something rare at his nephews' shop—something he knew would please the New York dealers—he would buy it, carry it back to his own shop, and mark up the price.

Taste is a difficult thing to teach. What separates dealers along the pyramid of the antiques trade is not only the ability to distinguish forms but also the sort of feeling for the things that Israel Sack meant when he said, "It speaks to me." One might know that a bowfront chest usually brings more than a straightfront, because bowfronts are rarer forms. That's the simple law of supply and demand. But to know the truly great straightfront is something that one either has the knack for or does not. When people said of someone like Fred Giampietro, "He has a great eye," they meant he could distinguish great things. The New York dealers generally had better eyes than those in Connecticut, and Harry Arons had a better eye than his nephews.

While the firm of Ginsburg & Levy remained in good financial shape, Israel Sack found himself increasingly in debt. He paid enormous sums at auction to repurchase things he had once owned, to support the prices for his goods. In the best of times, this practice can build a dealer's reputation. But few people considered the worst depression in American history the best of times. In 1932 Sack paid $400,000 for the inventory of a Boston dealer, and in the same year he sold many of his own things. As Harold Sack has written, Israel was "reduced to struggling for each day's survival."

Harold soon discovered that his father owed large sums of money to a great many people. He owed pickers. He owed dealers. He even owed such notable collectors as Mrs. Francis Garvan, whose collection came to auction in 1931. Israel Sack naturally made an appearance at this famous sale. After having bid successfully on a number of items, carried them away, and sold them, Sack had still not paid for them. When Harold asked about these debts, his father shrugged. When Harold worked out agreements to settle the debts, his father simply nodded. This air of resignation, together with the large number of creditors, led other New York dealers to wonder how long the firm could survive.

Fortunately for Israel Sack, his sons acquired his appreciation for the beauty of American furniture. Albert exhibited a talent for buying equal to Israel's own, while Harold understood better than his father how to sell. Throughout the 1930s, Harold cultivated a number of affluent collectors such as C. K. Davis, the president of Remington Arms. Harold formed a friendship with Davis that he held so dearly, in fact, he came to describe it as "authentic," just as he might describe a particularly fine Boston tea table. Davis responded to the lines of American furniture, and Harold helped him to refine his taste. The manufacturer built an impressive collection that included an especially desirable matching Queen Anne curly walnut highboy and lowboy. The patronage of C. K. Davis, along with that of others Harold educated, helped to save the business.

Harold Sack left the business during the Second World War. He made a lot of money in the plastics industry, and after discovering that his father's shop was losing money again, he returned to help. To the end of his life, Israel pretended to deal antiques. He lived alone in a room at the back of the shop and ate from cans that he warmed on a hot plate. One would have had trouble seeing, in this tired and frustrated man, the person who made our taste for American furniture. He died in 1959 at age seventy-six.

Rosen's sofa table arrived at Sack's a year later. This object had led a rather mysterious life. It stood in a great house in Salem, and then disappeared for many years. But a thing with good character generally survives longer than one without, and this table was such a fine piece of furniture that it seemed almost fated to pass through the Sacks' hands. It must also have been lucky to have lived so long a life.

Perhaps Albert inspected the table at a dealer's shop in Boston. Perhaps someone brought it to New York. Everything about this object—from its elegance to its rarity to its condition—assured Sack's interest in it. The firm of Israel Sack, Inc., bought the table. Harold placed it on a floor of the Fifty-seventh Street shop and waited for someone to walk in the door.

Eight

OVER THE YEARS, HAROLD SACK HAD OBSERVED THE HABITS OF
many American furniture collectors. Some of them ago-
nized over every acquisition. Some took things away on
approval and brought them back, while others returned day
after day to gaze at an object and to question him about it.
Sack encountered those with no money who pretended to
have a lot, and those with a lot of money who pretended to
have none. He dealt with the greatest collectors of his era.
Among all of Harold Sack's clients, however, one stood out.
No one bought antiques quite the way Joseph Hirshhorn
bought them.

Hirshhorn stood five feet, three inches tall and bore a
remarkable resemblance to the comedian Jimmy Durante.
Hirshhorn made one fortune trading stocks in New York
and another fortune discovering uranium in Canada. He
also amassed one of the greatest collections of contemporary
art in the country. By 1961, many people knew Hirshhorn as
a patron of the arts, but Harold Sack knew him as a col-

lector of American furniture. When the elevator door opened onto Sack's second-floor showroom and Hirshhorn stepped out, the collector invariably yelled across the room, "Hi, Schack!" It didn't seem to matter whether other customers milled around the shop or not. As Sack recalls, "He'd come in with his curator, who always accompanied him, and he'd go around and he'd say, 'How much is this? How much is this? How much is this? How much is that?' And we'd tell him, and he'd say, 'Well, how much for the whole lot?' I never held anything for him because he made up his mind that second."

Hirshhorn first bought American antique furniture from Israel Sack in the 1940s, while Harold was managing the Universal Plastics plant in New Jersey. Joe and Israel became great friends. They were small and intense men, both Jewish, who had immigrated to this country from the same part of the world. They shared a fondness for practical jokes of the kind in which a man might enjoy setting fire to the newspaper of an unsuspecting reader, or punching holes through the crowns of people's hats and then tossing them out the window. Despite the hard times created by the Depression, Sack managed to retain his reputation as the best dealer of American furniture in the country. Hirshhorn read the Parke-Bernet auction catalogs, marked them up, and employed his friend Israel as an agent for him. "His tastes mostly ran to New England, like ours chiefly does," Harold Sack once said.

Hirshhorn came to this country at age two. By the time he was twelve, he had a steady job with a Brooklyn jeweler. From there, his ambition took him to Wall Street, where he learned to buy and sell stocks. According to his biographer,

Barry Hyams, from the time Hirshhorn started trading at age seventeen, it took him ten months to earn a cash profit of $167,000. He married the first of many wives shortly after that. By 1926, at age twenty-six, Hirshhorn was rich enough to buy a house in Great Neck, Long Island, and staff it with a butler, a cook, two maids, and a chauffeur. In August 1929, on the advice of a friend, he cashed out his stock portfolio for $4 million. The market crashed two months later.

At work, Hirshhorn sat behind an enormous desk piled high with papers, stock quotes, memorandums, magazines, newspapers, and bottles of water. He occasionally held a telephone to each ear and shouted buy and sell orders to his associates while a manicurist worked on his nails, a barber cut his hair, and a waiter from the Savarin restaurant served him lunch. He smoked thirty-five Corona Belvedere cigars each day. Hirshhorn learned to dance a vaudeville routine known as the buck and wing, which he often performed in the middle of board meetings. Sometimes he sang, too. He bought a Pennsylvania mountaintop, named it Huckleberry Hill, and planned to erect a turreted French Provincial mansion with a handball court, a swimming hole, and guest rooms for sixteen. He grew so excited marching across this landscape with the engineers he'd hired to create his fantasy that he began to dance the buck and wing and burst into a rendition of "You Made Me Love You."

Hirshhorn lost much of his fortune from speculation during the Depression, and looked for a way to replenish his wealth. He grew interested in mining after a trip to Canada in 1933. Hirshhorn set up business in Toronto, a place then inhospitable to the presence of foreigners with his particular background and habits. He later claimed that each of the city's park benches held little signs that read "No Dogs and Jews Allowed." He recalled that when he phoned the brokers on the Toronto Stock Exchange to ask why they failed to place his orders, the brokers explained themselves with sentences that began with clauses like "Listen, you goddamn New York Jew bastard ..." Hirshhorn persisted with his business activities nevertheless, and eventually discovered the largest deposit of uranium on the continent of North America. By 1960, when he sold the last of his stock in the uranium mines, he had amassed nearly $100 million in cash.

Shortly after Hirshhorn made his first large profit, in 1917, he ordered two suits, some nice shirts, a pair of cuff links, and a Dobbs hat. He felt, as he later said, that "I became a gentleman." After buying two engravings by the sixteenth-century German artist Albrecht Dürer, he also became an art collector. Hirshhorn taught himself from books. When he bought the mansion in Great Neck, he filled it with the opulent Edwardian furniture, silver, and china then popular among the *nouveau riche.* "Soon thereafter, Hirshhorn became aware that old did not necessarily mean poor," Barry Hyams has written. "He discovered that with antiques, age increased their value." Hirshhorn bought vintage cars after coming to understand the depreciation to which a new Cadillac was subject upon leaving the showroom floor. By the late 1930s, antiques had replaced his imitation English furniture.

Americans began to show an interest in the artifacts of their history at about the turn of the twentieth century, probably because they only recently had much of a history in which to show an interest. This country was still very young. A few old men and old women still alive in 1900 had known some aging heroes of the Revolution. Collectors of American antiques tended to be doctors and lawyers who loved to find a chair that once belonged to George Washington, or the table on which Thomas Jefferson had drafted the Declaration of Independence.

Old furniture grew more desirable following the first major exhibition of American antiques in 1909, during New York's Hudson-Fulton Celebration. This extravaganza commemorated the three-hundredth anniversary of Hudson's navigation of the river he named, as well as the hundredth anniversary of Robert Fulton's first steam navigation. Henry Watson Kent, the secretary of the Metropolitan Museum of Art in New York City, suggested an exhibit of old American furniture. This notion perplexed most people. Before then, most Americans had thought of old American things as junk. The Metropolitan did not own a single piece of American furniture. By organizing the products of American craftsmen in a coherent and interesting manner, the Hudson-Fulton Celebration gave many Americans their first appreciation of American antiques. Just after the exhibition closed, the Met bought the collection of a man named Eugene Bolles.

Over a magnum of champagne at lunch in Boston, Kent handed Bolles a check for his antiques. The two men then discussed plans for a club to organize serious collectors of American furniture. They named it after the famous eighteenth-century English writer and collector Horace Walpole. The Walpole Society soon became the most prestigious club to which a collector of American furniture might belong. Many of these early collectors viewed antiques as a way to connect to a class of people whose families had passed down their heirlooms since arriving on the *Mayflower*.

The most interesting member of the Walpole Society was Richard Canfield, who once noted his occupation on a customs declaration as "Gentleman." In Elizabeth Stillinger's book on the first Americana collectors, no one emerges more vividly than Canfield. He ran elegant gambling houses in Providence, Rhode Island, and Saratoga Springs, New York. During a stint in jail in 1885—for operating a faro house—Canfield studied history, literature, and art. "Jail," he later said, "was my Harvard." Canfield's gambling houses were among the most exclusive in the country. Evening dress was required at the establishment in Saratoga, where Canfield employed a French chef who spent his off-season—about nine months of the year—touring Europe to find new recipes. James McNeill Whistler, who painted Canfield's portrait, called Canfield "His Reverence" and declared him to be "the best known and wealthiest individual gambler in the world." Canfield amassed a fine collection of English and American Chippendale furniture.

During the 1920s, men such as Henry Ford, Francis Garvan, and Henry Francis du Pont began to collect antiques in great quantities. All of them patronized Israel Sack. Sack met Henry Ford in 1923, after Ford acquired an inn in Sudbury, Massachusetts, that Longfellow had memorialized in his poem *Tales of a Wayside Inn*. Returning to his shop on Charles Street one day, Sack encountered a stranger who had been waiting for quite some time. "I'm Henry Ford," the man said. "I just bought the Wayside Inn."

"The whole country knows you purchased the Wayside Inn," replied Sack.

Over lunch, Ford asked how he should furnish the historic property. Sack told him to buy the best. "Go ahead," said Henry Ford, and Sack filled the inn with antiques.

In the twenties, Ford conceived the idea for a museum in Dearborn, Michigan. He wanted something close to the center of his automobile empire that would re-create the lives of American pioneers. At about the same time, John D. Rockefeller, Jr., decided to restore the colonial capital of Williamsburg, Virginia. These projects required enormous quantities of antiques, which Sack's, as well as Ginsburg & Levy, happily supplied. Henry Ford came often into the Ginsburg & Levy shop on Madison Avenue. He habitually walked through the three cavernous floors of antique furniture, pointing out what he wanted, while Isaac Levy followed behind, tugging off the price tags. Frequently Levy had pulled off forty or fifty tags by the time Ford had finished. Every December, the automobile manufacturer sent Levy a list of people to whom he wished to give Christmas presents, along with a check for $50,000 and instructions to "pick out gifts for these people."

Competition between the great collectors grew fierce. They fought with each other in shops and bid each other up at auction. This frenzy culminated in 1929, when Henry Francis du Pont bought a Philadelphia Chippendale highboy at auction, after a bidding war with William Randolph Hearst, for the staggering sum of $44,000. Prices did not again reach such levels until after the war, when men like Joe Hirshhorn began to spend new fortunes.

Like the gambler Richard Canfield, Hirshhorn collected art and antiques not to connect to a simpler past, but to secure his place in the present. Early in his career, such paintings as Bouguereau's *Madonna of the Lilies* had attracted him. "How does a nice Jewish man like you come to have this kind of art?" asked one of his Jewish painter friends. Hirshhorn began discarding paintings of the Crucifixion in favor of paintings by American social realists such as Jack Levine. It didn't seem to bother him that these painters were busy depicting the plight of people oppressed by men like himself.

Hirshhorn applied himself seriously to the study of art. He questioned artists, dealers, critics, and museum curators. As he taught himself, his passions for art became apparent to everyone who encountered him. After acquiring one painting at Parke-Bernet, he yelled at the top of his voice, "My name is O'Brien! I'm just a poor ballplayer out of left field from Yonkers!" He frequently left in the middle of board meetings to prowl around the lofts of undiscovered artists. After a sandwich at a Horn & Hardart Automat, he'd breeze through midtown galleries. Hirshhorn talked as Israel Sack did about certain pictures "speaking to me." He made instant decisions. "If you've got to look at a picture a dozen times before you make up your mind," he once said, "there's something wrong with you or the picture. You've got to buy what you believe in."

In 1961, following a divorce that came in the middle of a long series of such legal transactions, Hirshhorn bought an estate in the Round Hill section of Greenwich, Connecticut.

A Tudor-style mansion stood on the estate's twenty-two acres. The enclave included a tennis court, a swimming pool, a gardener's house, and a five-car garage. Hirshhorn had no trouble finding things to place on the walls of his mansion, but he found that he did not have nearly enough furniture to fill the massive spaces between them. He decided to go shopping at Sack's.

Antiques thrilled Hirshhorn somewhat less than the pleasures of uranium mining and the abstract expressionism of Willem de Kooning. No one considered Hirshhorn a great collector of American furniture. He did not care about the historical associations that give some owners of antiques their greatest pleasure. In Harold Sack's words, "Joe's collection of American furniture was to use and live with and love in his home. And that was it. If it was pleasant and it fit, he'd buy it."

Sack sold Hirshhorn a great many beautiful objects over the years. These included a Massachusetts Queen Anne highboy and matching lowboy, and a Simon Willard clock that he prized over all else. Before he mentioned the word "divorce" around his wife of the moment, Hirshhorn called Harold Sack. "Schack," he'd say, "come get the clock." Sack stored the clock until all legal claims were settled, and delivered it back when asked.

"He had a very fast taste," Sack recalls. "A very interesting taste. I think that what appealed to him was the simple elegance of American furniture, the clean line and proportion. He didn't respond to a lot of ostentation. That's the forte of American furniture—good form and proportion, simple elegance. Joe's interest in American furniture was completely instinctive and aesthetic. He knew what he liked. It didn't take him a second. He wasn't interested in construction or authenticity. He assumed that wherever he was going he could rely on them."

Like Henry Ford, Hirshhorn often acquired forty or fifty things at once. After he had made his selections and breezed out of the showrooms, Sack supervised the packing of these new acquisitions and followed the truck out to Round Hill. "What astonished me was the rapidity of his selecting something," Sack says. "And then what astonished me more was that everything had a place. I could never get over the fact that everything was placed when we got there, just perfectly."

As soon as he began buying furniture to fill up his house, Hirshhorn invited Harold Sack to spend the night. Sack discovered that the only other guest invited for cocktails that evening was the chief of the Greenwich Police Department. "He invited me up there to meet the police chief because he was showing me off," Sack remembers. "He wanted to make sure his house was protected. He said, 'This is Harold Sack,' and he'd say, 'Tell him how much that's worth, Harold. Tell him how much this is worth.' He was rather crude about the whole thing."

Sack and Hirshhorn became good friends and Sack often spent the weekend at the Greenwich house. While the antiques dealer found great beauty in the magnolia and forsythia blossoms, the trim hedges, and the lawn filled with sculpture, he described the interior of the mansion as "a craphouse." Sack was not referring to the art on the walls or to the lovely American furniture that he himself supplied, but to the papers, cups, bottles, clothes, and trash strewn everywhere, and to the paintings stored in the closets in such quantities, he remembered, that "You'd open the door and they'd practically fall on your face."

One day, possibly in the fall of 1961, Hirshhorn appeared at Sack's store on Fifty-seventh Street. "Hi, Schack!" he said. He was looking for furniture and knew what he wanted. As Hirshhorn roamed the floors, one item caught his eye among a group of Massachusetts Federal-style furniture. He stopped for a moment, glanced at the object, asked its price, and moved on. It was the Federal inlaid satinwood sofa table that Albert Sack had bought one year earlier. When he finished examining the hundreds of items in Sack's inventory, Hirshhorn ticked off a list of thirty-five or forty pieces he wanted. The sofa table was among them.

A truck delivered the sofa table up Hirshhorn's long driveway. The collector placed it behind his couch, and astonished Sack because it fit so perfectly. The sofa table was a rare and important object, as Harold Sack might have pointed out to Joe Hirshhorn if he had cared to know. But Hirshhorn did not. As Sack has said, "Joe's approach to the sofa table would have been, 'Well, that's an interesting sofa table and I can use it behind the sofa.' He would not approach it from, 'Well, American sofa tables are extremely rare.' There was a sofa table. It was American. He needed a table. In his mind's eye, he knew exactly where he was going to place it behind which sofa in which room."

Hirshhorn kept the sofa table until he died in 1981. He'd gotten rich and famous, and he lived an opulent life, but he never found the acceptance in the world that mattered to him. Many of the artists whose work he bought despised him for haggling over prices. Art and antiques led Hirshhorn into the homes of Wall Street financiers such as

Robert Lehman, who inhabited a world to which he always wanted to belong. When the industrialist Norton Simon acquired Rembrandt's *Titus* for $2.5 million, he gave a $40 reproduction of the painting to his friend Hirshhorn. This gesture so moved Hirshhorn that he hung the reproduction over his fireplace in Greenwich, next to genuine paintings by Picasso, Bellows, and Eakins.

People with old money thought Hirshhorn a vulgar *nouveau riche*. Those with no money found him just as strange. He couldn't understand that the people of rural Pennsylvania didn't want him on Huckleberry Hill, the estate where he had built his turreted French provincial mansion. He claimed the local inhabitants called him "the only Jew in captivity," and "the only one around for twenty-five miles." Hirshhorn believed that art could make the difference. "I tried everything," he once said. "I gave Guernsey calves to the agriculture clubs. I gave paintings to all the churches. But I couldn't reach them." Hirshhorn sold Huckleberry Hill in 1947, after local inhabitants sawed down two enormous trees that guarded his driveway.

A museum bearing Hirshhorn's name and filled with his collection of masterpiece paintings now overlooks the mall in Washington, D.C. Choices made in an instant decorate the walls of this space. Although art could not give him respect while he lived, it could give him immortality. Hirshhorn had asked questions and read books and done the hard work necessary to build a great collection of modern art. He didn't care so much about his antiques. He'd bought them just as impulsively, but with different results. His antiques are not masterpieces because he didn't care.

The sofa table didn't speak of his passions. He filled his

home with Queen Anne tables and Chippendale chairs, and when he bought a New England Federal sofa, he found he needed a table to sit behind it. Eighteenth-century sofas are rare, and the tables to go with them are even rarer. Imagining the sofa table in Hirshhorn's house, one could see that it had survived not because it was beautiful, but because it was unique. It survived because a man with a lot of money had a very special need.

Nine

JOSEPH PARI INHABITED THE WORLD OF AMERICAN ANTIQUES, but his precise occupation depended on whom one asked. In 1953, just as now, Pari lived in Hamden, Connecticut. While those pickers who stopped by his house knew Pari as a dealer, those dealers who stopped by knew him as a picker. For more than a decade, he had made the rounds of little towns around Hamden, knocking on doors, looking for things. When he found a nice antique, he brought it home, a place that stood on the regular route of dealers higher on the pyramid than he. Sometimes he sold his acquisitions quickly. Sometimes they lingered in his house, as such things will, for weeks or months or even years.

Pari stands about five feet, ten inches tall. He has a raspy voice and wears large square-framed eyeglasses. The voice undoubtedly owes some of its quality to the years since 1953 that Pari has spent as an auctioneer. He runs a small auction business from a structure built of concrete blocks that sits behind his house. This building is intended to resemble an old country barn. Watching Pari from across the room, as he conducts a sale in his blue blazer and gray slacks, one has trouble distinguishing him from a slimmer Merv Griffin. On auction nights, millworkers in their sneakers and housewives in print cotton dresses and secretaries who favor earrings in the shape of hearts fill this barn. A hundred signs on the walls tell these earnest clients where to stand and what not to touch, warn them of state smoking laws, and admonish them about where not to eat and drink. Pari has combined his affection for signs with his affection for antiques in the form of quotations grown dusty from age. "Any man can work and accumulate money," reads one, "but where is the man with another string of Persian enamel beads such as these?—George Dexter."

Pari doesn't sell Persian enamel beads. Men and women usually come to buy sets of china for $10 and paper cutters for $15, to acquire bargain boxes of tools, old motors, and Depression glass. For $25, a couple in need of a sofa can have one that purports to have been made in 1830. In case there is a mistake in identifying the date on such an object, one sign on Pari's walls states his "Conditions for Sale." Rule No. 4 reads, "The auctioneer will not be responsible for the correctness of the description, authenticity, genuineness, or any defect or fault in or concerning any article, and makes no warranty whatever, but will sell each lot exactly as it is, without recourse."

Rule No. 4 has surely held significance for Pari throughout the years, but it's possible that in 1953—when he was just starting in the antiques business—it stood somewhat farther down his list of commandments. Back then, real antiques filled the attics in the towns where Pari did his

picking. He could afford to buy them. Painted country furniture looked especially nice in the shops of antiques dealers
to whom Pari often sold. Other things that looked nice in
these shops included cigar store Indians, quilts, needlework,
schoolroom maps, and paintings by itinerant artists untrained in the techniques of the academies.

One day in 1953, while making his rounds of the towns
around Hamden, Pari discovered the blue blanket chest.
Pari does not remember anything about how he found the
chest, or where, or what he paid for it. Perhaps he stopped
at a tumbledown farmhouse. Such houses frequently held
examples of Queen Anne country furniture, which could
often be had for very little money. Elegant formal furniture
from the eighteenth century had reached such high prices by
then that many New England farmwomen could tell the
value of these antiques within $50. But most people failed to
distinguish rough country furniture from junk. A man like
Joe Pari couldn't make a very large percentage on a Newport lowboy—when he could find one—but he could make
a substantial profit on old painted tables, chests, and chairs.

Pari might have walked up the steps to this house and
knocked on the door. He did a lot of door-knocking in those
days. Perhaps a farmwoman laid down her housework,
turned, and saw this strange man standing on her porch.
"Do you have any junk?" he would sometimes inquire in
such circumstances. The woman probably hesitated. She
thought perhaps she might make a little money off this
harmless-looking man, and invited him in. Walking
through her house, Pari entered the bedroom, where he
might have seen the blue blanket chest and drawers. Pari

may not have stood high on the ladder of antiques dealers, but he knew a beautiful piece of Queen Anne furniture when he saw it. "What would you take for that piece of junk?" he may have asked her casually.

For two hundred years, the various owners of this chest had esteemed it for its usefulness to store linens, underwear, and pairs of socks. Its meaning hadn't changed much over the years. The blue blanket chest stood in a bedroom somewhere, among assorted other furniture. An eighteenth-century ladder-back chair might have stood nearby. Perhaps an Empire sideboard, a porcelain-topped table bought in the thirties, and a set of new chrome kitchen furniture inhabited the house as well. The chest sat in a context that was full, as the historian William Hosley has said, "of the historical resonant power of the objects." When an object moves into a new house, it makes a place with other things around it. It sits for years in the same spot, considered in the same way by its owners, and then suddenly something happens. In the lives of most things, important changes do not come frequently, but when they do come they can come quickly.

Now suddenly someone wanted to give the blue blanket chest a new life, full of new meanings and contexts. Joe Pari understood the utility of such an object, but that wasn't what interested him. What the farmwife had viewed simply as old, collectors in more sophisticated places had begun to appreciate for precisely the same reason. They wanted the chest because they'd learned to appreciate the spirit of its long passage through history. Survival can be just as attractive in things as it is in people. A picker could make money finding such things, and Joe Pari spent his days trying to do just that. Money brought the blue blanket chest out of its house, out of its historical context, and soon would give it a new job.

Americans had begun to appreciate their own folk art after Picasso and Braque pointed out the beauty in African tribal art. In 1914, the photographer Alfred Stieglitz placed African art in his Manhattan gallery. Soon people began to see the value of objects made by untrained artists in this country. Electra Havemeyer Webb filled her house in Vermont with hooked rugs, cigar store Indians, hand-painted wallpaper, and carved eagles. Her mother, Louisine Havemeyer, did not approve. Louisine was a friend of Mary Cassatt and a collector not only of Impressionist art but also of old masters. She gasped the first time she visited her daughter's house in Shelburne. "How can *you*, Electra," Louisine is once said to have asked, "*you* who have been brought up with Rembrandts and Manets, live with such American trash?"

Abby Aldrich Rockefeller's husband, John D. Rockefeller, Jr., exhibited no more sympathy for his wife's artistic inclinations. He so detested her contemporary art that he forced her to hang her Picassos and her Georgia O'Keeffes in a gallery on the top floor of their nine-story Manhattan town house. Rockefeller puzzled even more over her folk art, which Abby collected in New England and eventually donated to one of the museums at Colonial Williamsburg.

Objects painted with figures or geometric patterns had at least begun their lives as a kind of art. But by the 1950s, people began to see sculptural qualities even in such things as the blue blanket chest, which had probably been painted with a common house brush. People saw abstract qualities to some Queen Anne furniture. In the way we often bring meanings to things that their creators never intended, these people turned objects of utility into art.

A dealer from Brentwood, New Hampshire, named Roger Bacon helped Americans appreciate old painted surfaces. Bacon sold fine antiques to such collectors as Henry Francis du Pont, but he exerted his greatest influence over dealers of American country furniture. Bacon refused to refinish anything. He loved what he called a "crusty" thing. When he saw a thing with "good surface," he'd say, "It's right as rain." Bacon developed a following—something like a cult—of dealers who saw the tragedy of refinishing. Once one took the paint off the blue blanket chest, and sanded it down, and sharpened its edges, it would be difficult to tell from a thousand reproductions. The nice proportions would still be there, but much of what gave the chest its beauty lay in the evidence of its travels through the years. Once that evidence had vanished, its history would disappear.

Although Joe Pari believes he did not have the blue blanket chest long, his wife recalls that they had it "for at least ten years." Perhaps Joe Pari had intended to sell the chest but couldn't find a buyer. Perhaps his wife grew so fond of it that she refused to let it go. Neither of them remembers. The chest came into the house not as a member of the family, but as an object to be sold to the highest bidder.

By 1963, Pari had owned the blanket chest for nearly a decade. It is in the nature of things to stay put. They move when we will them to move—when they no longer serve our needs, or when they will serve someone else's needs better, or when the forces of money are brought to bear on them. When these forces are absent, objects that we once saw as temporary residents begin to belong. The Paris kept the chest in their bedroom and filled it with their things and thought about it as a nice antique as well as a useful piece of furniture. The blanket chest had a new life. It was not a piece of junk any longer. It was valued for the shiny surface that had mellowed through the years, for the worn spots, and for the places where fingers had dug, and occasionally it was also valued for its ability to recall another time and another way of being.

One day in 1963, shortly after the Paris had given birth to a daughter, Howard K. Richmond stopped by their house. Richmond sold antiques from his own house in Westport, Connecticut, where he lived with his wife, Priscilla, and their children. As a man who made his living selling old things, Richmond combed the landscape in his station wagon. He made a particular point of stopping at Joe Pari's house. The hierarchy of dealers is organized like a pyramid, with those possessing the most experience, knowledge, and intelligence at the top. Richmond knew people that Joe Pari didn't know—people who stood farther up the pyramid, people who could pay more for one antique than Pari earned in a month. An antique travels upward along the pyramid until it arrives at a place that people in the trade like to call its "appropriate level"—a place where a thing can sell for its highest price. Richmond spent his days sending things up.

Though new to the business of trading antiques, Richmond recognized a great object when he saw one. In the ten years since Joe Pari had bought the blue blanket chest, the market for rough country furniture had changed. Prices for beautiful untouched antiques had risen considerably. Richmond was a disciple of Roger Bacon, but he wasn't alone. Money drew great antiques out of the attics and barns of hapless farmers, and it also drew antiques out of the bedrooms of picker-dealers such as Pari. By 1963, a man such as Howard Richmond didn't often come across things as great as the blanket chest. It struck him by its rarity and its original blue paint and by the absence of the drawer pulls that cluttered many such objects.

Howard Richmond is dead now. From photographs, he appears to have been a pleasant, energetic man. A look of comfortable success filled his face. He was nearly bald and he wore a rakish little mustache. He favored suspenders with his pleated suit pants and crisp, plaid ties. He had been the first art director for *Life* magazine, and he had decorated windows at Bloomingdale's and Saks Fifth Avenue, but he had always dreamed of dealing antiques. Finally, in 1957, he was able to leave New York for good, and he opened up an antiques shop in Westport. Like Albert Sack and John Ginsburg and all the other dealers, Richmond made the rounds. He cruised State Street in New Haven. He stopped in Ansonia to poke around the shops run by the Arons family, and watched one day as Harry Arons's lame nephew, Benny, stepped in the middle of a Chippendale mirror and broke its original glass. He sold things to dealers higher up the ladder, to famous dealers such as Florene Maine, who owned a shop in Ridgefield, Connecticut.

Joe Pari's house stood on Richmond's regular route. Richmond might have paid $600 or $700 to take the blanket chest away. Like most good dealers, Richmond had a fondness for the things he sold, but this object felt different to him somehow. When he got the blanket chest home, Richmond thought it might make a nice permanent addition to the household furniture.

"I would love to keep it," he told his wife.

"We are in the business," Priscilla replied. "It's a good piece. Put a good price on it."

The price Richmond settled on—perhaps $700 or $800—was apparently good enough. Despite his connections, the blue blanket chest failed to sell. In 1965, when they moved to a farmhouse in Southbury, the Richmonds took the chest with them.

Priscilla Richmond still lives there. It's an unusually large farmhouse with unusually large windows for a place built in 1713. Fresh green paint covers its clapboards, and a redbrick chimney sticks out the top. A red schoolhouse, moved onto the property in 1840, stands next door. Richmond tried to keep an open shop inside the red schoolhouse, but he didn't have much patience for the public. One day he heard the shop's bell ring once too often. After running across the lawn in the rain, he found a customer who said, "I don't like antiques. My husband tells me I have to be out of the house three hours a day." With that, Richmond decided never to deal with the public again. He closed the shop, and from then on did business only with the dealers and collectors who knew where he was and who felt like part of his family.

The house filled up with things for sale and things Richmond wanted to keep. Frequently this distinction proved meaningless. Pilgrim chairs with worn armrests, early lighting devices, weathervanes, dainty chests, buckets, and hooked rugs were mixed among telephones and Zenith television sets. Richmond devoted one room to Queen Anne furniture and another to Pilgrim-Century. The blue blanket chest sat beside the door where kids, cats, dealers, pickers, and collectors wandered in and out.

In the summer of 1965, a few months after the Richmonds moved in, a picker-dealer named Skip Carpenter stopped by to inspect the merchandise. Besides selling old furniture, Carpenter supplemented his income by restoring old books. A family of rare-book dealers near Poughkeepsie often required his talents. As soon as the Richmonds moved into their house on Route 4, their shop became a regular stop on Carpenter's journey to Poughkeepsie from his home in Shrewsbury. "My way of dealing was to make a circle of all the dealers and pickers," Carpenter recalls. "I didn't deal with the public. Couldn't stand 'em."

Carpenter generally had a client in mind when he bought a piece of antique furniture, but some things appealed to him so much that he bought them without thinking. Like Howard Richmond, he fell in love with the chest the moment he saw it. He bought it on the spot, possibly for about $1,000, put it in his car, and drove it home. He didn't know how he would sell it, or when, or even if.

Ten

THE DAY AFTER SKIP CARPENTER ARRIVED HOME WITH THE BLUE
blanket chest, a folk-art dealer named Bill Samaha stopped
by his house. This visit did not surprise Carpenter. Samaha
held a position in the antiques world known as a "runner"—a position that stands just above the level of picker.
His visits to Shrewsbury had grown frequent enough that
Carpenter felt comfortable calling him "Sam." Carpenter
was known among runners like Samaha to have a good eye,
and his inventory frequently included choice examples of
New England country furniture. Some objects remain in a
dealer's inventory for years. Occasionally, though, moments
come in the lives of things when they change hands very
quickly. Carpenter had placed the blanket chest in his house
and told himself that he might own it for a long time. "Sam
came by the next day," Carpenter recalled years later. "He
saw the chest and he said, 'How much?' "

Bill Samaha was thirty-five years old. He had served
with the Marines in Korea until he was wounded at Inchon,

and he earned a bachelor's degree in business. In 1960, he moved to Cambridge, where he found a job at the Harvard Coop. In his spare time, he started working as a runner. Samaha performed all the duties of a picker with one notable exception. Unlike a picker, a runner never knocks on doors. Samaha bought his goods from pickers and traded them further up the pyramid. He was not new to the antiques business. His parents, George and Mildred Samaha, dealt antiques in Ohio, and had gained such fame that Bill found his good name as much a hindrance to his career as a help. In the hierarchy of dealers, those farther up move goods for higher prices, and some people believed that Bill traded on his parents' reputation to get more for some things than his position should have allowed.

Samaha today is a tall, balding man in his sixties, with rosy cheeks and a fringe of fine white hair that falls well below his ears. People must have thought him very dashing when he moved to Boston in 1960. Samaha tends to view a city from the point of view of its furniture. When he referred to Boston as "a good place," he meant it was a city where "the great stuff was going out, but there was very salable stuff coming in," or, more simply, that it was a "clearinghouse of antiques." He could buy things in Boston—things often made two centuries earlier in rural New England—and take them back to the country and sell them for a lot more money. He learned the business by watching dealers such as Katrina Kipper and Joe Carboni. Carboni sold fine china and porcelain, along with some English furniture, and he became a particularly helpful teacher. "He liked my family, so he guided me along," Samaha remembered years later. "He'd get a lot of stuff he didn't want in the shop. He used to give it to me at the right price."

Samaha did most of his buying in New England, but he didn't do most of his selling there. To Samaha, selling things in "the country" meant taking them to the heartland. His parents ran an antiques business from their farmhouse in Milan, Ohio, and they had discovered that while they could find a great many antiques made by Ohio craftsmen, few people who lived in Ohio actually wanted them. Collectors in the Midwest wanted folk art and painted furniture that came from the East. As a result, Ohio antiques dealers in possession of something made in Ohio often took a certain license with the object's point of origin. When clients asked about a piece, the dealers would sometimes say, "The people who owned it moved from Pennsylvania."

A great migration of antiques began after World War II. English furniture, imported to the colonies when new, sailed back across the sea to fill the homes of English bankers. Objects made in this country moved to places where people wanted them. Texans didn't appreciate their old Victorian furniture, but collectors on the East Coast did, so an endless stream of Texas Victoriana moved north. If New Englanders wished to sell antiques, Midwesterners wanted to buy. George and Mildred Samaha struggled to keep up with the demand for New England folk art and painted furniture. Luck had given them a son who could fill their endless needs—and luck had kept all but a few others from seeing the profit that can lie in great migrations. In Bill's opinion, not more than ten other antiques dealers made a habit of bringing antiques to Ohio. The Samahas had the market to themselves. That was why their son packed his truck with things and led them, something like Moses, to a place where they could belong.

George and Mildred Samaha owned a nineteenth-century farmhouse on a quiet country road, with a barn that held thirty milk cows. The house sat on a knoll under great maple and cedar trees, in perfectly untouched condition. Its lack of plumbing and electricity gave the Samahas the same satisfaction they drew from antiques with their original coats of paint. The best country antiques moved into and out of its rooms. Mildred held a fondness for needlework and Pennsylvania German frakturs, while George concentrated on furniture and ceramics. They sold tollware, chalkware, and spatterware, soft-paste porcelain, Pennsylvania redware, and furniture that ranged from the Queen Anne to the Victorian, from curly maple chests to Windsor chairs. Their clients included Abby Aldrich Rockefeller and Henry Francis du Pont.

George Samaha had arrived in this country from Lebanon in 1911. Though only fifteen, he was already an accomplished stonecutter. This skill drew him to Amherst, Ohio, a place that billed itself as "The Sandstone Capital of America." He saved his money and bought a candy and ice cream business. He met Mildred and married her, and together they saved enough to move to Akron in 1927. They built an apartment house and a restaurant with a tearoom, which Mildred began to decorate with antiques. This business might have succeeded if not for the ensuing Depression. The restaurant, Bill says, "went kapoof." They discovered the kitchen equipment for which they had recently paid $50,000 to be all but worthless. But they did notice that the knickknacks with which Mildred had so casually decorated the place held their value. The Samahas packed their things and moved to Worcester, Ohio, where George went back to work cutting curbstone, and, on the side, buying and selling antiques.

George was a short and stocky man with a nice smile. He had little schooling and he spoke broken English. Believing he could give his children nothing more important than a good education, George Samaha made them work hard in school. Bill says, "He used to tell us, 'Fix it. You been to school.' " The people in the Ohio countryside could never understand what Bill meant when he called his father "tough." Everybody thought him "the nicest guy."

George thrived in the antiques business. "He was a real cold-turkey door knocker," says his son. Rural Ohio during the 1930s was a poor place. In those days, one rarely sold any antique for more than a couple of hundred dollars. Not many buyers opened their wallets, but a great many sellers opened their doors. When someone arrived on the front porch to say, "I'm buying old stuff," this generally brought smiles to people's faces. George discovered that his relative lack of formal education and his immigrant's accent proved great assets in the antiques business. Some people liked George Samaha's Lebanese accent and some, believing themselves smarter than he, came to the mistaken belief that he could not, in his son's words, "take them."

An elderly farmwoman became one of George's first clients. Her name was Mrs. Emma Olds, and she always dressed in black. Mrs. Olds made a little money from the apple trees that stood around her property, and she made a little more by buying antiques from pickers and selling them from her home. George Samaha soon began to bring her

things. Though he had little formal education, George had
no difficulty solving the math problem that went, "If you sell
Mrs. Olds something for $20 and she sells it for $65, how
much profit has Mrs. Olds made?" He concluded that the
more he knew about antiques, the more money he could
make from them, and so he began to study the books on
antiques that Mrs. Olds happily loaned him. He studied
books and he studied the objects themselves. He never hesitated to ask questions of people with more knowledge than
he. In time, George Samaha became one of the best pickers
in Ohio. He traded on his knowledge, on his memory, and
on some other quality that is difficult to explain to people
who have not always loved things.

"It's like any other business," Bill Samaha says. "You
have to have the charisma, the knack. People begin to sense
if you know what you are doing. My father was a door
knocker. He just enjoyed it. He enjoyed people." Bill has
also said, "You have to be a gambler in the antiques business. A lot of people in the business have no confidence in
the merchandise. They look for a buyer first. My father said,
'If it's good enough to sell, it's good enough to buy.' " George
came to know the prices of objects he had never seen before.
He learned to distinguish between the $5 cruet, which he
found all the time, and the rare one he had never seen
before. "I've bought a lot of bottles," he'd say, "but this one
is different."

George and Mildred moved again in 1934, to a resort
community for wealthy Clevelanders called Vermilion.
Large summer homes stood on lagoons that crept out from
the pretty lake there. The Samahas bought a huge Victorian
house right on the water in the center of Vermilion, and

erected a sign on the front lawn that read, "Tourist Home & Antiques Shop." A couple could get a room there for $1 a night. Mildred went to work making pies and salads for Mr. Ogaki, a Japanese-American who owned the fanciest restaurant in town. George sold antiques to tourists. He also sold to Mrs. Olds, who would shake her head and say to him, "You learn too much. You've learned more in five years than I learned in a lifetime."

George came also to rely on a dealer named Rhea Knittle. She was a great scholar who wrote pamphlets on such subjects as Ohio silver. As a dealer, her clients included Abby Aldrich Rockefeller and Francis Garvan. In other ways she was, as Bill Samaha recalls, "too big, way up the hierarchy." Rhea Knittle's husband, Earl, ran an auction house, and the Knittles had what Bill remembers as "one of the strangest relationships. They lived separate lives. He didn't give her much respect, but he did like her contacts and the respect people gave her." George Samaha had not yet met the Knittles when he stopped by their house one day with a piece of eighteenth-century American glass. Earl would not let him inside the door, so George waited on the front porch while the husband took the small piece of glass inside to get his wife's opinion. "The pickers all knew the Knittles but most of them were afraid to go there," Bill recalls. "Dad wasn't afraid. After Earl paid him, Dad said, 'Someday you'll work for me.'"

After Rhea died, Earl Knittle did work for the Samahas. George had become one of the leading folk art dealers in the country. The Samahas left Vermilion in 1940 and resettled in Norwalk, Ohio. During World War II their business prospered. They exhibited at such prestigious venues as the White Plains Antiques Show in New York. In the summers, the family paid $25 a week to rent a cottage in Maine, where they took Bill and his three brothers and sisters, Bill's grandmother, and assorted children from their Norwalk neighborhood. George spent his summer days out in the Maine countryside picking antiques. He refused to come home empty-handed. "If he came in from all day in the country and he was carrying food, you knew he had a bad day," Bill remembers. "He had to buy."

George Samaha could always tell which of two similar objects would bring more money. He seemed to possess an innate ability to distinguish those the market thought merely good from those it approved as better. It's difficult to say whether he could see a quality that people call beauty. It's difficult to know whether a great piece contains what Jay Cantor has called a "certain logic"—a logic that pleases some innate sense of order—or whether its form merely fits a category that our culture has embraced. It doesn't really matter whether we find a thing beautiful because of an inner longing for the beautiful, or because our culture has told us what beauty is. The market demands that we distinguish one thing from the next, and so a great antiques dealer, like a scholar of French painting, must order all things on a scale. Most dealers move up the pyramid as far as their senses will carry them. Men like George Samaha move to the top.

The ability to discern beauty does not, of itself, make a man wealthy. To get rich in the antiques business, one must also have a head for business. Some dealers make good livings by buying ordinary things. Some who refuse to buy ordinary things can also thrive, just as John Ginsburg thrived when he found a partner who could sell. Those who possess a great eye for beauty, but lack either the skill to sell or the sense to share their businesses with those who can, do not make a lot of money. George Samaha lacked both. He never got rich. "My father," Bill says, "would have done much better if he didn't have an eye."

Bill Samaha, by contrast, has managed to make a great deal of money. Many consider him one of the country's leading dealers in American folk paintings, folk art, and painted furniture. Samaha has achieved this success through much the same business sense that has made Fred Giampietro so successful. But Samaha could not have done it without his eye for beautiful things. When he attends a show of contemporary art, Samaha regularly picks out what experts consider to be the best examples in the room despite knowing very little about the subject. He doesn't exactly understand this ability, but he knows he possesses it. Samaha says, "Some people can never tell the difference between the fine piece and the ordinary one."

When Bill Samaha saw the blue blanket chest in Carpenter's house, he thought its proportions might have been better, and he thought the scalloped base a little clumsy, but in every other respect he believed the blanket chest to be, as he later put it, "a hellish good piece." He considered the little cherrywood legs perfect and he was startled by the chest's condition—by its original coat of paint, its lack of drawer pulls, and the obvious care its owners had taken with it. Finding such a piece made from pine, instead of a harder wood such as maple, particularly amazed him. A hardwood chest in that condition would have brought more money, but Samaha would not have thought it so charming.

He asked its price and Carpenter told him. Neither man can recall the sum now, but such an object would probably have gone for more than $1,000.

Samaha lifted the chest into his truck and carried it to Boston. When he had another load ready, he drove it to the farmhouse in Milan, Ohio, where he and George carried it down to the showroom basement. The blue blanket chest was moving again. Since Joe Pari removed it from the farmhouse eleven years before, the chest had been looking for a home. It sat in bedrooms of dealers or by their kitchen doors—in places where someone might snatch it up at any moment. Things fare best in a stable environment. They appreciate sitting in a single spot, where they can stay out of harm's way. Things like to make their places, to sink their weight into carpets and rugs, to settle. They want to belong.

Eleven

IN A DECADE OF COLLECTING, PAUL AND ALICE ECKLEY CAME TO own many objects of American folk art. Their sophistication grew considerably. In 1964 the Eckleys lived in Palatine, Illinois, a middle-class Chicago suburb where Paul worked as a tax consultant. They had recently decided to build a New England-style house in Long Grove, Illinois, and had reached the conclusion that for the moment they could not afford to buy expensive things. This did not mean that they should deprive themselves of the pleasures of looking. Every fall, Paul and Alice vacationed on the East Coast, where Alice grew up, and on the way they stopped by George and Mildred Samaha's house in Milan. The Eckleys looked forward to such visits as much as anything else about their vacations, and so in the fall of 1964 they anticipated a pleasant interlude. They promised themselves that they would not buy, but only look.

The Eckleys had first moved to Palatine ten years earlier. They had started collecting by walking into what Alice remembers as "anyplace that had a sign." But they had a hard time finding things that interested them. When Alice says "It's very late up here," she means that one has trouble finding things in Illinois that date from any period earlier than the Victorian. Trying to furnish the house in Palatine proved so difficult that Alice was once "reduced," as she puts it, to buying a reproduction still-life at Marshall Field. Alice is ashamed to admit this fact. "That's how discouraged I was," she says.

Paul Eckley is a strong, self-confident man who chooses his words carefully and speaks them slowly. Alice has fewer inhibitions. She likes to tell stories and she tells them well. When Paul and Alice are together, Alice tends to do much of the talking. They met in New York and got married there. In 1948 they moved to Cape Cod, where they ran a guesthouse. Paul became a teacher and a guidance counselor at Yarmouth High. Each summer after school let out, the family spent its vacation antiquing in New Hampshire. The Eckleys grew addicted to antiques. They once found a Queen Anne table in a shop run by a man named Clyde Brown, who lived there with his hydrocephalic brother. Paul and Alice bought the table for $200 by borrowing money from Paul's mother and then paying her $20 a month. They loved it so much that they stripped off its original finish and put it in their kitchen. Even after knowledgeable people began to explain the value of original surfaces, it took years for the Eckleys to appreciate them. Alice believes she could never have gotten used to the rough, pimpled surface of that table. She had difficulty imagining it with such highly polished pieces as her Sheraton bowfront chest.

When they moved to Illinois—Paul's father had asked

him to take over his tax business—the Eckleys regarded themselves as collectors of some sophistication. Through a process of trial and error, they discovered the area's better dealers. They got to know Pat McCleary, who was backed by a local Ford dealer and who ran a shop from a farm called Stony Lonesome. They got to know Owen and Betty Smith, and they got to know the people in shops with names such as Town Hall Antiques and the Buggy Wheel. Poking around the nearby town of Geneva, Paul and Alice once noticed a couple carrying a nice antique out of a building where newspapers covered the windows. This intrigued them. When they made their way inside, they discovered an array of merchandise that included what Alice remembers as "things like red painted tin coffeepots, things that we didn't have the money or the sense to buy." A man named John Berryman ran this shop. "Berryman was very wealthy," Alice recalls. "He was kind of a recluse, who lived with his mother. He had covered the windows of his shop with newspapers to keep out the ladies who came to Geneva for lunch. He didn't want the women looking for their painted china."

Dealers with the habit of keeping browsers out appealed to the Eckleys. They met Louis and Sarah Santany, who had moved their operation from Long Grove to Geneva because, Alice remembers, they couldn't stand the tourists who poured through their former location. The Santanys also exhibited what Alice considered "marvelous things," such as textiles, pottery, and country furniture—in other words, just what the Eckleys wanted. Paul and Alice looked a lot. They bought from McCleary, from the Smiths and the Santanys, from what Alice refers to as "the Old Town boys" and "the Buggy Wheel people." They bought a refinished trestle table. They bought a refinished Pilgrim chest, a pewter cupboard, and a set of bannister-back chairs. They bought Wheeldon plates and Delft bowls and blown glass bottles.

Alice remembers these years as a time when their taste was "developing." The more she and Paul looked and the more they inquired of knowledgeable dealers, the more refined their taste became. Like most collectors, the Eckleys wanted to know where their things came from. But a curious thing happened: Whenever Paul and Alice asked about the provenance of a piece they thought particularly beautiful, nobody seemed to remember. One day, after the Eckleys had paid for a brown chest at the Buggy Wheel, one of the Buggy Wheel people told them, "George saw this chest and wanted it, but he already had too big a load." The dealer had let George Samaha's name slip out.

The Eckleys made inquiries about George Samaha. They discovered that every dealer from whom they'd bought not only knew him but also had dealt with him for years. The Smiths acknowledged knowing him. So did the Santanys. When the Eckleys asked Pat McCleary about him, the dealer at Stony Lonesome cheerfully admitted that he had a key to the Samahas' house. He further informed them that the Samahas treated him like a son. He told them that he regularly made the six-hour drive to Milan, combed the house while the Samahas were away, and found the best things—the things George wanted to hide from him—in the attic. The Eckleys also discovered that McCleary habitually raised the prices of the things he brought from Milan to levels they could not afford.

Dealers who rely on other dealers for much of their best merchandise must keep their sources secret or else soon lose their customers. Collectors rise in the hierarchy of the antiques world as their knowledge, sources, and incomes grow, in the same way dealers do. Just as dealers can outgrow their clients by offering more sophisticated merchandise, so collectors sometimes outgrow their dealers. The Eckleys had spent much of the 1950s poking through the shops around Chicago. They had slowly abandoned those that sold lesser things. The Eckleys had paid inflated prices to McCleary for the bottom of the Samahas' line— for the things that Alice calls "the cream of the refinished crop." The moment they discovered McCleary's source, they outgrew him.

The Eckleys first visited Milan in 1958. Alice remembers that the sight of George and Mildred Samaha's house "stunned" them. They observed a collection of antiques that included not only paintings and furniture but also quilts and other textiles, objects made of iron, candlesticks, and a range of ceramics in what amounted to every conceivable color and design. "Their whole house was one of the most amazingly lovely places, because they had so much," Alice recalled years later. "They had so damned much that we liked. We'd just say, 'It's time to go to Milan.' It was a cheap trip. There was nothing involved in terms of meals and staying over."

The Eckleys loved collecting antiques so much that they made annual antiquing pilgrimages to the East Coast in their Pontiac four-door sedan. After they met George and Mildred Samaha, Milan became a regular stop on these journeys. George recommended that they stay in the town's motel, rather than the more elegant Milan Inn, because, he used to tell them, "It's really clean, and a whole lot less money."

A tour of the Samahas' house required several hours. The Eckleys entered through the kitchen door and walked past the large round hutch table, where the family ate many of its meals. Paul and Alice moved slowly, from the living room to the dining room, stopping to examine each new object. They passed through the basement, whose windows overlooked a long hillside. George and Mildred used the basement to house what Alice describes as "the things that didn't look as good." They passed through the four bedrooms that stood on the second floor, and contained objects like a Chippendale secretary with carved shells. Years later, Alice tended to remember either those things she and Paul had bought, or those things like a nineteenth-century field bed with which the Samahas would never part.

"Your first impression of the Samahas was that they were great people," Alice remembers. "He was a little man, very Lebanese, dark. He had a slight accent. He always got down to brass tacks. He didn't try to misrepresent anything. He'd always tell you, 'This has the knobs replaced,' or whatever. He tried to buy things in their original condition."

The Eckleys had begun their trip back East when they visited the Samahas in the fall of 1964. They moved slowly through the house, cataloging those items they could think about while they traveled east. On this trip, they knew, they would buy nothing. They needed to save their money. Like many couples who have lived together for years, the Eckleys shared the same tastes. Perhaps Alice liked baskets more than Paul, and perhaps she also had a greater affection for what she calls "the earlier things"—seventeenth-century, or Pilgrim-century, furniture. But over the years, their collection had assumed a character all its own, so that sometimes people looked at an antique for sale in a shop or at an auction, and said of it, "That's an Eckley piece." The union of marriage had produced a union of taste. This union also produced in both Eckleys the habit of finishing each other's sentences.

On that day in 1964, the tour ended as usual in the Samahas' bedroom, where the country field bed was about the only thing not for sale. "We came upstairs and saw this blanket chest," Alice remembers. "It just knocked us out. We'd never seen anything like it before. It was the . . ."

". . . condition," says Paul.

"The wonderful legs. The fabric on the bed was an early blue India print that went wonderfully with the chest."

George Samaha had moved the chest from the basement to the bedroom because he wanted to see more of it. He told the Eckleys that their son Bill had just brought the chest from Massachusetts. He stated its price at $2,500. This amount staggered them. Paul and Alice had never spent so much on one antique, had never seen a blanket chest of its kind for anywhere near that sum, and, in any case, could not afford to buy it. But they had fallen in love with this object. Paul explained to the Samahas that he thought $2,500 a high price. This left George unmoved. "I want the chest," Paul remembers telling George, "but I gotta think about this one."

As the Eckleys examined the chest, their dealer friends from Chicago, Owen and Betty Smith, stopped by the farmhouse. The Smiths had heard from another dealer about the wonderful new blue chest that the Samahas had just acquired. "Betty and Owen came upstairs," Alice remembers. "Betty said, 'Where is it?' and she started right at it as if she was going to eat it up." Since the Eckleys had expressed a desire to own the blue blanket chest—even though they had not made a commitment—George told the Smiths that the Eckleys had the right of first refusal. "She was madder than a wet hen," Alice says. "You know how people get touchy when they think they want something."

Such tensions occur frequently in the antiques world, a place that nurtures competition and where passions run high. Once the combatants have released their energies, however, they usually find themselves friends again. George Samaha gave the Eckleys overnight to make their decision, and then the Smiths, the Eckleys, and the Samahas spent a pleasant evening over dinner at the Milan Inn.

Paul could not sleep that night, an event without precedent in the Eckley home. He paced the tiny motel room for most of the night, trying to decide whether they should acquire the thing they wanted so badly but did not have the money to pay for. In the end, they found a way to have it. "We worked out a deal to put a little down, and at the end of three months George wanted it all," Paul remembers. "No quibbling. He wanted it guaranteed." They arranged to leave the chest with the Samahas until they finished building the house in Long Grove. Then they left for their vacation in the East, and in the car they dreamed of living with their most recent acquisition, thought of it as a member of the family, and wondered where to get the money to pay for it. "We denied ourselves things in order to own it," Alice says.

Paul and Alice did not pick up the blue blanket chest for more than a year. Building the house occupied them throughout 1965. Alice had dreamed of owning such a house since a childhood trip to Colonial Williamsburg. She had wanted something with exposed beams and wooden floors and large fireplaces, and they settled on a plan for a half-gambrel house like one they'd seen in a book called *Old Houses of Nantucket*. After they finished building, the house reminded her of the one in which they had lived on Cape Cod. They could fill this house with all the furniture they'd acquired but that had not fit inside their town house. They drove to Milan to pick up the blue blanket chest, separated its top from the frame with the scalloped base and the stubby Queen Anne legs, and placed it in the backseat of their Pontiac.

The Eckleys moved the chest from room to room in their new house. "It looked good wherever you put it," Paul recalled. At first they placed it upstairs in the guest bedroom, where they had put what Alice describes as "a number of other chests and chairs in nice reds that went with the blue." When Paul complained that he didn't get to see it enough, they moved the chest downstairs to the front hall. They brought it into the kitchen. Wherever the chest landed, it looked as though it belonged.

The Eckleys could hardly contain their enthusiasm for the new acquisition, but the friends who visited had no such trouble. People smiled and said, "Oh, what a lovely house," or they said, "That's an interesting chest." Alice saw that often they didn't mean it. People looked puzzled when the

Eckleys tried to describe the beauty of the blue blanket chest. They shook their heads at the object with no handles on its drawers, and when, after discreet inquiries, these people learned its price, they called it "the most expensive blanket chest in the world."

Twelve

A LARGE WOODEN CRATE, FORGOTTEN FOR SIXTY YEARS, STOOD IN the musty basement of a building owned by the First Pennsylvania Company. Someone at this prominent Philadelphia bank had placed it there in about 1898. Over the years, records of its existence were misplaced or destroyed, so that the only clue to its provenance lay in two names stenciled on its side.

Through one of those coincidences that often shape the lives of things, a man whom we will call Tom Hughes entered the basement in 1964. Although he is dead now, old snapshots of Hughes portray a tall gentleman with an aristocratic nose, a square jaw, and eyes that conveyed something of his reputation for scrupulous honesty. The Hugheses come from the sort of old Philadelphia family that prefers not to see its name printed in any context besides those of marriage and death, and asks researchers to oblige. As someone with an interest in the Philadelphia Maritime Museum, Hughes had led the search for new and larger quarters to house the museum's collection of marine paintings, scrimshaw, whalebones, harpoons, and ships in a bottle—a search that brought him first into the building, and then into the dark, dry basement where the crate with Thomas Willing's card table had stood for half a century.

Coming unexpectedly upon this box, Hughes observed among the inscriptions on its side the words "Phebe Barron Willing Newhall." This struck him as interesting, since Phebe Barron Willing Newhall was his grandmother. When he opened the box, its contents startled him even more. He saw a trove that included paintings, silver, pewter, jewelry, and furniture. Hughes happened to collect antiques, but it did not require an expert to see that the things nestled inside had been made during Philadelphia's grand colonial period. Their value, Hughes understood at once, was staggering. He could see beautiful chased silver trays and fine oil portraits of those with whom he might share blood ties. One large object especially intrigued him. Though a blanket covered most of it, Hughes could see a ball-and-claw foot that promised some as yet undetermined object of Chippendale furniture.

Like most collectors, Hughes appreciated antiques for their ability to connect him to the past. He liked to make excursions with his wife to the Pennsylvania Dutch country. They frequented antiques dealers with names that Mrs. Hughes would later remember as "Hattie Bruner" and "Mrs. Mussleman." They spent lazy summer afternoons in Berks County underneath the tents at Pennypacker's Auction. They traveled to New York City so Hughes could poke about the shops that carried lines of marine-related memorabilia. Antiques connected Mr. and Mrs. Hughes to a rich past, but always to an indefinite one, and always to indefinite owners. Nothing can give a collector the pleasure Hughes got in the basement on Walnut Street, when he discovered an array of objects that connected him to a specific past—to a past that belonged to him. An ancestor had once owned these things. They were, so to speak, members of the family like his children.

Though the goods inside this crate tantalized him, Hughes did not remove them. Being a scrupulous man, he didn't even peek underneath the blanket. After consultation with the bank, he delivered the crate to the department of American decorative arts at the Pennsylvania Academy of Fine Arts, on whose board he had sat for ten years. As the staff unpacked this box, he discovered the magnificent Chippendale card table. Shrouded by a blanket for more than half a century, this table had escaped the hard effects of time. No one had nicked its clawed feet in those years, or placed a sweating glass on its top. No advocates had fought over its possession, and no adversaries had sought its destruction. The table had stood as if in suspended animation, waiting to resume its life. Of all the things inside the box, this one most struck Hughes by its beauty.

Tom Hughes believed that all things benefited from the enlightenment of further knowledge. He was, as his wife would say, "big on research." He had turned his talents to the study of marine crafts, American paintings, and pottery, and now he turned them to the study of his family tree. In the course of his research into the fabulous treasures inside the box, Hughes traced his ancestry to his great-great-great grandfather, Thomas Willing. From the design of the things inside the crate, Hughes felt certain that they had once belonged to Willing. He discovered that Willing had died in 1821 at age eighty-nine and that he'd been quite famous. Hughes's interest in genealogy had previously extended to names, but as he pieced together the puzzle of Phebe Newhall's crate, he learned facts that brought the names to life. Later, historians would uncover other facts of Willing's biography.

In 1775 Willing began to supply arms to Philadelphia's Secret Committee. Though his friend Robert Morris signed the Declaration of Independence, Thomas Willing did not. This mistake haunted him for the rest of his life. "I voted against this declaration in Congress," he wrote years later, "chiefly because the delegates of Pennsylvania were not then authorized by their instructions from the Assembly as a voice of the people at large, to join in such a vote." One saw in this defense everything Willing ever was—the moderate politician, the shrewd businessman, the precise and literal lawyer. He remained in Philadelphia during the British occupation but refused either to take the oath of loyalty to the crown or to socialize with British officers. He saved his great fortune, so that after the Revolution he could ease his guilt with a loan of more than $100,000 to his new government. He joined with Alexander Hamilton to organize the United States Bank, and became its first president.

Willing married Anne McCall. Together they had thirteen children, who appear to have regarded their father fondly. Invitations to parties at the Willing house remained among the most sought after in Philadelphia. As soon as the new Federal style appeared, Thomas undoubtedly redecorated this house. His fine rococo card table, once an object of much admiration, had by the 1790s become another tasteless thing, unfit for use inside the home of a modern man. He probably banished the table, along with most of his other Chippendale-era furniture, to the servants' quarters that stood above his carriage house.

After Willing died, someone drew up an inventory of his belongings, which included a portrait of Willing's mother by Robert Feke, together with silver, pewter, jewelry, and furniture. Beside each thing, someone had listed its value. Portraits were inventoried at two dollars each. A bottle of Madeira was worth a dollar. One item on the inventory, described as "1 Mahogany Card Table," was listed at a value of fifty cents.

The city of Philadelphia, like the city of Salem, Massachusetts, made its way through the nineteenth century as a place that dreamed of its past. New York replaced Philadelphia as the country's center of international finance and commerce. Fashion began someplace else. Perhaps the card table remained in the carriage houses or the servants' quarters of those who inherited it. It passed to one of Thomas Willing's sons, George, who left it to his son Charles. Though Charles died in 1868, his wife, Salena Watson, lived much longer. She kept the things that once belonged to her husband's grandfather—not for their beauty, but for their sentimental attachments to her husband's past. She kept Thomas Willing's silver and his pewter and the family portrait by Feke. She also kept the card table. Before she died, in 1898, she packed these things into the crate, deposited it in the bank basement, and left this box to her daughter Phebe.

Phebe Barron Willing Newhall did not want these things. She thought the card table old-fashioned and had no use for it inside her home. But though Phebe chose not to live with the table, neither could she part with it. A small piece of her own history lay twined inside the leaves and curling vines that her relative had loved so long ago. She left the table packed away until the day that one of her children might appreciate it, or one of her children's children, or someone else who lay at the other end of her history. We sometimes value junk in the same way that we value more admired things, for its ties to our futures as well as to our pasts. And so she left the large crate in the basement of the bank in Philadelphia, where her mother had sealed it up, and where her grandson found himself one day in 1964.

A great deal had happened in the world of American antique furniture since the card table began its residence in the crate. Though no one had seen this table for more than sixty years, or even known of its existence, it had nevertheless acquired the status of a beautiful thing. Israel Sack and John Ginsburg had made decisions about what was beautiful and what was not, the market had responded to their choices, and prices for things like the card table had risen accordingly.

Sometimes when we say of a person, "She has good taste," we mean to refer to something highly personal—to some innate gift that no amount of education could have given her. Such gifts no doubt exist. In admiring her good taste, we have seen what belongs especially to her. But we have naturally acknowledged our own good taste as well.

We have found something we share—something not so highly personal. We have found what our culture has sanctified as good. In this same way, Sack and Ginsburg brought highly personal gifts to bear on the appreciation of American furniture. But for their taste to seep into our culture, these men required an American aristocrat to endorse it. They found this person in a man named Henry Francis du Pont, who possessed his own highly personal and equally magical gifts.

Du Pont was born in Delaware in 1880. His family had grown rich on the manufacture and sale of gunpowder, and when, in 1902, his father sold his interests in the company to some cousins—the people who went on to establish the huge chemical concern—one might then have described Henry Francis's family as fabulously rich. Du Pont grew up in a house named Winterthur, after an ancestral home in Switzerland. As a boy, he collected birds' eggs and minerals on the property. At Harvard, he studied horticulture, and developed a lifelong love for gardening that made him as famous to gardeners as to antiquers. In 1923, the first time du Pont visited Electra Havemeyer Webb's house in Vermont, he was, as he later wrote, "fascinated by the colors of a pine dresser filled with Staffordshire plates." The mix of colors reminded du Pont of his gardens.

A visit to the Gloucester, Massachusetts, home of an architect and decorator named Henry Davis Sleeper also helped to shape du Pont's future. Sleeper liked to mix his colors and his textures and to create contrasts between dark walls and light objects. He set his rooms around such themes as strawberries or the sea. Du Pont was captivated by these rooms. He liked the objects and he loved the way they fit together. Du Pont developed a highly regarded sense of decoration. He liked to say that if he walked into a room and immediately noticed something, then that object didn't belong. "When it comes to arranging furniture," he once wrote, "somehow I seem to feel where each piece should go." His obsession for decoration grew so strong that he could not walk into a friend's house without rearranging the furniture.

Du Pont, a tall, lanky, man, was hopelessly shy. He stuttered badly. People remembered him as a "warm man," or a "generous man," or a "very gentle man." Soon after his father died in 1926, du Pont decided to make a museum out of his house. He added a wing and began to import interior paneling from old mansions, each from a different place, each from a different era, to create historical "period" rooms. In the same way that other wealthy heirs who built museums had achieved, as Nelson Aldrich has written, "the triumph of the family's history over time," Winterthur would survive as du Pont's greatest legacy.

Du Pont then began his search for the things to fill his house. Objects pulled du Pont to dealers' shops, and du Pont's money pulled the dealers to his front yard. They would arrive by truck, one of them remembered, and spread their wares across the hillsides. Du Pont bought in such prodigious quantities that the dealers began to call him "Mr. Big." No one sold a great antique without first offering it to him. By the time of his death in 1969, du Pont had bought nearly 100,000 objects. They filled the 196 rooms at Winterthur.

Du Pont once told Bernard Levy that the hair on his neck stood up whenever he saw something "wonderful." If

he walked into Levy's shop and saw a fine table—a table
other collectors had overlooked—he held his arms before
him in the manner of Dr. Frankenstein's monster, and his
hands began to quiver. "It's mine! It's mine!" he would say.
"I'll talk price with you later. I can't talk now. It's mine!" If
he made an appointment at Israel Sack, Harold learned that
he and his father could "set our watches by his arrival." Du
Pont sometimes invited the dealers to lunch at his house.
Thirty years later, some of them shook their heads at the
memory of eating while a footman stood behind each chair.
Bernard Levy and his wife, Laura, occasionally went down
for the weekend. They always stayed in a room that Levy
refers to as "the one with the maple secretary." In Levy's
words, "You woke up in the morning in the room with the
maple secretary, and on the little secretary was a little tray
with the breakfast we had ordered the night before. White
peaches and figs and all sorts of things. He had a staff that
gave you the feeling that when you turned over at night they
fluffed the pillow."

Du Pont was a product of the upper class. He generally
kept the world of antiques dealers separate from the world
he inhabited with aristocratic collectors such as Electra
Webb. He was a man of upper-class sensibilities. He acquired his taste from his parents in the same way Thomas
Willing had from his. This taste came to him in the natural,
unconscious way that taste is passed down among people of
any class. He had the freedom not to have to learn the code,
not to strive to know. He had the power to decide what was
good because he came from a world that decided what
"good" was.

Du Pont had the good taste that his parents gave him—

but he had something else as well. He had an extraordinary sensibility that others of his class did not share. Some people are born with special gifts for seeing things, in the same way that some are born with gifts for playing music or gifts for learning languages. Du Pont did not acquire his taste in furniture from his parents or from any of the dealers with whom he did business. He arrived on his own at an estimation of American furniture forms. What was more, the decisions he made—on the right proportions for a cabriole leg, or the best arrangement of a carved shell—happened to coincide almost exactly with those made by Israel Sack. Perhaps the two men responded to similar pieces for the same reason that we might sometimes know what note will follow another in an unfamiliar piece of music.

Du Pont tried to make his house historically accurate, but he failed. Too many fine things sit together in one room to illustrate the way people actually lived. These things represent the tastes of a man who lived most of his life not in the eighteenth century, but in the twentieth. He put them together in such a way that a woman like Electra Webb, and not Thomas Willing's wife, Anne, would appreciate. Winterthur is not accurate, but it's difficult to enter this house and not see the beauty that shimmers all around.

Experts now consider the proportions of du Pont's chests to be great proportions, the legs of his chairs to be great legs. The dealers feel the same way about things once sold by Israel Sack. When Bill Stahl finds an antique similar to one at Winterthur, his catalog description will include this fact. Books filled with the things bought by du Pont or Sack fill the shelves of those dealers who want to sell the best. These books are useful, but they fail in one important respect. They contain only objects of uniform magnificence. Collectors in the 1940s found themselves wishing for a book that compared great legs to mediocre ones. Harold Sack's brother, Albert, answered their needs.

Albert wrote this book in 1950. It's called *Fine Points of Furniture.* In its foreword, Israel Sack wrote that the book filled him with the "natural pride of a father who sees his son carry on his life's work of preaching the importance of Early American craftsmanship." Albert laid out *Fine Points of Furniture* with photographs of two or three similar objects on each page. Short captions underneath each photo noted whether he thought a thing "Good" or "Better" or "Best." On one page stood three highboys, all of which looked the same to an untutored observer. Under the "Good" highboy, Albert pointed out that he found the legs "especially clumsy." Under the "Better" highboy, a reader learned that it had "fat knees abruptly tapering into too thin ankles." Albert attributed the "Best" piece to John Goddard of Newport, Rhode Island, and described it as "a beautifully proportioned example with graceful, well-formed cabriole legs."

Although Albert wrote this book more than forty years ago, its significance remains incalculable. People in the trade refer to the book as *Good, Better, Best,* in a way that lets one know they forgot its actual title long ago. It made such an impression on the marketplace that people began to make fun of it, as when they referred to it as *Good, Better, and in Stock.* Dealers may say snide things about this book, but no great dealer lives without it. When a dealer sees an ordinary object and says of it, "That's 'Better,' " he means to make fun of the trivialization to which Albert Sack's book has reduced the state of his business, while at the same time to describe accurately the object's undoubted fate in the marketplace. *Fine Points of Furniture* became a bible. Here for the first time someone had laid the code out in nice, easy steps: one-two-three. Now a person didn't need to be born the scion of a gunpowder fortune to understand these concepts. Now one could see what a clumsy leg looked like next to a truly great leg.

Albert talked about "quality." He talked about the "essential merit of the piece." He talked about furniture in the same terms in which he talked about masterpieces of art. Rarity is not a useful measure of quality, he said. It didn't matter that other Dutch paintings were rarer than Rembrandt's. If one knew the code (and who did not when it came to old master paintings?), one preferred a Rembrandt to a Van Ravesteyn. It was the same with furniture. Once one had a cabinetmaker's name—the Goddard family of Newport, Rhode Island, for instance—one had a Rembrandt. When Israel Sack wrote of his antiques, "I did not care who made them," one knew that this could not be true—or at the very least one knew that his son did not believe it. Albert littered *Fine Points of Furniture* with attributions to the Goddards.

Albert Sack wanted to make sure that American furniture entered what he called "Art's permanent Hall of Fame." He wrote with such conviction that one instantly believed schools of cabinetmaking such as Boston Queen Anne or Philadelphia Chippendale "far surpassed the best English or French [schools] by their originality of form." This opinion was naturally not shared by connoisseurs of

French or English furniture, who frequently held the opinion that American things were plain and ugly. It was a question of taste and it was a question of culture. The Sacks preferred New England Queen Anne furniture because it was simplest of all. Albert Sack spread the word, and one believed.

When a person discovers a great artist's work through the eyes of someone who has studied it, that painting suddenly comes to life. Suddenly one notices how the atmosphere inside Fitz Hugh Lane's paintings appears to have been sucked out, how the sails on the ships hang limp, and how it is that the still water and the quiet air evoke a moment of calm in the years preceding the Civil War. When Albert Sack describes a piece of furniture, the object comes to life. One can never look at another hotel-room reproduction without feeling offended, on a deep level, by its ugly, shiny newness. One wants patina after reading Albert Sack. One wants age and mellow wood and the evidence of human hands rubbing the edges of a thing. One wants a perfect curve to its leg.

Taste is a curse as well as a blessing. Sack and Ginsburg and du Pont have condemned us even as they have endowed us. Once Alan Miller has shown us Thomas Willing's card table, we will never see another one in quite the same way. We will miss the fat leaves full of rainwater, the tension of the shells, and the luxuriant twisting of the vines. Some things will now thrill us, while others will offend us. The appreciation of American furniture has required years to develop. It has taken education and publicity and the weight of staggering sums of money to make such things beautiful.

It has taken money and it has taken time. The blue blanket chest and the sofa table each made their journeys through more regular channels. They passed from mother to daughter, and from dealer to dealer, and acquired a le gitimacy slowly, through each new estimation of the marketplace. Collectors had owned these things, and this gave them famous histories. But the card table had arrived out of nowhere. It had not, like the sofa table, received the benediction of Israel Sack, Inc. It was a stranger to the world of antiques, and people required time to get to know it.

Tom Hughes spent months tracking down each of Phebe Newhall's descendants. In 1964, he dispersed the contents of the crate to near and distant cousins. He chose to bring the card table home with him and to place it in his living room, with its top folded over, as an object not of use but of admiration. Most people who dropped by for gins and tonic and a game of bridge, however, could find little in it to admire. "The table was so much more ornate than anything else we had," his wife recalled years later. "A lot of people thought it was too fancy."

The friends who frequented the Hughes's house preferred the clean lines of sixties modern to the rich carving of Chippendale furniture. But even though the table was not a thing they would bring into their own homes, neither did they mistake it for junk. Money makes some things beautiful, and the card table, they knew, was worth a lot of money. It was valuable because some people wanted it in their homes and because museums wanted examples in their

American wings. It was valuable because someplace a market existed for it and because out in the world of American furniture—where the dealers fought and lied and stole things from their friends—some people could tell a great card table from a good one.

Thirteen

FOUR MONTHS AFTER JOSEPH HIRSHHORN DIED, SOTHEBY'S HELD a sale of his American furniture collection. The inlaid satinwood sofa table, which had decorated Hirshhorn's house for nearly twenty years, now waited with most of its companions behind the curtains of the saleroom stage. As the hour of the auction approached on this Saturday afternoon in January 1982, antiques dealers drifted into Sotheby's large saleroom. The dealers greeted each other like cousins arriving at a family reunion. They talked of the successes and failures of their colleagues, of deaths and of debilitating illnesses.

The sofa table stood beside an enormous lazy Susan, which waited to spin this object like a prize on a TV game show to face the crowd in Sotheby's saleroom. The table was well made, pretty in its own way, but it lacked something that one couldn't quite put a finger on—something like charm, perhaps. It was not what people in the business would call a "winner." It possessed just enough character and just enough luck to have kept it alive, but not quite enough of either to have made it magnificent. Sotheby's had estimated the sofa table would bring as much as $35,000, not because anybody there thought it especially beautiful, but because it was rare. The table did not excite many of the dealers who wandered into the saleroom. They considered it—just as they considered most of Hirshhorn's things—a "quality home furnishing."

Harold and Albert Sack arrived at Sotheby's shortly before three o'clock, when the sale was scheduled to begin. Harold wore a dark suit and walked straight to the chair he always occupied near the front of the room. On his way he drew smiles from his friends, nods from his acquaintances, and respectful glances from those who had never met him. Hirshhorn had bought all but fourteen of the seventy-five items for sale that day from the Sacks, so that on page after page of the catalog, under the heading of "Provenance" beside each item, a reader saw the words "Israel Sack, Inc., New York." A dealer makes his reputation on how his things fare in the marketplace. When one of his collections comes up for sale, he often bids on many of the things he once sold in order to sustain high prices and preserve his reputation. The other dealers at Sotheby's took an interest not so much in the things themselves as in how many of them the Sack brothers would have to buy back.

The Sacks had once hoped to acquire these things by other means. Entering into private negotiations with the estate, Harold had offered what he thought a reasonable sum for the entire collection—a sum that included $100,000 alone for a Massachusetts Queen Anne highboy and matching lowboy. But he had not succeeded. His rival at Sotheby's, the auctioneer John Marion, had persuaded Hirshhorn's last wife that she could get more by selling her things through him. Ten years earlier, Sotheby's might not have even heard about Hirshhorn's furniture. Though the firm regularly sold off the contents of estates, few widows would have thought of sending a significant Americana collection to auction. Harold Sack would not have found himself waiting to buy back his own merchandise at retail prices. In fact, his presence at Sotheby's that day owed largely to the efforts of the auction house to compete for just such merchandise.

A London bookseller named Samuel Baker founded the enterprise that became Sotheby's in 1744, while Thomas Willing was studying at school in Bath. It remained a small firm even after the Sotheby family bought it and gave the business their name. For more than a century, Sotheby's sold off people's libraries while the rival firm of Christie's, which held its first auction in London in 1766, sold the other contents of their homes. Sotheby's only began in this century to compete with Christie's for paintings and furniture from the great English country houses. Until a man named Peter Cecil Wilson came to Sotheby's, both firms did most of their business with dealers. Wilson changed the nature of the auction business by selling to ordinary people—by turning a wholesale trade into a retail one.

Sotheby's furniture department hired Wilson as a trainee in 1936. Three years later, he acquired a partnership in the firm—a circumstance that owed to his aristocratic background, to his social connections, and to a recent inheritance that had come to his wife. Much of what we know about Peter Wilson comes from Nicholas Faith, who wrote a book about Wilson's effect on Sotheby's. Nearly everyone called Wilson "PCW." He reminded Faith of the actor John Gielgud. He worked from early in the morning until late at night, out of a shabby office where papers and old sandwiches stacked up on his desk. He dedicated so much of himself to the firm that a friend said at his retirement, "He had no real life except Sotheby's since he was young."

Many considered Wilson the best auctioneer of his day. People said that after he prepared for a sale, he knew exactly who would buy what and for how much. He mastered the art of saleroom hype. He charmed everyone he met. He televised an auction for the first time in history. He hired Sotheby's first public relations adviser. In 1958, his first year as chairman of the board, Sotheby's sales doubled to £5 million. Wilson bought the New York firm of Parke-Bernet in 1964 and thereby established a presence in the United States that no other auction house could match.

Wilson understood that to make Sotheby's a retail business, he needed to sell things that an average housewife could afford to buy. In 1971 he opened a low-end saleroom called Belgravia, where one could find Victorian knick-knacks for next to nothing. He soon expanded the areas of collecting into such specialties as antique pornographic postcards and old saltine cracker boxes. He started education programs to teach people what to look for in art and antiques, and "Heirloom Weeks," when the hopeful might bring their treasures in for free appraisals. He extended credit to his best customers. He dispatched sales figures to the accounting offices after every twenty items had sold, so that customers could pick up their goods, pay for them, and carry them home even before the sale had ended. Wilson made it possible to shop at Sotheby's the way one shopped at Macy's.

By the 1970s, average citizens had begun bidding against the dealers, and widows like Joe Hirshhorn's had begun taking their collections to John Marion. Men like Harold Sack might have found themselves without any merchandise—and without any customers—except for one critical advantage. These dealers possessed a vast knowledge that auction houses often failed to match. The market does not penalize an auctioneer the same way it punishes a dealer for making mistakes. If an auction house believes a reproduction Queen Anne tea table to be genuine, the auction house loses no money by miscataloging it. But a dealer who makes the same mistake—who pays $10,000 for a thing that's worth only $1,000—loses everything. The market teaches hard lessons and disciplines dealers to take great care. Watching the auction houses encroach on their territory led the dealers to scorn them for selling goods with questionable reputations, misleading histories, and inaccurate descriptions. In the 1970s, Harold Sack told his clients, "Don't go near the auctions."

Sack nevertheless found himself at Sotheby's on the January afternoon in 1982. He was there quite regularly of late, because John Marion often beat him to the goods. As Sack recounts the tale of Sotheby's success, one imagines how things had been and how they might be now. One can hear the frustrations of an altered world. "I would have had the collection," Harold would say, "except for the fact that John Marion put his two cents in with the last widow, and agreed to appraise and catalog six thousand lots in another collection, free, if they'd give him the Americana collection."

As Harold Sack took his seat in Sotheby's saleroom, one pair attracted the glances people reserve for eccentric members of a family. A short man with black-rimmed glasses, a crunched-up face, and a cigar stuck in his mouth had arrived in the company of a much younger man. This second man might have weighed three hundred pounds. He was so much taller than the first, and so often found in the other's company, that people sometimes called them Mutt and Jeff.

Every dealer in the room recognized this large man as the collector Richard Rosen. They knew the small man with the cigar even better. He was a dealer named John Walton, and he was a familiar sight at Sotheby's. Walton bought so much at auction that he had come to be known as an "auction animal." He thrived in a climate where one might find great things mislabeled. Auction houses usually place the most expensive goods at the end of the sale—a tactic meant to ensure the continued presence of the buyers at the top of the market. Walton believed that one found the best deals among the goods described in the front of the catalog—the rare table, miscataloged out of ignorance as ordinary, for example, or the fine dish thought to be junk. As a result, Walton bought a lot of great things at what his client, Richard Rosen, liked to call the "ungreat portions of their sales." Rosen enjoyed this spirit no less than Walton. They could be found together at obscure country auctions in Maine and Pennsylvania. They regularly met in New York. Few things could give Walton so much pleasure as a large New York sale, and when he came to New York, he came eagerly to Sotheby's.

Walton ran an operation in Jewett City, Connecticut. His compound there included a colonial farmhouse, a barn full of antiques, and an icehouse where he kept his cabinet shop. He stood five feet, six inches tall and had a large smile. He was so powerful that when asked to describe him, one person said, "He would have made a great muscle match with a gorilla, and I think he would have won." He spoke loudly, used vulgar language, and cheated his friends at every opportunity. Like many dealers, he commented unfavorably on the very things that he himself wished to buy. He often left his wife at a sale to bid on a piece of furniture while he, feigning disinterest, dragged his competitors outside to chat. Walton reveled in the seedy side of things. He loved to make deals, to find things for nothing. He saw what took Harold Sack longer to see—that times had changed— and found ways to use the auction houses to his advantage. He taught clients like Richard Rosen to do the same.

Walton was born in 1907. He grew up around his father's cabinet shop in Westport, Connecticut. Few skills serve a dealer of antiques better than a knowledge of cabinetmaking. Furniture begins its life in pieces, and the pieces fit together in such a way that after a couple of centuries, like all long-term relationships, they come to belong with one another. Sometimes it happens that a table loses its top, or breaks a leg, and needs repair. It's important to know whether the parts of a thing all started with that thing, and John Walton could tell as well as anyone who dealt American antiques.

In the late 1930s, Walton and his third wife opened an

antiques shop in Wilton, Connecticut. She sold Staffordshire and early glass from their seventeenth-century farmhouse, while he concentrated on furniture. He dealt in country chests and elegant tea tables, from all periods of colonial history. So much furniture cluttered Walton's home that visitors had to pass through narrow alleys. To keep the house filled, Walton would set off in the afternoons with a wallet full of cash to scour the countryside from a battered half-ton pickup. Few homeowners in the 1930s respected the value of a check. If Walton found a New Hampshire birch chest for $200—something he suspected that the famous Dunlap family of cabinetmakers had made in the 1780s—he brought it home, cleaned it up, and inspected its construction to assure its authenticity. He figured he might get $450 for it. If he paid $62 at a country auction for a box filled with china, wooden spoons, and antique pots and pans, he sometimes discovered a rarity inside—a Lowestoft porcelain tureen, say, which he could sell for $550. Like most dealers of the day, Walton scraped the original paint off of eighteenth-century pine chests to sell them to the antiques departments of New York stores such as Lord & Taylor. The customers of such stores liked refinished country furniture. If Walton had found Fred Giampietro's blue blanket chest and removed its coat of paint, its value today would be closer to $15,000 than $245,000.

Israel Sack occasionally stopped by Walton's shop on his Saturday morning expeditions to Antique Alley. John Ginsburg and Florene Maine and other dealers showed up, too. Such collectors as Miss Ima Hogg and Mrs. Francis Garvan came to see if they could find great antiques before the expensive New York dealers did—in the words of Walton's son, "to beat the dealers out of their livelihoods." Those who loved antiques exhibited a charming camaraderie around one another. When two dealers could not agree on a price, they flipped a coin to see whether a thing would sell for $425 or $475.

Walton spent a lot of time around Florene Maine. "God save ya' if ya' ever mentioned it," his son John E. Walton recalls, "but Florene taught him more about antiques than anybody." If Walton found a piece he knew to be good, but lacked the capital to acquire it, he called up Maine and brought her in as a partner. The antiques business respects those dealers whom the market has approved, and when someone like Israel Sack or Florene Maine called an object "a masterpiece," others respected their opinions and paid their prices. A young dealer—even one with an eye for the best things—did not get so much respect.

Walton and Maine became lovers. This fact was apparently unaffected by the succession of women who cosigned marriage licenses with him or by the succession of women who did not. Those who knew Maine have described her variously as "a continental beauty with auburn hair that was four or five feet long," as "a real *signora*," and as "a Renaissance woman who could curse like a truckdriver and then listen to a Bach concert." Walton's son John E. once called her "the great love" of his father's life. When Walton said he was going someplace to look at antiques, he generally intended to snoop around the small shops along Route 7, or to pick houses in the country, or to visit an auction. When he told his son, "I'm going over to Florene's to look at antiques," he usually meant something else.

"They were battling constantly," John E. remembers.

"Mostly over ownership, or who's going to buy that treasure." Walton, Sr., would say, "Why won't you sell it to
me?," to which Maine would reply, "John, you can't have
everything!" "I had to stand on the sidelines of this," his son
recalls. "From where I stood, it was very humorous, but they
were deadly serious." John E. also says, "A good definition
of their relationship would be love-hate. Because on one side
of the coin, she detested him with his business tactics. Anyone who had a long and lasting relationship with John S.
Walton had to be pretty tough. She could brush it off fairly
easily, or at least give you that impression, with some of the
knocks and kicks she received."

Walton brought this same rough attitude to bear on his
competitors. "There's only one winner," he used to tell his
son. Walton lied to people about whether he had decided to
attend this auction or that. Everyone who knew Walton
remembers him as "tough."

"He was a very ambitious guy trying to arrive, clawing
his way to the top," recalled Harold Sack.

Bernard Levy had similar memories. "I had many deals
with him where he did his best to screw me. It didn't bother
me. It bothered the Sacks. The Sacks were afraid of him, but
I screwed him back. He got away with one, I got away with
three."

By the 1950s, Walton had opened up a shop on Park
Avenue that sold antiques of the same quality as those inside
Sack's. Other dealers respected Walton's eye for beauty and
his broad interests. He regularly dealt in areas to which the
Sacks paid little attention. He traded in country furniture
and in accessories such as bed warmers and andirons. He
sold a wide array of candleholders. He dealt in paintings,

watercolors, needlework, and folk art. His passion for rare treasures was so great that it could lead to violence. He drank Jack Daniel's straight from the bottle. When another dealer beat him to a great object, he occasionally threw the bottle. Walton did not discriminate. He cursed men and women, ladies and gentlemen. He sometimes called the next day to apologize.

Dealers thought of Walton as a dealer's dealer. He knew what he wanted and he got it. From the Park Avenue shop, Walton traded things with Albert and Harold Sack's father, Israel, and paid record prices for American furniture. He smoked a huge cigar wherever he went. Long after he finished examining the goods in an auction showroom, dealers who followed behind Walton could tell what antiques had interested him from the quantity of cigar ashes that lay about their feet. Boys growing up in the business wished to be like Walton. The boys carried big, fat cigars, just like his, and imitated his odd, gorilla-like walk. Wayne Pratt, the dealer at the Winter Antiques Show who sold a $1 million desk on opening night, dreamed of being like Walton. Bill Stahl wanted to become Walton. "Absolutely. I wanted to be him. Or I wanted to be playing in his league." When Walton died of a heart attack in 1985, something passed in the world of American antiques—something besides the charisma of the man and his intensity and his toughness.

One of Walton's most famous customers was a Milwaukee department store magnate named Stanley Stone. He employed Walton to build a great collection for his house, which he called Chipstone and which he intended to turn into a museum. Stone grew so dependent on Walton that he proudly admitted having bought things—a rare Queen

Anne stool, for example—sight unseen. Other collectors adored Walton just as much as Stone, but none grew more devoted to him than Richard Rosen, the engineer from Belmont, Massachusetts, who had taken up antiques as a hobby.

Rosen first met Walton at a New Hampshire auction house run by a man named Ron Bourgeault. Rosen remembers that the first words spoken to him by one of the country's greatest dealers were, "The hell you doin' here?" Rosen explained that a rare eighteenth-century American piano had intrigued him. "Listen," Walton had said, "you got a lot a taste, but you don't know what the hell is goin' on. First of all, you don't want to buy any of those goddamned pianos. You can't play 'em. They all have broken soundboards. And they ain't worth a shit as antiques. This goddamned Bourgeault auction, you have to pay for shit in this sale just like it was down in New York. You'll pay more for it than you would down in New York. Everybody comes up here thinking they're gonna get a bargain or something, and a lot of the stuff here is *crap*. Fake antiques, modern reproductions. What the hell do you want to get involved with this kind of thing for?"

Rosen had rarely come across anyone with more bluster than himself. A couple of months later, he and his wife, Marguerite, drove down to Walton's shop in Jewett City, Connecticut. Walton treated the couple to a five-hour tour of the premises, moving from one carefully selected object to the next. Before buying his first object, Rosen had spent seven years studying antiques. He thought he knew a lot. But until he met John Walton, he did not have any idea how much he still had to learn.

In May of 1980, Rosen and his wife traveled to the

six-day exhibition and sale of Edgar William and Bernice Chrysler Garbisch's Americana collection. Sotheby's conducted this sale on the grounds of the Garbisches' Maryland estate. The Rosens spent a couple of days there, wandering about the grounds in a shock of disbelief. Richard would later call the sale "an extraordinary event." Many people in the world of American antiques agree with him. Every famous American furniture and folk art dealer showed up for this event. It changed the price structures of entire categories of objects.

Richard Rosen spent much of his time at the sale in the company of Walton. When Rosen describes the event, one senses his own powerful, emotional—almost sexual—response to the things. Neither he nor Marguerite had ever felt such a charge from a group of objects. The furniture and folk art, the china and glass, the silver, the porcelain, the paintings—all evoked a covetous desire he had never known before. The Rosens spent money with abandon. They bought a Chippendale side chair. They bought a slate-top tea table that Walton had found miscataloged at the beginning of the sale. They bought a pier table. They bought a porcelain mug decorated with the picture of a ship, and a set of eagle-decorated china.

Rosen could see in Walton the same passions that he himself felt, and stood in awe of the vast knowledge that Walton willingly imparted. After the Garbisch sale, the two men soon saw each other constantly. A week rarely passed without their getting together. Rosen would spend a couple of hours poking around Walton's barn to see what recent acquisitions might entice him, and another couple of hours over dinner with his mentor. They drove to auctions in New

York, New England, and Pennsylvania. The closer they grew, the more Walton surprised him. Walton obviously knew cabinetwork, construction, and wood. But he knew other things as well. He enjoyed historical research. He handled documents with great care. "He was a fantastic historian," Rosen recalls. "I've known a few scholars. If you have a Harvard Ph.D., you run into a few scholars. He was one of the best I have ever known."

Collectors want to buy things that reflect their tastes and their desires, and gravitate toward those dealers who appreciate them. Passions require the nurturing of those who understand. Rosen liked to call Walton a *dealer*, a title that the collector bestowed with special emphasis. A *dealer* belonged to a rich tradition, and found himself with special obligations. Walton disdained those who kept the good things for themselves in the front rooms of their houses. Real dealers *sold* the things just the way he sold them. All dealers loved the chase and all of them loved to possess fine objects, but real dealers loved the things they found so much that they didn't need to keep them. "He really believed in the beauty of the objects," Rosen remembers. "He said if something wasn't beautiful, don't buy it. I think the people who make good livings have access to great merchandise. Some dealers have it. Some don't. John Walton would buy a thing because he loved it."

Walton had a great many rules. Collectors like Rosen learned them by heart. One was, "If it don't look right, it probably isn't." A second was, "If it looks right, it may not be. The only way to tell is to take it apart"—a rule that led Rosen and Walton to remove the tops of countless lowboys. A third rule was, "If an object is totally great, even if it's imperfect, buy it." Rosen learned other rules from Walton. "I learned never to buy chairs unless they had rounded knees and balloon seats. I learned never to buy chairs unless they had seat frames rather than overupholstered seats. I learned never to buy country furniture unless it had its original paint."

Buying rare things thrilled Rosen in a way that he had not thought possible. To prepare for a sale, he and Walton spent hours with the catalog. They'd discuss each object's merits and each one's flaws. They'd argue over the soundness of the estimates. They'd decide what to try to acquire. Rosen and Walton approached Hirshhorn's collection in the same way. "He'd studied the catalog in great detail," Rosen recalls. "He taught me to read cataloges. For example, when a description includes the evidence of repairs, you have to know when to pay attention. Some are serious, some are subtle."

The pages of the Hirshhorn catalog revealed photographs of such things as a matching Queen Anne highboy and lowboy estimated to bring as much as $150,000, a serpentine-front chest of drawers, and an inlaid tall clock. A couple of other objects attracted their attention, and they decided to try to buy two things: a gilded Chippendale mirror and the Federal satinwood inlaid sofa table. Their decision to buy the table was not surprising, since among the things they could afford, it was by far the rarest.

The dealers at the Sotheby's sale exhibited none of the excitement, the tension, the heightened anticipation common when they expected spirited bidding. The dealers didn't think much of the objects for sale that day. They later said, "These things were not masterpiece level," and "There was not much great stuff in that sale." They seemed more interested in seeing what Harold and Albert Sack would do than in the objects themselves.

Having lost the entire collection to Sotheby's, the Sacks now tried to pick up the pieces. On that January day in 1982, Harold and Albert bought seventeen items that had stood inside their shop once before, and paid a total of $392,000 to do it. Luck had followed Hirshhorn's last widow. The matching highboy and lowboy—a lot for which Sack had offered Mrs. Hirshhorn $100,000—sold for $190,000. This sale made big news in the world of American antiques, for it was then a record for any pair of objects. The firm that paid this tremendous price was Israel Sack, Inc.

When the sale of the sofa table began, John Walton bid for Richard Rosen against a single, anonymous competitor. Walton began with a great flourish, bidding up to the low estimate of $25,000, and then he kept bidding in increments of $1,000. Walton eventually acquired the table for $43,000, almost $10,000 more than Sotheby's highest estimate. With the 10 percent buyer's commission, Rosen would pay $47,300 for it. The sofa table would be coming home with him now, would hold the vases for his flowers, and would reflect his sensibilities to the world. Rosen and the sofa table would not have met at all if not for the intimate bond he had formed with Walton. "The sofa table was a good example of John Walton telling me to buy something," Rosen remembered later. "I wouldn't have bought it otherwise."

Fourteen

PAUL AND ALICE ECKLEY STILL OWNED THE BLUE BLANKET CHEST in the summer of 1986, even though they had left their house in Long Grove, Illinois, for the convenience of an apartment. The smaller space required them to sell off some of their collection, but they hadn't thought of parting with the chest. It stood in their new living room and gave them as much pleasure there as it had in Long Grove for more than twenty years. One object in a collection generally stands out among the rest, and in the three decades during which the Eckleys had accumulated antiques, no piece came to represent their taste more than the blue blanket chest. A dealer who knew the collection once said of it, "That was their claim to fame, that piece."

In the course of their collecting, the Eckleys befriended two antiques dealers named Bert and Gail Savage. Bert had started the antiques department at Marshall Field and earned wide respect as a dealer of American folk art. The Eckleys bought a number of things from the Savages. They shared their taste in things. Bert believed the Eckleys to have an important collection, did his best to impress this fact on others, and generally earned the title Paul Eckley once gave him as "the leading promoter of the Eckley collection." Through Bert Savage's connections, curators at the Chicago Art Institute saw the blue blanket chest and thought it important enough to include in a 1969 show of New England colonial furniture. Few events sanctify an object more than an exhibition in a museum, since the approval of scholars confirms a thing's authenticity and its beauty. The blessing of so prestigious an authority as the Chicago Art Institute transformed the chest into a work of art.

The blue blanket chest began a new career. Now that it had sat in a museum, the chest had acquired a kind of celebrity. People thought it attractive because others had approved it, and the more who approved it, the more attractive it became. People now appreciated the qualities of simplicity that had once made others regard this object as junk. As each year passed, its charm increased. Its destiny seemed to follow its successes.

One day in 1972, Bert Savage brought a man named Cyril Nelson by the Eckleys' house. Nelson edited folk art books for E. P. Dutton. He often published on subjects whose significance many collectors—and other editors—had not yet seen. Nelson was just then going to print with a new book called *American Painted Furniture*. This book was written by Dean Fales, a former director of the Essex Institute in Salem, Massachusetts. It was the first serious treatment of the subject and its pages included some of the finest examples of painted furniture in the country.

Seeing the blue blanket chest in the Eckleys' living

room, Cyril Nelson immediately thought it was "a great piece of work." He was struck by its "sculptural or architectural beauty," its "wonderful color," and its "very early form." He liked this object so much that he would have urged its inclusion in the text of *Painted Furniture* if Fales's book had not already gone to the printer. The chest amazed Nelson. For weeks afterward, he couldn't get it out of his head. He finally concluded that the chest was so distinctive he had to place its photograph on the back cover of Fales's book. When *Painted Furniture* appeared, it elevated the status of every object pictured inside—and even one that was not. In this way, a single photograph turned a work of folk art into a folk art icon.

Only a handful of people then appreciated objects like the blue blanket chest. Even books like *Painted Furniture* did not reach a large audience. The chest's career was further advanced in 1974, when the Whitney Museum of American Art put on a show called "The Flowering of American Folk Art." This show did so much to change the country's perception of folk art that dealers have come to talk about the world "before Flowering" and the world "after Flowering." The Whitney introduced a wide public to the beauties of paintings by Edward Hicks and to exquisite early watercolors by Jacob Mantel and Joseph H. Davis. Woodcarvings of George Washington, ships' figureheads, and weathervanes also filled the exhibition. After "Flowering," families brought a new appreciation to the quilts left by their grandmothers, seeing them for the first time not only as heirlooms but also as objects of beauty. Merchandisers began to knock off reproductions of folk art. The people who came into the Eckleys' house began to see their things differently after "Flowering."

Folk art inhabits a small niche in the art world. For $3 million—a price that might buy a single good Impressionist painting—a person can put together one of the finest folk art collections in the country. The market for this material breaks down into smaller submarkets such as oil paintings, watercolors, and painted furniture. The blue blanket chest stood somewhere far down the pyramid of the art market, but in the market for painted furniture it stood somewhere near the top.

Some things prosper in a home. By 1986, the blue blanket chest, which the Eckleys had bought in 1964 for $2,500, had become a great work of American folk art. Dealers coveted it. When they saw the Eckleys at antiques shows they explained how much they would like to buy it. By 1980, prices for painted furniture had risen to such levels that one dealer—the Eckleys cannot remember who—offered them $60,000 for it. Bill Samaha never mentioned a price, but he told them, "Anytime you want to sell, I'd be delighted to buy it."

One summer day in 1986, Bert Savage stopped by the Eckleys' house and kidded them about selling the chest. "Sure I'll sell it," Paul joked, "if I can get $150,000 for it." Bert Savage did not find this number outlandish. "I wouldn't mention prices," he warned, "because you might have sold it already." Bert soon called the Eckleys to say that two dealers named Peggy and David Schorsch had offered $125,000, and that, furthermore, they wished to see the chest immediately. The Schorsches wanted to make a deal. "That knocked us over," Paul recalls. "We knew we'd never see that kind of money again."

The Schorsches were a mother and son who lived to-

gether in Greenwich, Connecticut. Peggy Schorsch, a slen-
der, stylish woman with blond hair, was in her fifties at the
time. Her son, David, was twenty-three. They were among
the strangest but shrewdest dealers trading American folk
art. Their reputation rippled to the far corners of the American antiques community. They had made a few enemies,
but they had made more friends, and of the latter among
their oldest were Bert and Gail Savage.

David had left for a vacation in Aruba when Bert
Savage called to ask if the blue blanket chest held any interest for the Schorsches. Peggy knew this object, as every
other folk art dealer did, from the back cover of *Painted
Furniture.* She knew it furthermore to be exactly the sort of
masterpiece that she and her son excelled at trading. Within
a few days, Peggy Schorsch had flown to Illinois, examined
the chest for damage or repair, and handed Paul a certified
check for $125,000. With the 10 percent commission she
agreed to pay the Savages, the blue blanket chest cost her
$137,500.

For the first time in twenty years, the blue blanket
chest stirred from its place in the home of those who cared
mostly for the pleasure it gave them. The distinction between people and things had changed considerably since
Abraham Lincoln abolished slavery. Even though Americans have come to treat human beings less often as things,
they have come to treat objects more often as people.
Through personal attachments to things for reasons of aesthetics or family history—associations that the first owner of
the blue blanket chest never thought of making—owners
endow some things with the qualities of those who once
touched them. By placing pieces of their tastes and their

desires inside a thing, these people give it life. The things they treasure become parts of their families, and they feel pangs of loss at stories of family heirlooms auctioned to the highest bidder. Selling off such treasures seems like casting out a member of one's family.

Paul Eckley had quit working. He and Alice planned to sell their things to pay for their retirement. Their children had no special attachment to the beautiful antiques they had accumulated. A thing in a collection is different from a family heirloom. New antiques connect people to the past, but not to their own pasts. The Eckleys' children held no more attachment to their antiques than to the modern things their parents bought. Like a child adopted as a teenager, the blue blanket chest was no longer secure in this family. One day it was safe and the next it was gone. The sum of $125,000 appeared to be enough to ease the parting.

David Schorsch cut short his vacation on Aruba. He wanted to examine the newest item in his inventory. Like his mother, David first saw the blue chest on the back cover of *Painted Furniture,* and like many other dealers he dreamed of owning it. Most of the country's folk art dealers were adults when *Painted Furniture* came out in 1972. David Schorsch was nine years old. "In your mind you kind of put together a pantheon of great works," he says. "And in the world of painted Queen Anne country furniture, this chest falls into that category. It was always in the category if it was in the book or not, but the fact that it was in the book sort of elevated it to icon status."

Schorsch had a knowledge of mahogany furniture that stood on a level near Harold Sack's. No one possessed a greater understanding of American folk art, from Pennsylvania German watercolors, to the paintings of Edward Hicks, to painted furniture such as the blue blanket chest. Schorsch lived the sort of life that Hollywood finds it profitable to romanticize. In those days, informality ruled his wardrobe. He liked to wear T-shirts with logos such as "Indian Village Magic Forest—Lake George, New York" emblazoned on them. He spent much of his day on the telephone, doing business with auctioneers and other dealers, pickers, decorators, and clients.

On business trips to California with his mother and his sister Maggie, David took a suite at the Beverly Wilshire Hotel. He refers to this time in his life as "my Beverly Wilshire period." He found the suite to be "a little slice of heaven," and more beautiful than the hotel room pictured in the movie *Pretty Woman* because it had real antiques in it. He ate cracked crab by the pool. He shopped at Mr. Guy of Beverly Hills because that's where Alex Trebek, the host of *Jeopardy,* got his clothes. During Schorsch's Beverly Wilshire period, a masseur ran an electric vibrator up and down his back as he took incessant telephone calls. His telephone style suited the milieu. Even in New York, he would say, "Harriet, darling, how do you think *I* feel? I like cash flow, babe."

Antique objects and folk art paintings occupied a place in Schorsch's life on a level with the friends and family who surrounded him. He viewed movies from the point of view of the antiques that sometimes inhabited them, and he startled visitors with such questions as, "Did you see the highboy in *Rosemary's Baby?*" Schorsch says, "Some people, myself included, absolutely get a physical, chemical reaction in our bodies upon seeing great works of art. It's the same thing that athletes get. It's like sex and fear and music. Food, beauty, auctions, and gambling. Some people get it selling and some get it buying."

David Schorsch got it buying. Certain objects held magical attractions for him. He saw them and he desired them and he felt he must possess them. The blue blanket chest was one such object. Upon his return from Aruba, David discovered the chest sitting in the dining room of his mother's house. From the photo on the *Painted Furniture* book, he had come to love its color, its condition, and the fact that no one had replaced its leather hinges. As he put it later, "It's amazing that somebody years ago wouldn't have gotten pissed off, and stuck some knobs on it." Objects have a power over David Schorsch that no photograph can match. Some objects have greater power than others. "I was speechless," he recalled of seeing the blue blanket chest for the first time. "It was smaller than I thought. For some reason I was expecting something like a highboy. It was much more diminutive because I had never encountered it personally. Which I thought was delightful."

The Schorsches often had a client in mind when they paid more than $100,000 for something. But they had bought this chest because, as David says, "We believed in the piece." The Schorsches numbered among their clients many important collectors of American folk art and Shaker furniture. These included Ralph Esmerian, an international jewelry broker who occupies a space in folk art much like the space Henry Francis du Pont once occupied in American furniture. Along with Esmerian, the Schorsches had also sold to the actor Bill Cosby. The Schorsches had the blanket chest photographed, and they sent the pictures to all their best clients. To arrive at a price they applied the formula standard to most retail operations. They doubled their cost. The blue blanket chest, which had sold in 1964 for the then staggering sum of $2,500, was for sale once again. This time, twenty-two years later, it would cost a client one hundred times as much. David's generosity was such that his "best clients," as he later remembered, "could have had it for $200,000."

The blue blanket chest, which had sat for so long in the Eckleys' house with no other duties than to hold some linens and give its owners pleasure, was now made to perform. The Schorsches carried the chest into the homes of those clients who expressed an interest in the piece. They shipped it back to the Midwest, from where it had only recently arrived, to a home filled with what David describes as "the greatest Shaker collection." Collectors often want to live for a time with the things they wish to buy, and dealers like the Schorsches are happy to oblige. David believed that the Queen Anne chest of drawers, though not a Shaker object, had what he called "a Shaker-like aesthetic." After placing the blue blanket chest in his client's living room—a room filled with nothing but Shaker objects—he believed that in that context "it looked like a billion dollars."

Paul Eckley believed the blue chest had an odd way of looking good no matter where it sat. Unfortunately, the clients from the Midwest did not agree. Perhaps they felt uncomfortable mixing Shaker and Queen Anne, or perhaps it simply cost too much. To a collector of folk art such as the midwestern client, $200,000 represents an amount budgeted for an entire year of buying objects. Collectors like to buy, and most find that buying only one object in the course of a year requires a discipline they don't have. "I told him I'd give him a really long time to pay for it, so that it wouldn't feel so hard," Schorsch remembered later. "At any rate, it didn't work out."

Failure does not daunt Peggy and David Schorsch. They packed up the blue blanket chest, shipped it back East, and let it stay for a time in the houses of other clients. Something always seemed to sabotage the deal. One client suffered a temporary financial setback. Another didn't like it. The chest moved from house to house, and David slowly came to realize that nobody wanted it. "I think it is such a sophisticated aesthetic—its not having brasses, the simplicity of the piece. It couldn't find a home because it was such a sophisticated aesthetic. Every one of my clients turned it down. The most important collectors in the field turned the piece down."

The blue blanket chest had entered the market at a price at which the Eckleys felt comfortable parting with it, but now it couldn't find a home. The appreciation of this thing lay in the minds of very few individuals. People place value on beauty and believe a thing that's beautiful at $25,000—a price at which the Schorsches could have sold a hundred such chests—was not so beautiful at ten times that price. Only a few people who could appreciate so unusual a thing had the money to acquire it, and they had decided that this thing wasn't worth it. One could see that the beauty of the blue blanket chest, at $250,000, lay not in the object itself but inside David and Peggy Schorsch.

David Schorsch was born in Philadelphia in 1963. His father, John, had inherited a scrap metal fortune. Peggy and John Schorsch began to collect Chinese porcelains, Delft, and American furniture for the opportunities to socialize with other collectors. Whenever the family took a vacation, it came back with antiques. The children named their German short-haired pointers Chip and Dale, their maltese Antique, their yorkie Lowboy, and their two boxers Queen Anne and Windsor. David began to accompany his parents to antiques shows, and by age four he knew the difference between a Chippendale side chair and a Windsor. He became expert on the subject of antique paperweights. When he was six, Peggy gave him a nineteenth-century hatbox. This object so overwhelmed him with its beauty that each night, when he was supposed to be in bed, he pulled it off the shelf to stroke it as one might a cat. He quickly saw that what one box could do, twenty could do better. He began to collect these hatboxes, not as his brother collected Lincoln memorabilia, or his sister dolls, but obsessively. He learned to tell the genuine from the fake and to see subtle distinctions. Antiques dealers looked at the little boy in awe, the way one looks at a violin prodigy. The appreciation of beauty, like the love of music, is revealed very early in life. By age seven, Schorsch was among the most knowledgeable people on the subject of blockfront furniture from Newport, Rhode Island. By his eighth birthday, he owned the most important collection of hatboxes in the country.

One of David's favorite pastimes was to play antiques dealer, a game in which he employed his G.I. Joe doll as a customer while he ran the shop. His heroes were antiques dealers. Each month, he ran to the mailbox to grab the family's copy of *Antiques* magazine, the most prestigious publication in the field, so he could study the ad placed by Sack's. Strolling about the fields of country antiques fairs, he sometimes carried a big cigar the way John Walton did.

David's father and his uncle sold the scrap metal business when David was nine. Three years later, the family moved to Greenwich, Connecticut. Their new house possessed eight bedrooms and stood on a thirty-six-acre estate. Butlers and maids moved quietly about the house, while a gardener patrolled a domain that included a stable and a heated garage with its own gas pump. This life appealed to David Schorsch. By the time he was eleven, he had learned to tell the best objects from the merely better ones and to understand that fine furniture gave him pleasures that hatboxes could not. He decorated his room with a Queen Anne youth-size pine desk (worth about $3,500), a Lancaster County Windsor chair, a blue painted wardrobe, and a dome-topped Rhode Island blanket chest.

This life came to an end a couple of years after the move to Connecticut, when his parents divorced. All but one of the servants left the family after discovering that paychecks would not be forthcoming, and the one maid who remained sometimes paid for their groceries herself. David went into the antiques business at age thirteen and began to support his mother, his two brothers, and his two sisters. A friend with a van drove him about the countryside, where he bought and sold furniture. Pickers such as Fernando, a

Greenwich butler with a sideline in antiques, waited outside the house until David returned from school. He bought and sold objects worth as much as $20,000 and occasionally made $10,000 in a month.

Each object tells its owner a story, and collectors like to hear their constant chatter. But a roomful of murmuring objects is not enough to gratify a dealer. David found through necessity that he could take as much pleasure from having things for a short while, and then passing them on, as he could from keeping them. He learned that age and history are commodities like any other. He learned to see the profit margins in beauty.

Some dealers resented this child, who not only claimed to know more than they but who also often did. He told them that their chests were fakes, or he told them that their chairs had replaced legs, and these truths did nothing to endear the boy to them. Those who watched him dismiss adults of fifty on subjects in which they considered themselves expert usually ended by saying things like, "He was right, unfortunately." His friends in the business recalled how he might buy a weathervane for $5,000 and sell it in the same weekend for $15,000. They thought him brilliant but wondered at the sadness with which he filled them. They'd say, "How does he relate to another kid his age who's equally intelligent but who's getting $25 a week for an allowance?"

People saw that David was "a man when he should have been a child," or that he "didn't do the fun things kids do," or that he "missed his childhood." His love for objects consumed him in a way that it consumes many collectors and dealers. Those who called him "obsessive"—dealers such as Marguerite Riordan, who had known him all his life—generally admitted, as Riordan did, that "We're all neurotic. We're bugged. People involved with objects are compulsive. They care more about objects than they do about people sometimes. Their relationships with people are difficult."

David testified at the divorce trial of his mother and father. Because he had ignored a court order against selling any of the family antiques, the judge told him, "You know, I could send you to jail." He was thirteen years old. His father never spoke to him again. Clients and friends didn't believe this until they watched John Schorsch pass within a few feet of his son without acknowledging David's existence.

During the school year, David attended Rye Country Day School. He accompanied his mother on buying expeditions and became so expert that she needed his opinions. "Do you want to go to school?" she'd ask him in the morning. "Or do you want to go to the White Plains Antiques Show?" At age fourteen, David was invited to exhibit at the Connecticut Antiques Show, second only to the New York Winter Antiques Show in importance. He spent every summer dealing at flea markets and buying at auctions. During the school year, he often skipped class. Though he made up his schoolwork, an English teacher told him at the start of his senior year that he would fail if he missed another class. "Probably I would have gone to college," Schorsch says. "I know other people who dealt in college. But I quit high school. I started dealing full-time. That put me in the center and I've been there ever since."

David spent most of his waking hours with Peggy and his sister Maggie. When he believed his mother to be wrong, he told her to shut up, or used even stronger language that revealed the evidence of a troubled childhood. He could be even harder on his sister. She worked in the business but did not quite possess David's love for, or knowledge of, objects. "WHAT, MAGGIE, WHAT?" he would scream at her. "Don't interrupt me, FOR GOD'S SAKE!" Bad moods sometimes lasted for days, and when a mood overcame him the skin tightened up around his eyes, as it will on someone with a migraine headache. Though he yelled at his mother and sister, he was closer to no one else. He shared with them his innermost desires, bought them thoughtful presents, and in other ways exhibited an extraordinary love for them.

David and Peggy both tried to run antiques businesses on their own. They found that each needed something in the other. His emotional responses to objects—especially when bidding at auction—often carried him away. Only his mother could restrain him from his habit of paying far more for certain objects than he could ever hope to recover. Sometimes, when even her presence did not suffice, she told her friends, "He went crazy." Peggy depended on her son's deep knowledge of antiques and on his willingness to gamble—a trait that, as often as not, resulted in spectacular profits.

David Schorsch had acquired the blue blanket chest because he made it his business to sell the best. He believed in the concept of having "an eye" for beautiful things and felt that while this eye could be trained, it was, as he said, an "innate gift." This gift is critical to the success of any antiques dealer. But the price structures for most categories of formal furniture have been set for a long time, and except for extraordinary objects, these prices increase at predictable rates. Folk art, however, is a young field in which prices are not so predictable. Dealers with a gift for seeing great things possess the power—like that Israel Sack once possessed—to make taste.

One man who has astutely analyzed the folk art market is the art dealer Alexander Acevedo. He runs a shop on Madison Avenue, and over the past decade he has sold, among other things, paperweights and antique toys, jewelry, pre-Columbian art, Orientalia, arts and crafts, American Indian artifacts, Old Master and European paintings, gems, coins, and baseball cards, as well as Shaker chairs, American quilts, and American formal furniture. Each one of these areas generally requires a lifetime of study to master. Acevedo has mastered them all. He deals at the top levels of every field, and has come to be regarded with a kind of awe by dealers throughout the world. David Schorsch has said of Alexander Acevedo, "If he died tomorrow he would be a legend. He is unique in the world of art dealing."

Acevedo has noticed distinctive traits among those who deal in different areas of antiques. Toy dealers are the most fun, dealers in paintings the stuffiest, coin dealers the most neurotic, and furniture dealers the most unscrupulous. Acevedo is especially contemptuous of those who inhabit a world where prices are not stable and where small fortunes can be won or lost in an afternoon. "Folk art dealers are the most vicious," he says. "The folk market is like a bunch of sheep and we follow them. It's the most gossipy business I know. Who's to really say what constitutes a great piece of folk art? There are a few people who get together, they're in the forefront. They may even have a great collection. And they make their taste, and we all follow them."

No one was more adept at making taste than David

Schorsch. One method he employed, after coming to prefer one object to another, was to pay far more for it than any similar item had ever brought. At an auction in East Dennis, Massachusetts, at age eighteen, Schorsch once outbid John Walton on a set of six painted Windsor chairs of the sort that are often considered folk art. The $61,000 he paid for these chairs far exceeded anything a set of similar chairs had brought, and the effect of Schorsch's gamble was to earn him recognition as a star among folk art dealers. This result so infuriated Walton that he telephoned Peggy Schorsch, and, in David's words, "called her a cunt nineteen times." David believed Walton had spread a rumor—a false rumor—that his check for these chairs had bounced. Walton was so upset at the publicity the boy received from buying them that he told a friend, "You know, he just got ten ads in *Antiques* magazine for free."

Some dealers prefer a strictly private business, but wide publicity suited David Schorsch's personality. He liked to bid at auction and had the habit of sticking his hand in the air and not taking it down—the habit Peggy Schorsch meant when she said, "He went crazy." Dealers who knew his habits called him "daring" or "impetuous" or "irresponsible." He paid record prices—outrageous, unheard-of prices —for folk art paintings and painted boxes, Shaker tables, cigar store Indians, and trade signs. This method guaranteed that people would sit up and take notice of categories of objects that had theretofore remained unnoticed.

Sometimes the method backfired. David once saw a pair of nineteenth-century andirons with the faces of suns cast on them. He had never before seen such sunfaced andirons. Their beauty struck him as remarkable. These andirons had come from the famous Harold Corbin iron collection. David recognized them as having been made by the Meriden, Connecticut, firm of Bradley & Hubbard, a well-known andiron maker. When they came up for sale he bought them for the astonishing sum of $13,750. The news of this stupendous purchase spread throughout the folk art world. Trade papers such as the *Maine Antiques Digest* and *Antiques and the Arts Weekly* reported it with bold headlines, and dealers and collectors talked about it. Then a curious thing happened: David Schorsch discovered that these andirons were not so rare after all. Once the news of his record price reached the collecting public, sunfaced andirons began, as David puts it, "coming out of the woodwork." The market for them dropped to $1,500.

David and Peggy Schorsch would not have prospered long if such mistakes occurred frequently. More often than not, David sold his objects for modest profits and gained the publicity that had so infuriated Walton. Like many antiques dealers, David had read and reread the S. N. Behrman biography of Joseph Duveen. In 1933, Duveen had acquired the British title of Lord Duveen of Millbank through his reputation as the greatest antiques dealer who ever lived. His clients included Andrew Mellon and Henry Clay Frick, and he had mastered the art of making these American tycoons pay staggering sums for masterpiece paintings. Like Duveen, Schorsch made it a practice to outbid the greatest collectors of American folk art—men and women who happened not to be his clients—in the hope of teaching them a valuable lesson. If they wanted the best, they would have to come to him.

Despite David's talent for spotting beauty, and Peggy's

talent for selling it, the blue blanket chest remained unsold throughout much of 1987. The Schorsches showed it to every client they had. What David called "the most interesting response" came from Bill Cosby, who owned one of the most significant collections of American furniture and folk art in the country. Schorsch had met Cosby only once. Usually he dealt with Cosby's agent, and after Schorsch had sent a letter, he received a phone call from this man. Cosby had "loved" the blue blanket chest, the man said.

"Cosby saw a photograph and he said he thought the piece was great," Schorsch remembers. "He thought it was so great I should keep it, that in a few years it'd be worth a million dollars. The agent told Cosby, 'You know, the fellow who has it is a young dealer. He can't afford to hold it.' "

Antiques are most valuable when they are fresh to the market. The longer they remain on the market and unsold, the harder it is to sustain their prices. Dealers do not happily discount their merchandise. The market for antiques is not like the market for new dresses. One expects toward the end of a season to find even designer dresses on sale at Bloomingdale's. But with antique items like the blue blanket chest—with works of art—dealers like to create the illusion that price rests inside the thing itself. They want their customers to feel that value, like beauty, is innate. Discounting one item puts into question the prices of all that dealer's items. Nothing about an antique that's lingered in a shop makes it inherently less valuable than a more recent acquisition. An antique is supposed to grow more valuable with time. No dealer can afford to have his or her price structure questioned.

Searching for a larger audience, Schorsch placed an

advertisement for the chest in the November 1987 issue of *Antiques* magazine. He knew that if he couldn't sell the chest with this ad, he would have to take it off the market for several years to make it fresh again. Every time a client rejected it, its luster faded, and little by little, in the minds of those who knew it, the chest grew tarnished. Word that it had failed to sell spread through the antiques community. The chest went to David's shop in Greenwich, where it stood not as a thing that pleased the Schorsches but as a source of irritation. A total of $137,500 stood inside this object, unable to generate new cash. Such objects often sit with a dealer until the dealer grows tired enough to unload them at any price, or until they've come to serve the role—the way the chest did in Joe Pari's house—as a member of the family.

On November 12, 1987, Schorsch returned from an auction in San Francisco to his mother's house in Connecticut. He recalls the events of that day as "the single most profound thing in my life, aside from my parents' getting divorced." A snowstorm left the roads nearly impassable, but he found himself wanting a good meal. "I drove to town and got as far as the bridge on the Merritt Parkway," he recalled. "The bridge was frozen. I did a 360-degree spin and hit a guy oncoming head-on. I never lost consciousness." Surgeons later discovered that the femur of his right leg had, as he describes it, "exploded." The resultant surgery left him with an eighteen-inch steel rod in his leg, two bolts in his knee, and one bolt in his hip. "When you have a near-death experience it changes a lot of things in your life," he says. "This stuff isn't that important. I like the action now as much as the objects."

David Schorsch's accident also changed the destiny of the blue blanket chest. His operations cost huge sums of cash and he needed to find a way to pay for them. In January 1988 he sold a folk art painting at Sotheby's—a painting by John Brewster—for $852,500, realizing a profit of nearly $500,000. This might have alleviated his financial woes except for the lawsuit filed by the people from whom he bought this work of art. Though they had employed an expert to advise them on the sale, the litigants believed that Schorsch had somehow cheated them. The ensuing legal battle left Schorsch in what he would later call "a bad way."

In the spring of 1988, Schorsch decided to sell some things both from his personal collection and from his inventory—a large volume of antiques that included a tall clock, a Queen Anne chair, a Philadelphia ball-and-claw chair, and a pair of Philadelphia andirons. The blue blanket chest was among them. Schorsch might have chosen to sell this group of objects at auction. "But I wanted the money in my hand," he says. "Furthermore, I wanted to keep it discreet. I wanted this shit to go away. It was no one's business in the trade that I needed the money."

A number of people—a number of his friends —would have grabbed up individual items. But among those friends with whom he did business, and who usually had plenty of cash on hand, Schorsch knew only one person who could buy them all. His name was Wayne Pratt. Pratt ran a shop in Marlborough, Massachusetts. He had grown up in the antiques business and for years had worked as a picker for John Walton. Pratt's specialty was blockfront furniture. He also handled other brown furniture, folk art objects like Windsor chairs, paintings, and pinball machines. Because of his habit of appearing at scenes of distress, like the scene in which David Schorsch found himself, Pratt was sometimes known in the world of American antiques as "The Undertaker." Schorsch sold him the entire lot for a sum the young dealer has described as "hundreds of thousands of dollars." For bookkeeping purposes, Schorsch figured a price for each item in the lot, and the price at which he figured the blue blanket chest was $100,000. This was a $37,500 loss.

Fifteen

WAYNE PRATT THOUGHT OF ANTIQUES MORE AS CAPITAL THAN as art. Pratt's clients felt the same way. Long after he had bought the blue chest and sold it, Pratt always kept in mind where it fit into the market. He said, "I liked the blanket chest, but I figured it was in the collectible furniture area." Or he said, "I felt it was helped by being on the back of the *Painted Furniture* book."

Pratt figured each object's value differently from Schorsch. He thought the blue blanket chest to be worth $125,000, and was certain he could unload it for that. Schorsch had hoped by the force of his aesthetic judgment to sell this object for twice that much—to change its price structure. But the sum Wayne Pratt allotted to the chest— the same $125,000 that the Eckleys had received two years earlier—represented its true retail value. Now that Pratt had the chest, he hoped to dispose of it as quickly as possible.

Pratt lives in a neat and tidy house, in a town where small farms, light industry, and suburban developments meet in the tucks of low, rolling hills. Marlborough lies only about twenty-five miles west of Boston. It is a place where young men and young women smoke a lot of cigarettes, drive Pontiac Trans Ams, and rarely get to the big city. Across the street from Pratt's house, neat rows of white pine trees shield his view of a factory owned by Digital Equipment Corporation. A large barn that serves as a cabinet shop and warehouse stands next to Pratt's house, and five enormous maple trees shade the circular driveway where he parks his new Mercedes station wagon.

Pratt sells highboys, lowboys, and secretaries, Windsor chairs, weathervanes, and antique toys. The cash that moves in and out of his bank account each year amounts to more than $6 million. His expenses regularly reach $80,000 each month. "The best antiques dealers," he says, "are good businessmen."

Pratt grew up poor, in a tiny town on the Massachusetts south shore. He began collecting old toys at age seven and bought his first Windsor chair at eight. In high school he ran the 100-yard dash and the 440 not so much for the thrill of victory as for the economic rewards that ensued from team bus trips to neighboring schools. After completing his races, Pratt often knocked on a couple of doors, found a chest or a couple of antique chairs, and tied them to the back of the school bus. By his senior year he owned a '55 Plymouth whose trunk lid and backseat he had removed. He made a habit of registering as a peddler with the police in surrounding communities. He drew elaborate street maps and formed a strategic plan to knock on every door in town. "I buy old things," he'd say, an introduction that seemed to elicit the same reply from every grandmother in eastern Massachusetts. "Oh, I'm the only old thing here," they'd say. Pratt kept elaborate records in thick books—"Mrs. Jones has highboy. Called on her. Offered $200"—and every six months returned inquiringly to Mrs. Jones's. He sometimes came across a rare object for which he knew he might get tens of thousands of dollars. Because people grew suspicious at large numbers, he found that an offer of a few hundred dollars was more likely than one of a few thousand to result in a sale. Old people made the best prospects because they tended to have, as well as to be, old things. He could tell from the old lace curtains and the neatly trimmed yard whether a house promised treasures.

After high school, Pratt attended a business college, moved to Marlborough, and started an office supply company. But he never quit dealing. When he sold the office supply business in the mid-1960s, he began trading antiques full-time. In these early years, Pratt sold his things to a number of dealers who stood farther up the pyramid than he. He commonly sold to John Walton. The two men spent long days together at auctions and on the road. Both loved to hunt for antiques. In the days when Walton ran his shop on Park Avenue, these two friends occasionally combed the countryside together in a beat-up van, acquired a load of Victorian furniture, and tied it on the top. Each man might make $500 on such a venture. Each was just as happy as if he had sold an expensive Chippendale tea table. Pratt enjoyed this line of work. He could ride around in a van all day, wear jeans, and stop for a beer if he liked. Buying junk from Mrs. Jones and selling it to Mr. Walton, he could make a couple hundred thousand dollars a year. Pratt will never forget that Walton called him "the greatest picker that ever lived."

Rare, painted Queen Anne blanket-chests-on-frame are tricky merchandise. Such things did not ordinarily appeal to Pratt. His idea of a good market was brown furniture, a market, he explains, where "prices are pretty stable, have been for thirty years." Pratt distinguishes between markets for old toys, Windsor chairs, and Federal furniture by the different types of customers who buy these things and the different price structures for each market. In Wayne Pratt's world, items of brown furniture from the Queen Anne and Chippendale periods occupy the same market because their prices stand at about the same levels and rise at the same rates. They also interest the same people.

Pratt believes many of the things that David Schorsch has specialized in—Nantucket baskets, Shaker rocking chairs, painted furniture—to be "collectibles." Collectibles fit into what he calls "fluctuating markets," where "all of a sudden you get prices shooting up," and he learned long ago to stay away from them. Pratt makes a few exceptions—he likes to "play around" with Windsor chairs—but he does not like things so speculative as the blue blanket chest. Though made in the Queen Anne style, the chest belongs to the painted furniture market. Things whose value one might miscalculate by $100,000—as Schorsch had evidently miscalculated when he bought the chest—scare Pratt.

Pratt allows his clients to trade any merchandise they have bought from him for anything he has in stock. He has also discovered the advantages of sometimes giving his clients good merchandise at cost. Pratt knew that one of these customers, a New Jersey contractor named Bruce Wilt, had a taste for things like the blue blanket chest. He offered it to Wilt for $125,000. "I didn't want to overprice it to him, because I didn't want to hang him with it," Pratt remembered. "He was a good client. I wanted to price it so two years from now I could get it back and sell it. If you're dealing with a client consistently, you can't gouge them with one particular article. It'll come back to haunt you. They'll want to trade it back. They'll want to sell it. You'll end up hurting yourself. You have to put them in the article at a price level that you could resell it from at a later date. You have to think about that."

Bruce Wilt's father was a sheetrocker, and after college Bruce started his own sheetrocking business. In time he came to employ as many as five hundred men and became what he describes as "the biggest sheetrocker in the state—or *one* of the biggest." Wilt is now in his midthirties. He has a flattop haircut and intense blue eyes, and he often goes to work in a leather jacket, a flannel shirt, and soft leather deck shoes. He lives with his wife and two daughters in the upper-middle-class community of Basking Ridge, New Jersey. This is a town of old trees but new houses, of sweeping lawns with split rail fences, of BMWs and Saabs.

A couple of years earlier, the Wilts had built a two-story house on a plan of eighteenth-century saltbox construction. Pretty green paint covers its clapboard siding, large brick chimneys rise from either end of the roof, and an authentic antique bull's-eye window sits above the front door. The Wilts plastered the downstairs walls so that an artist could cover them with landscapes of a simple farming life like those depicted by the eighteenth-century muralist Rufus Porter. The Wilt house shows the remarkable progression of a man's taste. The living room in back features a fifteen-foot ceiling, a gargantuan stone fireplace, and contemporary furniture. It seems at odds with the rooms at the front of the house. The Wilts have filled their front rooms with painted Windsor chairs, Oriental rugs, and weathervanes. Painted boxes rest on antique cupboards, and folk art portraits by such luminaries as Jacob Mantel and William Matthew Prior decorate the walls. Wilt estimates that in the course of his short collecting career he has spent more than $1 million on antiques.

Bruce Wilt knew nothing about antiques until 1984, when he met his wife. Her parents collected what he calls "primitive stuff—more toward folk art," and they took him to his first antiques show. He became interested in antiques, and when he furnished his saltbox house, he brought in "truckloads" of antique furniture—what Wilt calls "country stuff. Stuff that you use for a house. Something you're going to need anyway, like for your bedroom you're going to need a chest of drawers."

Like most collectors, Wilt only discovered over time how much he had to learn about the antiques business. People warned him, "Watch what you do. You're going to get burnt one time. You're going to get burnt." But Wilt didn't want to listen. The method Wilt first employed is known to antiques dealers as the "shotgun approach, where you just sort of buy." Then he began to learn. He talked to dealers and he liked it when people told him, "Geez, you got a pretty good eye." Besides finding antiques interesting, Wilt liked the way they held their value.

Wilt soon came to know a number of dealers and found that they wore him out because, as he explains, "they keep bullshittin' and bullshittin'." He discovered that every piece a dealer had in inventory was "great" but that anything belonging to another dealer was "a piece of shit." Dealers bad-mouthed their competitors and they bad-mouthed the things they wanted to acquire but could not. The antiques business, he discovered, was a lot different from the sheetrock business. As a contractor, Wilt was happy when he could make a profit of 6 percent, but he soon learned that antiques dealers never hesitated to make 1,000 percent when they could. This led him to identify most antiques dealers as "crazy people, crazy people." He found the business to be populated by what he calls "a bunch of whore gypsies just screwing each other whenever they can."

Wilt did learn that while some antiques dealers might not have what he considered a proper set of scruples, the best ones knew a lot about their merchandise. He made the acquaintance of these more knowledgeable dealers and questioned them whenever he could. He saw that when the best dealers came to his house, they would offer to buy some things from his collection but disdain to buy others. It wasn't a question of the antiques being fakes. A collector quickly learns to ask for a receipt with the word "genuine" written on it in bold letters, and that this habit usually keeps fakes from entering his house. But to buy things that would rise in value—to buy the $2,000 thing that will soon be worth $6,000—was a question of aesthetics. He learned that only the best things appreciate greatly in value. He learned that "the market knows crap."

Wilt at first grew very attached to his things. He'd started getting catalogs from auction houses, and when a Sotheby's catalog arrived, as he explains, "I'd go, 'Holy shit, I gotta get that, I gotta get that,' you know? Very compulsive eye. 'I gotta get that, what is it going to cost me?' And I would go for it. I would pay for it, because I was afraid I wouldn't see something like that again. But as it ends up, every year there are beautiful, beautiful things coming around."

Wilt knew the blue blanket chest from the back of the painted furniture book. He had long coveted this object, and believed he knew what David Schorsch had paid for it. Schorsch was famous in the world of American folk art. Though Wilt had never met Schorsch, he knew of Schorsch's unsurpassed reputation for knowing quality. Wilt believed he knew for certain that the chest would be a good investment, and that was why he bought it from Pratt sight unseen.

The blanket chest arrived in New Jersey in the summer of 1988. For the first time in two years, it had a real home. Wilt placed it in the dining room, where his dinner guests could admire it. "When you got a consensus on a piece like the blue blanket chest, it's just right," he says. "It's just great. Nobody will deny it's great. So this piece became a real figurepiece. This was a great, great piece."

Sixteen

THE CHIPPENDALE CARD TABLE THAT TOM HUGHES HAD FOUND in the basement of the First Pennsylvania Company grew very expensive to insure. By the spring of 1990, Hughes's widow faced a dilemma. Her husband had died eight years earlier, and Mrs. Hughes did not feel as strongly about the table as her husband had. Her idea of a nice antique rested more in a piece of strawberry pottery that she'd found in the Pennsylvania Dutch country. After her husband died, Mrs. Hughes moved into a smallish, two-story, French provincial house in a pleasant Philadelphia neighborhood. English and American pottery filled this house, which was also decorated with nautical paintings, scrimshaw, and the other marine-related memorabilia that had so taken her husband. The Willing card table stood beside the door in her front hall.

In consultation with her children, Mrs. Hughes decided to sell the table, and with this thought the family turned to the New York auction house of Christie's. The

Hugheses' association with Christie's dated back many years, to Tom's friendship with Paul Ingersoll, the head of its Philadelphia office. Tom's wife and children felt comfortable with Ingersoll. He often visited the Hughes house, knew the card table well, and seemed the logical person to approach. Christie's agreed to place an estimate on the table for the sake of appraisal, and in time its New York office dispatched the head of the American furniture department, John Hays, to look at it.

Hays is a friendly, straightforward man, who at the time was thirty-one years old. Compared to people such as David Schorsch, or Leslie Keno of Sotheby's, Hays came rather late to the study and appreciation of American furniture. He grew up in a family that appreciated the arts—a cousin, Arthur Upham Pope, was a leading scholar of Persian art—and took a job out of college at the Peggy Guggenheim Museum in Venice. But he had never studied antique furniture until Christie's Americana department hired him at age twenty-four. He was, furthermore, a man not given to great displays of excitement, and who therefore fit well into the genial, gentlemanly world of Christie's.

Hays traveled to Philadelphia to look at the card table. After he left, Mrs. Hughes's daughter Elizabeth felt, as she reflected later, that "his enthusiasm was not great." In the way that owners usually form an idea of what their things are worth, the Hugheses had decided to value their table at $1 million. The difference between expectation and reality often causes distress and people in distress generally take measures to do something about it. In this case distress led the Hughes family to contact Christie's chief competition—Sotheby's.

As it happened, Elizabeth Hughes had a friend at Sotheby's named Barbara Deisroth, head of Sotheby's Art Nouveau and Art Deco department. One spring day, Deisroth appeared at the door to Bill Stahl's office. Although she was Elizabeth's good friend, Deisroth also served as a member of Stahl's broad intelligence network. Whenever she returned from a visit to the Hughes house in Philadelphia, where she had remembered to glance at the Willing card table, she made a point of telling Stahl, "It's still there." On the spring morning in 1990, Deisroth lingered by Stahl's door somewhat longer than usual. She explained that Mrs. Hughes might be interested in selling her treasure. "You ought to go see this table," Deisroth told him.

When expensive objects appeared on the market, Stahl often found himself in competition with Christie's. Some people think of Sotheby's as a place where auctioneers try to be gentlemen, whereas Christie's is regarded as a place where gentlemen try to be auctioneers. Christie's employs men like Paul Ingersoll and Ralph Carpenter, whose bloodlines run back to the country's early history and who regularly drink Bloody Marys with those whose families have owned Chippendale furniture for a couple of centuries. When a Rhode Island family decided to sell the Nicholas Brown secretary—the one Christie's would auction to Robert Bass for $12.1 million—a daughter of the family led Stahl to believe that they'd have preferred to sell it through

Sotheby's. But Stahl knew he would never get it. The daughter summed up Ralph Carpenter's connections to the family with the question, "What would Uncle Ralph say?"

Since first hearing about the card table, Stahl knew that the Hugheses' friendship with Paul Ingersoll would give Christie's an advantage. The auctioneer understood that Ingersoll lived around the corner from Mrs. Hughes and occasionally visited her house. Yet none of these facts daunted Stahl. He is a man of unusual energy and optimism, and though he figured Sotheby's to be "slight underdogs," he immediately made plans to see the table.

Stahl intended to bring along Deisroth. Although she knew little about American furniture, she was a good friend of the family and would lend the visit a comforting social atmosphere. He also invited Wendell Garrett, the former editor of *Antiques* magazine. Garrett, Stahl explained, would "add some scholarship, add some gray hairs, add some contacts."

Garrett had edited *Antiques* for eighteen years. In that time, he had acquired great respect in the world of American furniture. He's in his early sixties, a gentlemanly, soft-spoken man whose intelligence, sobriety, and honesty put those whom he encounters immediately at ease. A nerve disorder requires him to move about in an electric cart. *Antiques* magazine has published continuously since 1922. Garrett followed a tradition set by the magazine's previous editors, who liked to mix popular themes with scholarly articles, to print exquisite photographs, and to appeal to a broad range of interests. He encouraged academics and dealers to write about their favorite subjects, from Chinese export vases to the lives of itinerant painters, and managed by such means to appeal to about sixty thousand devoted readers each month.

As the final member of the party, Stahl invited Leslie Keno, head of the American furniture department. Stahl's most important job in Philadelphia was to arrive at an estimate of the table's worth. This task required deep knowledge of and experience with Chippendale furniture, and Keno had been studying American antiques for about twenty years—ever since the age of twelve. Keno had the further advantage of having once himself inspected another Philadelphia Chippendale turret-top card table with carved rails.

It's difficult to mention Leslie Keno in any context without also naming his identical twin brother, Leigh. Leigh Keno deals American antiques from a shop just off Madison Avenue and is no less highly regarded than Leslie as an Americana expert. The twins grew up on a farm in the town of Mohawk, New York, and became interested in old hinges and the shards of stone pots that they could dig up in the woods around their house. They formed a taste for better things at the home of a dealer named Myrtle Dicker, who would point to two Canton jars and say, "Which is the better piece?" Both boys could generally pick out the better object. "One was incredibly powerful," Leslie remembers. "The designs were vibrant. The shape was more ovoid. It was a much more powerful thing in the decorative arts. The other one was a little bit off, you know. The design didn't quite work. It was a little busy." Leslie speaks of an object that is not beautiful in the same language he and his brother use to describe people with bad habits, as if embarrassed to mention this aberration of what they consider to be the goodness of the human spirit and the goodness of the inanimate object. The brothers found that they could both usually pick the better piece, but occasionally they failed Myrtle Dicker. "She was very staunch, like a schoolteacher," Leigh recalls. "She'd get mad. If you picked the wrong one she'd say, 'You're wrong about that!' and almost rap your hand with a ruler."

The twins did everything together. They rode their dirt bikes together, played in a rock band together, and looked for antiques together. Sometimes they walked into mirrors believing the other brother to be approaching. They dressed alike until the eighth grade. When their mother is asked about their attachment for each other, she says, "They were so close, it's scary." By age seven, Leigh and Leslie had begun to buy and sell the American stoneware that Leslie calls "our first love and first connection." They studied stoneware, pestered dealers with questions about stoneware, and soon became among the country's leading experts in this small corner of the Americana market. Leigh made intricate drawings of the jugs and bowls they had acquired. "What we were drawn toward were these almost timeless ovoid shapes," Leigh says. "Every night after dinner we'd get a cup of coffee and go back and look at what we'd bought. We'd go back and pick them up and hold them, almost as you'd hold a—a baby."

At age thirteen, the twins began accompanying their parents to a flea market in Brimfield, Massachusetts, where Ron and Norma Keno operated a booth. Brimfield is among the largest flea markets in the world. Five hundred dealers set their wares out on a dozen different fields and sell everything from old toys to Depression glass. The Kenos themselves sold Christmas ornaments, quilts, jewelry, and wicker chairs, together with a collection of ceramic figurines that might at any one time have included teddy bears, cats, parakeets, snails, and elves perched on toadstools.

Each year when they returned to Brimfield, the twins would bring stone jugs they'd bought for $200 and for which they hoped to get $400. Leslie remembers the dealers with flashlights who approached their car late at night in the search to find treasures before anyone else. He remembers the days of hunting through the aisles, when he'd ask about a thing Leigh had just inspected, and the dealer who thought it the same persistent child would try to run him off. Their passions for objects consumed them. One year, after Leigh had broken his wrist, he found a beautiful stoneware jug with the image of a deer on it. He told the dealer to hold it for him while he found his brother. When they returned, and discovered that she had sold the jug, Leigh grew so furious that he slammed his fist into her trailer, smashed his cast, and rebroke the wrist.

Brimfield taught the Keno brothers a lot. It taught them to distinguish markets and it taught them to evaluate vast quantities of merchandise at a glance. They came to call this operation "scanning," and they quickly learned how to scan a booth in a couple of seconds. Everyone at Brimfield employs this method, but the twins were experts at it. The act of scanning a booth and spotting an item of genuine interest is also known to Leigh and Leslie as the "Terminator Effect," referring to Arnold Schwarzenegger's manner of scanning the landscape and zeroing in on his prey. They could spot a chair from ten yards away and determine in seconds whether it was really old or merely made to look old, and if it was really old, what sort of wear it had, what ratio the number of its spindles bore to its value, and what it might bring in their parents' booth on Main Street. Brimfield taught Leigh "to appreciate the great stuff from seeing thousands of baroque chairs." It taught Leslie the great understanding of things that he would later bring to bear on such objects as the Willing card table.

After eight years at Sotheby's, Leslie knew that Philadelphia Chippendale card tables were extremely rare to begin with, and that few have survived to this century. He also knew they almost never come to market. When Stahl asked him to make the trip to Philadelphia, Keno grew excited. Evaluating such merchandise is among the greatest pleasures that any auctioneer looks forward to. It is also one of the trickiest. Experts generally have no trouble evaluating the condition of a thing, but they can have a harder time certifying that all its parts are original. If someone had once left a cigarette to burn on a tabletop, or for any other reason its top had been replaced, the value of such an object would decrease by hundreds of thousands of dollars. A table might not in fact be very old at all, since people in the 1920s began to make reproductions of colonial furniture. A great demand for antiques led some cabinetmakers in the 1920s to make fakes as well, usually from the old parts of real ones. Stahl and Keno can usually recognize recently faked merchandise, but time has allowed the pieces of older fakes to fit snugly together, to shrink at the same rates, and otherwise to look as though they might have fit together for a couple of centuries. Experts learn to tell the genuine from the fake by looking at thousands of objects. After one has examined several hundred Boston highboys, the questionable highboy stands out.

So few turret-top card tables exist that many American furniture experts have never seen even one. Wendell Garrett had never seen one up close. Neither had Bill Stahl. Sotheby's advantage over Christie's lay partly in the fact that on a recent trip to Philadelphia, Leslie Keno had appraised a similar table on loan to the Philadelphia Museum of Art. He had turned this table upside down and studied its construction. He remembered details of its carved rail. There is no substitute for such intimate knowledge of a thing. Together with Garrett's broad background and Stahl's long knowledge of the table's existence, Keno's experience gave Stahl an edge over Christie's.

Though the world's largest auction houses recorded similar sales in 1990—Sotheby's brought in $2.5 billion, while Christie's did about $2 billion—these two operations could not have approached their jobs from more different points of view. Christie's tends to behave like a small museum, to nurture personal relationships, and to create an air of refinement and good taste. Sotheby's generally behaves more brashly. It is a more free-wheeling sort of place—more corporate, more self-confident, and less afraid to risk new ventures. Sotheby's owns a large real-estate operation and loans money to its customers on such a scale that many people treat it as a bank. Like those in charge of other departments, Stahl and Keno love the excitement of the hunt. They hold a passionate regard for objects, display their passions easily, and work well with those drawn to uninhibited expression of emotion.

Sotheby's owes much of its ambience to John Marion, the chairman of its North American operation and its chief American auctioneer. His father, Louis J. Marion, once conducted auctions from the podium at Parke-Bernet, the operation that Peter Wilson bought for Sotheby's in 1964. John Marion grew up in the business. He stands over six feet tall, weighs more than two hundred pounds, and gives the impression of someone who might have once possessed enormous upper body strength.

Marion realized in the late 1970s that dealers still held a couple of advantages over the auction houses: Dealers could pay cash for art, and they could pay immediately. A seascape by Winslow Homer might not bring as much from a dealer as from Sotheby's, but the collector in need of money did not have to wait for the next American paintings sale to find out. Marion saw that if he made loans to consignors, he could compete with the dealers for those who needed to raise cash. He decided to start a finance company, and in 1979 hired two bankers, Diana D. Brooks and Mitchell Zuckerman. The tactic of loaning money to customers might not seem strange to most people—General Motors, after all, has financed its cars for years—but people who knew the art business thought Marion's plan bizarre. Some viewed the work of Brooks and Zuckerman as a "black art."

After Peter Wilson resigned as chairman in 1979, and despite Marion's innovations, Sotheby's began to lose money. This circumstance led some to the paradoxical conclusion in 1983 that it was well worth buying. A famous takeover battle ensued. The man who came to its rescue—in the language of the eighties, a "white knight"—was A. Alfred Taubman. Despite his possessing assets of more than $1 billion, not a great deal is known about Taubman. It is known that he once claimed his first initial stood for "Alfred" (so that his name was supposed to be Alfred Alfred), while in fact it stands for "Adolph." It is known that he has built some of the fanciest shopping malls in the country, that he owns a great many department stores, and that he runs the A & W root beer chain. He flies about the country in a private jet. He owns enormous houses in Bloomfield Hills, Michigan; Southampton, New York; and Palm Beach. Some think him arrogant. Taubman summed up his attitude toward art in a speech he once made to graduates of Harvard Business School. "There is more similarity in a precious painting by Degas and a frosted mug of root beer," he said, "than you ever thought possible."

Taubman ordained a standard of financial discipline that Sotheby's had never known. Marion's scheme to lend money began to generate profits. Before 1983, the front office had left many accounting procedures to the experts in its various departments. These men and women held large loves for Manets and fine Persian rugs but no love whatever for spreadsheets. Bill Stahl himself admitted that he is "not the best administrator in the world." Taubman knew the value of expert knowledge. He didn't care whether the heads of his departments appreciated the nuances of an annual budget. He brought in people who did. Under A. Alfred Taubman, Sotheby's began to flourish.

The card table that sat in the Hugheses' front hall had seen a long life of inactivity. For nearly one hundred years, those who owned it had considered it a quaint but ugly reminder of the life led by a father or a grandfather. No one moved the table unnecessarily. In fact, no one bothered enough to move it at all. No one dealt cards, spilled cocktails, or dripped ink on its pink baize playing surface. The table was cared for, if not cared about. A blanket shrouded it for sixty years. Once it saw the light of day, it stood inside the home of people who admired it.

When Bill Stahl walked into the Hugheses' house and saw the Willing card table for the first time, he thought, "It's right."

Leslie Keno compared it to the other table he'd seen and thought, "This one is more successful designwise. It's much more delicate." The condition of the table astonished him. Keno had seen many Chippendale tables whose carvings had lost something through clumsy restorations, but this one "still had its crispness." As Keno explained later, "It had been refinished, but it had not been sanded. What was amazing was that everything had knife edges. All the acanthus leaves were knife-sharp. They weren't worn. They usually lose their crispness with refinishing. It was just like the refinishing dissolved all the dirt and crud, but everything was intact."

While Barbara Deisroth entertained the family in another room, the three men turned the table over, as Keno remembers, "to make sure the top was original and it all made sense." They looked for what Stahl considered "all of the conventional things—that the gradation of color on the underside of the top looked good, the shrinkage looked good, the blocks were basically intact."

For each item it puts on the market, Sotheby's estimates the price range in which it believes the item will sell.

It then prints these estimates in its sale catalog. To assure customers that their things will not sell for too little, the auction house employs another figure known as the "reserve" price—the figure below which an item will not be sold. Stahl had long since discovered that these reserves often determined whether an owner would part with his or her goods. The auction house can place the reserve at or below the low estimate, but by law this reserve can be no higher. With an estimate of $10,000 to $15,000, for example, the reserve can't be above $10,000. Sotheby's does not guarantee to sell a thing when it figures the reserve, only to protect the seller from a weak market. If a table has a reserve of $10,000, and the bidding never rises above $9,500, then the object will not sell. Sotheby's will pack it up and ship it back, and the consignor can wait for better times.

An auctioneer is unusual in that he acts as an agent not only for the seller but for the buyer as well. Stahl had learned that sellers responded better to high estimates, and that offering a high estimate sometimes helped him to secure a thing. But he had found that this tactic worked against him when he tried to sell it. He thought it useful to remember the equation that the lower the estimate, the more spirited the bidding. With lower estimates, so this argument ran, more people could believe that owning an object was possible. Those who think they can buy something begin to study it and to dream of where it might sit in their houses and so become connected to the piece. Sometimes they enter the skirmish of bidding and cannot help themselves from spending far more than they had expected. It's sometimes true—however paradoxical it might sound—that lower estimates can result in higher selling prices.

"It's a tricky business, estimates," Stahl once explained. "I hate it. My standard line is, I can tell you—any one of us can tell you—what we think the client wants to hear in order to get it in here. But that's not what we're all about. The estimates have got to reflect the market, as best as possible in an imperfect world."

The three experts discussed estimates in the privacy of Mrs. Hughes's hallway. The appraisal of fine furniture employs the method of finding recent selling prices for similar objects and then calculating their relationships to the one in question. This method of comparable values is no different from that employed by real-estate agents to fix the price of a house. The success of this approach depends, however, on accurate information, a commodity Stahl and Keno found conspicuously absent in the category of high-style Philadelphia card tables. The dearth of hard numbers left them to consider a table the collectors George and Linda Kaufman had bought privately in the early 1980s. Though he didn't know for sure, Stahl guessed that the Kaufmans had paid about $200,000.

In the absence of nearly identical objects, Stahl and Keno also considered other high-style pieces of furniture. They thought about a wing chair that had sold to Eddy Nicholson for $1.1 million. They thought of a piecrust tea table that had brought just over $1 million, of a suite of furniture that had sold in that same range, and of a pier table for which Harold Sack had paid $4.6 million. Considering the rarity of the turret-top card table, and the potential market for such a piece, Stahl and Keno believed they could accept an estimate in the $800,000 to $1 million range.

As different as Sotheby's was from Christie's, Stahl nonetheless acquired objects like the Willing card table just as Ralph Carpenter did—more often as a result of personal relationships than of things such as estimates. Parting with an heirloom can stir the emotions, and in the sorts of homes that usually contain heirlooms, such emotions can run deep and hidden. People from old Philadelphia families learn discretion at an early age. Even in the middle of negotiations, they generally don't mention the competition. Stahl never heard whether Christie's had seen the table, or what sort of estimate the rival firm might have given to the family.

Stahl and Keno usually consult each other to evaluate the things they sell. "Quite frankly, we work very well together," Stahl says. "In the whole scheme of things I tend to be a little more aggressive in the estimates. He tends to be more conservative. We take what he says, what I say, and average them." At lunch with the Hughes family, the men from Sotheby's discussed how their firm might market such an object. Stahl explained an ad campaign that would include expensive color spreads in *Antiques* magazine. He also promised to feature the card table on the cover of the sale catalog. "I think they were fairly impressed with that," Stahl remembered later. "We *save* the cover, my friend."

In Stahl's experience of estimating merchandise, "It isn't as much greed as it is ego. They have predetermined what their father's thing must be worth." Again and again during lunch that day, the seriousness with which the family held the $1 million figure struck Stahl as remarkable. He concluded that, as he later said, "the $1 million figure had to be worked into the estimate."

Sotheby's impressed the Hughes family. Elizabeth found Stahl and Garrett especially to be "much more enthusiastic going in" than she had found John Hays. "John doesn't get excited," she says. "Bill and Wendell were excited. They were just really up. It was very refreshing. It made us feel very nice."

Negotiations ensued with both houses. Hays returned to study the table with Dean Faily, the head of the Americana department at Christie's. Stahl planned a lunch with the Hugheses at Les Pleiades, an ornate French restaurant just off Madison Avenue that was then a favorite spot for the art crowd. He submitted a proposal in which Sotheby's offered to place an estimate of $800,000 to $1.2 million on the table. At lunch the conversation covered many topics, but none recurred more than that of the estimate. "I could sense that there was a magic to $1 million," Stahl says. "It was a recurring theme right to the night before the sale."

As Stahl drove to the airport two days later, the telephone in his hired car rang. It was Wendell Garrett, who said, "I just talked to Bill Hughes"—Elizabeth's older brother. Garrett explained his feeling that an estimate of $1 million to $1.5 million—where the reserve could be as high as seven figures—would probably close the deal.

Christie's submitted its own proposal. Elizabeth later remembered that the firm "was definitely not going to let us have a reserve over $750,000," and it was this fact, together with what she considered to be Christie's "waffling" as opposed to Sotheby's "enthusiasm," that determined the fate of

Thomas Willing's card table. Stahl drove to Philadelphia. He picked up the thing whose value an inventory might once have recorded at fifty cents but for which he had recently agreed to get a million dollars, placed it in the back of his Chevy Blazer, and returned to New York.

Seventeen

THE BLUE BLANKET CHEST STOOD IN THE DINING ROOM OF
Bruce Wilt's house in Basking Ridge, New Jersey, where
he had placed it two years earlier. On its top sat two of
his favorite objects: a miniature yellow chest and the
small figure of a dancing black man. Among the other
folk art and painted furniture in this room—the graceful trestle dining table, the Windsor chairs, the painted
corner cupboard—the blanket chest found a home. Wilt
liked it as much as any object he had ever bought, and
months later, after the chest had left his house, he smiled
when he remembered it. He had even adopted the language of the antiques dealer. "It showed great there," he
said.

Wilt wanted to buy some property in Pennsylvania
from a developer who had not been able to finish a subdi-
vision. Wilt believed he could acquire the project cheaply,
construct the remaining forty-four houses, and in the process, as he said, "really make some real decent money." He

did not have the cash to acquire this property, but he thought he knew where to get it.

After he began to collect antiques, Wilt saw that the market did not always conform to his own instinctive tastes. He had learned to train his eye, to digest his mistakes, to integrate his own tastes with the tastes of the market. In the past five years, Wilt had come to suspect the wild promises of one antiques dealer and to check them with the skepticism of another. He learned to take antiques on approval and to place them in his home. This allowed him not only to see whether he wanted to live with the object but also to get the casual advice of other dealers who drifted through. He learned what the dealers knew: Some objects are merely capital in a handsome suit. Two years earlier, Wilt had paid $125,000 for the blue blanket chest. Now that he needed some cash, he would try to sell it for $150,000.

Wilt recalled that Wayne Pratt, the dealer who sold him the chest, had told him at the time, "Look, if you sell it, you gotta give me a chance to get it." Wilt had transacted enough business with Pratt to know that the dealer held the firm opinion that he didn't so much sell his things as lease them. "See, Wayne feels that every piece is his piece," Wilt says. "That's the way it works for him."

Pratt is not alone in this belief. To ensure a steady supply of goods, many dealers want their clients to remain loyal sellers as much as loyal buyers. Pratt has perfected the technique he learned from John Walton, of providing a guarantee to each client that he will accept any piece he has sold in trade for anything he has in stock. He will also occasionally pay cash to buy back objects that he feels he can move quickly. But when Wilt called him, a curious thing happened. Wilt told Pratt, "I'm going to sell this blue chest. You wanna buy it?"

"Oh, Christ, don't sell it now, it's too early," said Pratt. "Wait a while."

Wilt did not believe Pratt had the money to buy the chest back. "He was going through some tough times, too, I could tell. I said, 'Look, I want a hundred and fifty. You gotta let me know.' "

Pratt asked for some time to gather the $150,000, but Wilt did not sit idly by. He put the word out through the network of pickers and dealers who came and left his house regularly. Soon a great many dealers throughout the Northeast had learned that this famous icon of American folk art was for sale. In time the news reached Fred Giampietro, the dealer from New Haven whom Wilt knew casually from attending antiques shows where Giampietro exhibited. Like many people who encountered Giampietro, Wilt had trouble pronouncing Fred's last name. In Wilt's vocabulary, "Giampietro" came out sounding something like "Giam-ee-peetro."

When Giampietro phoned to inquire about the chest, Wilt told him: "Look, Wayne's got first shot at this, but if he doesn't buy it you can buy it if you want."

"Aah, I'd *love* to buy it," said Giampietro. "Let me look at it."

"I'll let you know on Wednesday," Wilt told him. "Wayne's going to let me know Wednesday what he can do."

On Sunday Wilt got another call from Pratt. "Look, don't do anything," Pratt pleaded. "I'm working on this."

Pratt called again the next day and once more on Tuesday. On Wednesday, Pratt's pleas began to sound desperate: "Look, I can give you fifty now."

"I need the money," Wilt told him. "I got something I'm going to do."

"Ah Christ, ya fucked me on this one," Pratt said.

"I'm not fuckin' you on this one. I told you the deal."

"Who you going to sell it to?" Pratt asked. "Giampietro's going to buy it?"

Wilt denied that Giampietro was interested in the chest. As he explained later, "If I told him that, he'd call Giam-ee-peetro and start breakin' his balls about it."

Wilt himself phoned Fred on Wednesday. "Thursday Giam-ee-peetro was at my house. Boom, he bought it. So that's how I moved the piece."

Losing one of the most famous objects of American folk art did not please Pratt. He had sold the chest under the assumption that Wilt would hang on to it for a few years, then sell it back. "If I sold it to Bruce at 125, I would've bought it back at 125," Pratt later recalled. "I could've given him a little more. It depends on how tight you are at a given moment. I could've given him a little more, but he wanted 150 for it. So I didn't do it. I misjudged Bruce. I wish I'd sold it to somebody else. I didn't think he'd have to sell it."

Wilt told Giampietro that Pratt had until five o'clock to make his decision. Giampietro arrived at Wilt's house at six. Unobserved by Wilt during the course of his ownership was a small blemish—Wilt called it a "mark"—that, had it appeared recently, would have greatly diminished the chest's value. "When Giam-ee-peetro came, he's like, looking at that mark. He's going over it all. He says, 'You got the book?' " Giampietro wanted to examine a copy of *Painted Furniture,* on whose back cover the chest had appeared years earlier. He wanted to see whether this blemish had long been associated with the object, or whether it was a more recent addition. "I'm going, 'Oh, shit.' 'Cause I wasn't sure. I said to myself, 'I hope the kids didn't use a Magic Marker on it.' So I brought the book out and there was the mark. I said, 'Whoah.' He would have said, 'Oh, I gotta take 20 off on this.' "

Standing in Wilt's dining room, Giampietro reduced the blue blanket chest to its constituent parts. He examined the drawers. He inspected the chest's interior walls. "I knew I was going to buy it or I wouldn't have taken it apart," Giampietro recalls. "I just wanted to see if there was any restoration. There wasn't any. If there had been restoration it would have depended on how much. If one of the side moldings was missing or replaced I still would have bought it, but if the leg was replaced I would not. At that level, you're getting into a place where you don't want problems."

Giampietro wrote a check for $150,000, loaded the chest into his van, and drove it back to New Haven. He placed the chest in his bedroom, where he and his wife, Kathy, used it to store their socks, underwear, and sweaters. Giampietro had a couple of clients in mind for this object. To figure a price, he recalled that David Schorsch had once offered the chest to him at a dealer's discount of $185,000. Giampietro never knew Schorsch's retail price, but he suspected it was well over $225,000. Giampietro believed in the blue blanket chest. He believed in it as much as Schorsch.

He thought it deserved to be sold for a lot of money, and hoped to make a lot of money on it, too. He decided on a figure of $245,000—somewhere around Schorsch's price— and then he tried to sell it.

Fred Giampietro only began to have an understanding of what antique things might mean to his life in about 1974, soon after he and Kathy began selling junk toys and Depression glass and other used merchandise. At the time, they were both studying music at Stetson University in De Land, Florida. The antiques business, they discovered, was fun. Sometimes they couldn't believe how easy it was. They could find toys dating from the 1950s, for example, on shelves that lined the old five-and-dime stores along Collins Avenue in Miami Beach. All they had to do was buy the toys for their original prices, mark them up, and then take them over to the flea market in Coconut Grove, where they could sell the toys as antiques. Fred believes that starting at the bottom gave him an edge, since he knows suppliers at all levels of the trade. "We went into business with $30," Giampietro says proudly. "One thing that's sort of unique with us is we really started with nothing."

Fred began working weekends as a picker after finishing his graduate work at Yale. During the week, his real job was playing the string bass for the New Haven Symphony. But he found himself spending more and more time in the company of people who loved old things. He looked at things. He touched them. He smelled them. His eyes dilated at the sight of a beautiful new object.

When he touched something rare, he felt connected to the human past, and his heart beat fast. He connected through the smooth and glossy places touched by many hands, but also through the beauty of a form, and through its uniqueness. These qualities allowed him to see the hand of its creator.

One day in the course of their weekend travels, Fred and Kathy stopped into Harold and Florie Corbin's shop in Falls Village, Connecticut. As well as selling antique furniture, Harold Corbin was known in the trade for having fabulous collections of duck decoys and iron implements. The Giampietros had never heard of him. They entered the cluttered house that also served as the Corbins' antiques shop, and Fred was astonished to find an array of goods that included Indian moccasins, bird decoys, country furniture, weathervanes, iron, porcelain, oil paintings, watercolors, and eighteenth-century glass. "We walked in that shop and said, 'Aha,'" he remembers. "We knew when we saw something we liked, but I had never seen it all together like that. I was so totally turned on by it. I was just consumed by it."

Giampietro began to work as a picker every moment he could spare. He loaded up his old Ford van and went on the road to buy and sell and trade. He stopped at shops along the way and asked the dealers, "Hey, you want to see something?" He bought the same way. When he stopped by Harold Corbin's shop, he sold the old man five things and bought one for himself. He learned the pricing structure of the business by trial and error. He would buy a pair of moccasins for $75, without knowing its true retail value, and find to his surprise that he could sell this item for $95. The next time he saw a pair of moccasins for $75, Fred's self-confidence had grown.

After his second year with the New Haven Symphony, Giampietro's heart told him that was going to be a full-time antiques dealer and not a professional player of the string bass. He had auditioned with the Buffalo Symphony, where he discovered that he would be performing the same program of popular classics for the rest of his life, at an annual salary of $12,000. In the antiques business, Giampietro could make $12,000 in a weekend. Though he continued to play with the New Haven Symphony, his heart wasn't in it, and after a couple of years he quit. His dealing improved and his ambitions grew. Every January, Fred visited the New York Winter Antiques Show and thought how much he would like to exhibit there.

Giampietro cultivated the dealers he had known since his days in the Miami flea markets, when he was selling things for less than $20. He knew a lot of people. He knew people who dealt in garden furniture, people who dealt in Victorian furniture, and people who sold rolltop desks. If he bid on an estate and got a load of garden chairs and tables—the sorts of things in which he himself did not deal—he would call a friend from the old days and sell the lot for half its retail value. Fred did this because he knew that when his friend ran across a great piece of country furniture, or a great folk painting, the man would call him. That sort of thing happened all the time. For example, a dealer once saw a painting on sale for $20,000 and called Giampietro, who was known to have that kind of cash on hand. Giampietro bought the painting, sold it for $100,000, and gave the man *half* the profit. He just appeared out of nowhere one day with a check for $40,000. The dealer couldn't believe it. "That guy calls me once a week," Fred says.

Fred Giampietro discovered that the antiques business was a lot like the music business. Both required self-discipline. He had learned such discipline playing for a symphony orchestra. He had learned to hold back when it was somebody else's turn to be heard. Antiques were the same way. When a man bought and sold things worth tens of thousands of dollars, he had to discipline himself *not* to buy a candlestand for $350, even when he knew he could sell it for $1,500. If he wanted to be a great dealer, he had to have great things. When a $1,500 candlestand entered his shop, everybody knew it. It was a lesser thing, and lesser things made lesser dealers. One didn't get invited to places such as the New York Winter Antiques Show by selling crummy candlestands.

Antiques dealers have the reputation of people who love their objects a great deal but have no love at all for the technicalities of business. A vagueness inhabits their account books. Patient long-term plans have a way of evaporating into the dry and dusty air around them. Many dealers prefer to think of nothing other than the pleasures of profit, but Fred Giampietro is not among these. He is a businessman who knows also how to love his things. Besides antiques, Giampietro invests in real estate, stocks, and bonds, and his long-term perspective helps to prevent the discouragement that prevails in weak economic climates. He had the confidence to know that if he didn't sell the blue blanket chest by

Saturday, by next week, or even by next month, he would sell it someday. "The art business," Fred likes to say, "is a discipline business."

Giampietro gets nearly as much satisfaction from discussing the business of antiques as he does from talking about the objects themselves. All dealers have particular interests that lead them to socialize with others who share those interests, and Giampietro's idiosyncracies have led him to a friendship with a Connecticut real-estate developer named Allen Katz. Fred had seen Katz from time to time at antiques shows around the East Coast. He knew something about Katz's collection of weathervanes, cigar store Indians, and other sculptural objects, and once even sold Katz something. But Fred had no idea that they shared an interest in research. He learned this one day when Katz appeared at his house in New Haven to explain that he had, as Giampietro puts it, "watched us for three or four or five years and finally decided, 'Okay, now I'm going to deal with them.'" From that day forward, the two men became friends. "We basically built his collection for him," Fred says. "He's still buying. He has a great collection. It's a known collection. I think it's one of the best in the country."

Dealers like to turn collectors into friends. In a business full of charlatans, a dealer trades as much on his trust as on his knowledge. Katz got into the habit of stopping by the Giampietros' brick carriage house, a place filled with examples of American folk art that are almost all for sale. One day, while the two businessmen were, as Giampietro remembers, "just sitting around saying, 'Gee, it seems the dealer always loses,'" Fred observed that dealers cannot normally afford to hang on to pieces for the number of years required to realize large profits from them. He pointed out that he would sometimes sell Katz something for $20,000, turning a profit of about $5,000, and that Katz could hold the piece for three years. If he chose to sell it, Katz could then make $20,000 more. Because of their backgrounds in real estate, both men understood the concept of a limited partnership. "So, together we just had this idea of doing a limited partnership of Americana," Fred explains. "Sell shares. Buy a couple million dollars' worth of stuff and hold it for five years, just as an experiment."

Giampietro and Katz took their idea to a law firm in 1989, and created an enterprise called Artvest. They sold shares at $50,000 each—it was possible to buy half a share—in a portfolio of antiques. The partnership would buy objects in a dozen categories, from quilts and hooked rugs to Windsor chairs, and in a wide range of prices. In the category of $750 quilts, for example, they would include what Giampietro calls "the best $750 quilt you can buy." The partnership would sell out within five years, and in-vestors would share any profits. This idea, it turned out, had a great appeal among Wall Street investors interested in something that sounded like fun. Giampietro and Katz quickly sold out.

Now they had $2 million to spend on folk art. This sum might seem small to investors familiar with limited partnerships, and it would not have taken the two men very far with the sort of fine Chippendale highboys that Harold Sack likes to sell. But people with folk art on hand quickly took notice. Giampietro believes prices for great

American folk art to be low when compared to prices for other great works of art, which means that $2 million goes farther than it otherwise might. To people in the folk art world, $2 million sounded like a lot of money. People with goods to sell found Artvest to be an alternative to the auction houses. "When I open the floodgates and say I've got the money now, we're buying, the phone doesn't stop ringing," Fred says. "The letters and photos and videotapes don't stop coming. Al and I were on a plane every day. We were all over the place. We were flying and buying and looking. I wasn't really prepared for it. Collectors that want to sell. Dealers that find something great they think is for us."

Believing Giampietro to have all the money in the world, people would sometimes try to sell an object, as Giampietro says, "for a quarter of a million dollars when it was only worth a hundred." Another way Fred sometimes identified such absurd offers was, "You know, f-you prices." Artvest got the right of first refusal on any object Fred encountered, and one problem was that his own inventory fell by 40 percent.

Fred Giampietro was not daunted. "I look at it as a much longer picture," he says. "First of all, it's a great discipline. I enjoy doing anything that's a discipline, where I have parameters and I have to fill those parameters. Secondly, it gives people a chance to invest in this type of material—people who don't know what to do other than to go to an antiques shop and buy something and hang on to it. For $50,000 they can own a piece of these objects. It fills their investment portfolio section out. Thirdly, it brings an incredible amount of cash into the antiques business, the folk art business. That's fresh money. So much of our money is recycled. It's the same money coming in and out. I sell to the collector, who resells it. Back and forth, back and forth. We used to say, 'I sell it to a dealer, who sells it to another dealer, and then it goes into a dealer's collection.' It's just so incestuous. Every once in a while the business needs a fresh infusion of cash."

Fred was buying for Artvest when Bruce Wilt called him in the spring of 1990. Since the asking price for the blue blanket chest was too much for Artvest to spend on a single object, Giampietro bought the chest for himself. Fred knew the chest's history. He knew that David Schorsch had shown it to a number of people and that it had seen, as Fred said later, "a lot of exposure in the marketplace." Schorsch had tried to sell the chest for about $250,000, and then he'd been forced to get rid of it at a fire-sale price. Fred understood that this history of rejection would not help his own chances with the chest. "It never helps when you undersell something," Giampietro says. "It's the wild swings in prices that hurt a piece." The idea that Schorsch, and Giampietro himself, had priced the chest too high never once occurred to him.

Giampietro had not found a buyer when the New York Winter Antiques Show's exhibition committee asked him to participate. He carried the blue blanket chest with him to the armory, placed it at the center of his booth, and hoped. That was how an exquisite object of American folk art, which nobody seemed to want at the price at which he wished to sell it, arrived in January of 1991 at the most prestigious antiques fair in the country. Fred Giampietro hoped to find someone who had not yet seen the blanket chest, someone who had the money to buy it. He hoped a thing that looked shopworn to those who had seen it would look fresh to those who had not.

Eighteen

A SOFT MURMUR FILLED THE PARK AVENUE ARMORY ON TUES-
day afternoon of Americana Week. The armory swallowed
up each of the sixty-six dealers with a booth at the show, all
of their assorted helpers, and the three or four dozen visitors
who had come that afternoon to look at things. Most of the
patrons were women, and many of these wore skirts and silk
blouses with scarves pinned to their shoulders. Few if any of
them had attended the opening of the Winter Antiques
Show on Friday night. They appeared to have arrived from
Connecticut in the morning, shopped along Madison Avenue, and then treated themselves to splendid lunches. Some
of these women wore leather pumps and some wore Reebok
tennis shoes. The atmosphere of the armory seemed to require that they speak to each other softly, almost in whispers.

A few real collectors showed up that Tuesday as well.
They gave the impression of people killing time before the
four-day spree of auctions at Sotheby's, which would begin

with a silver sale on Wednesday. Prominent among these aficionados, Richard Rosen sniffed like a hound among the booths of brown furniture. Sotheby's had scheduled the auction of Rosen's things for Friday morning. He seemed slightly hyperactive, the way one might expect to feel if the contents of one's house stood ready for sale a few blocks away. Rosen spoke in confidential tones to Wayne Pratt. It was Pratt who, on opening night of the Winter Antiques Show, had sold a Newport kneehole desk for more than $1 million.

Rosen chatted also with Leigh Keno, who ran his booth from a prestigious location at the front of the room. The market in antiques depends on subtle distinctions between forms, on the peculiar histories of such craftsmen as the Garvan carver, on a knowledge of woods, and on an eye for the smallest details of construction. Dealers tend to have such information. Collectors want to get it. Sometimes by imparting an hour's worth of lessons, a dealer will feel a nibble, just as Keno did that afternoon with the collector from Belmont, Massachusetts. Rosen was so taken with a set of six New Hampshire ladder-back chairs that he asked Keno to place a hold on them for him.

The actor Harrison Ford also strolled about the room that day. Though he is usually esteemed for other talents, Ford was regarded by dealers of American furniture as a collector of some sophistication. When they thought about Ford in connection with antiques, however, what usually came first to the dealers' minds was his money. Everyone knew Ford had a lot of it. On that afternoon, he wore a tweed sport coat and a pair of eyeglasses, and wherever he went, a small group of fans followed discreetly behind. He seemed to have a taste for the same kind of brown furniture that attracted Richard Rosen. Ford wandered into one exhibit after another until he came to a stop at a booth where a young helper asked to have her picture taken with him.

Across the aisle, not ten feet away from the closing camera shutter, stood Fred Giampietro. He looked distinguished in his new suit and his wire-rimmed glasses. After four days of talking politely to customers, Giampietro had sold a lot of things, but he had not sold the blue blanket chest. This object drew many people to it on opening night. One couple even placed what Giampietro called a "semihold" on the piece. Fred himself had trouble distinguishing a semihold from the regular kind, but he was of an optimistic nature and regarded any sort of hold as preferable to no hold at all. The chest remained standing where he first placed it, against a stark white wall at the center of his booth, underneath a sign that read, "Fred and Kathryn Giampietro. New Haven, Connecticut."

Fred seemed unconcerned by the small commotion that Harrison Ford's presence was causing across the aisle. Giampietro does not often go to the movies, nor does he watch much television, and he believes, furthermore, that stars wish to be treated like anyone else. Fred's things gleamed under recent polishings. In a moment, Harrison Ford turned on his heel, glanced up at the sign with Giampietro's name on it, and began to examine some of the things for sale there. "Are you Fred Giampietro?" the movie star asked. "Yes," Fred replied. "Who are you?"

Although the blue blanket chest caught the eyes of many who encountered it for the first time, it did not hold the gaze of Harrison Ford. An eighteenth-century oxbow-front chest drew Ford's attention. He asked the sort of questions that Giampietro had come to expect of those with some experience with old furniture. Ford wondered whether Giampietro knew where the oxbow chest had been made, where the dealer had found it, and how much less than the stated price he might take for it. In the hierarchy of the antiques world, a dealer like Fred Giampietro stands near the top of the pyramid, and a collector like Harrison Ford stands in the middle. Having asked a few simple questions, the rich movie star moved on. His point in stopping appeared to have no other cause than letting Fred Giampietro know that Harrison Ford knew what an oxbow-front chest was.

Women in black tights and lizard-skin cowboy boots and women who carried Gucci bags on their shoulders paraded in front of Giampietro's booth. He met people at the Winter Antiques Show whom he would otherwise never encounter. Sometimes these people exhibited a knowledge that surprised him. More often, though, those who inquired knew nothing at all about antiques. Giampietro did not discriminate. He believed that almost anybody could be educated to covet the blue blanket chest. One needed only a willingness to learn and a large supply of money. In the fifteen years since he had become a dealer, Giampietro had exhibited in perhaps 120 different antiques shows, and believed he knew what to expect from the crowds at each different one. But he had never seen anything like the money that strolled past his booth at the Winter Antiques Show.

All large indoor spaces create an odd atmosphere. There is something of a vacuum created in such places, where the sounds of conversation never entirely disappear. The energies of visitors tend to rise as they would outdoors, but instead of being lost into a blue sky, they are trapped by a ceiling high overhead. Moods have no place to go in a room like the Park Avenue armory. Besides the ordinary energies caught inside such spaces, there were as well the energies of gleaming polished surfaces, the energies that beauty can create, and the energies made by money. These were the sorts of energies that, to Fred Giampietro's mind, helped to turn disinterested spectators into curious clients. In the old armory building, the stillness in the air seemed to capture desires. After one stayed inside this room for several hours, the world outside ceased to exist. In the armory, people could eat and drink and work and browse. After a while, they came to think of antiques the way Giampietro did, as among life's most important realities.

The man most responsible for bringing this sort of atmosphere to the Park Avenue armory is Russell Carrell. Though he no longer takes an active part in the affairs of the Winter Antiques Show, Carrell's long tenure as its manager has left a lasting imprint. Without him, the show might never have come to represent the supreme moment in the lives of those objects that made it there, as it had for the blue blanket chest.

Carrell took over the show in 1959, four years after its inception. Its success over the next three decades secured his place in the world of American antiques. At the height of his career, he operated twenty-three fairs around the country each year, ranging in quality from the armory show to the junk sales he ran on a field near his home in Salisbury,

Connecticut. Russell Carrell not only brought elegance to the armory, he also invented the flea market.

Carrell lives in a two-story farmhouse that was built, as he will happily explain, in 1742. Salisbury is a quiet, pretty town in Litchfield County, which lies in the northwestern corner of Connecticut. Wealthy New Yorkers spend their weekends in Salisbury. Enormous maple trees line its streets, and large clapboard houses—the kind with wraparound porches and gardens full of rhododendrons—stand on a succession of rising, perfectly clipped green lawns. Rivers of antiques pass through the town. Salisbury's antiques shops sport enticing hand-lettered signs, and promise enough objects to last a lifetime of looking.

Like everyone else who inhabits the world of American antiques, Carrell dwells among the echoes of our history. He knows that Alexander Hamilton once studied surveying in his house and that the first book on surveying published in America was written there. The windows of this house are small, the ceilings low, and the exposed beams dark and heavy. Not much light enters his small front parlors, so it can sometimes be difficult to appreciate Carrell's American Empire sofa and his Federal tables, the eighteenth-century country chests, the antique carved busts, the wooden eagles, old maps, jug lamps, portraits-in-silhouette, Staffordshire plates, and gold-lettered trade signs. Though such a catalog of possessions begins to describe Carrell's passion in life, it cannot quite account for Carrell's bachelor habits—for all the junk that spreads across his dining table, the piles of magazines, newspapers, and posters that sprout from every corner, the stacks of documents that rest on every stair, or the ceramic bear who presides over a kitchen frequently strewn with pots, pans, skillets, plates, knives, and half-eaten honeydew melons.

At the time of Americana Week, in late January of 1990, Carrell was seventy-two years old. He is a short, somewhat odd man who reminds one of a figure from Tolkien. He wears Top-Siders with his fluorescent green Bermuda shorts, and is especially fond of pink polo shirts, which tend to emphasize his large, round belly. He has clear, sad, blue eyes, and a habit of gazing directly at those he is talking to.

Carrell was born in Morristown, New Jersey, but he grew up in New York City. His father was a famous society decorator and his mother collected Americana. Carrell's parents raised him in what he refers to as "an atmosphere of antiques." He began to collect antiques as a child by buying old things at the Salvation Army and other secondhand stores. From an early age, Carrell knew he wanted to go into the antiques business. During World War II, while stationed for a time with the Navy in Jacksonville, Florida, he befriended an old antiques dealer. Selling things was not the primary concern of this woman, but buying them was. On an extended visit to Baltimore some years earlier, the woman had bought and bought. She placed her new possessions into enormous wooden barrels, shipped them home to Florida, and stored them in her garage, where they remained until Russell Carrell was able to peek inside. "It was stuff," Carrell remembers. "Pewter teapots, china, glass—everything. There were nine or eleven barrels. I paid her out of my Navy pay by the month. I thought it was good stuff, and it was, it turned out. They were bargains. It was my first real capital and it set me up in business."

After the war, Carrell shipped the barrels home to the

basement of his mother's new house in Sharon, Connecticut. Having decided to deal antiques, Carrell discovered that he knew nothing about running an antiques business, so he moved to New York City for a couple of years to learn it. He worked for a time in an antiques shop on Third Avenue. This shop was run by a man he remembers as "an old drunk, long gone now, I think his name was Brower." In addition to helping Brower, Carrell met an old picker named Pop Loy, whose father had once been an editor at the *Baltimore Sun.* In Carrell's words, "Loy knew all kinds of characters," and, believing that knowing the characters of the antiques business was just as important as knowing the merchandise, Carrell began to follow Pop Loy around town. Carrell discovered that drunks in great numbers populated the New York City antiques business. "Pop Loy was a white-haired old man who was living in a rooming house on Fifty-fifth Street," Carrell recalls. "He used to get so drunk, he'd give his money to the bartender at P. J. Clarke's, and the bartender would keep it for him till the next day. He'd pick along Third Avenue, Second Avenue, the Bowery. First he'd buy an antique, then he'd stop in a bar, then he'd stop someplace else to sell the antique." Carrell does not believe that his experience of selling antiques in New York City helped him much, but he did learn one thing: "I learned to stay sober," he says.

When Carrell returned to Connecticut in 1947, he rented a building in Salisbury where he could run an antiques shop on the first floor and live above it on the second. This building had no hot water—Carrell was forced to bathe at his mother's house in nearby Sharon—but it was located directly across the street from a place called the Ragamont Inn, a popular luncheon spot with well-to-do matrons. "After lunch, the ladies would come in and buy things, snoop around," Carrell remembers. "We had a group from Poughkeepsie called the Jolly Snoopers. The whole purpose to their club was to see, say, a table in a shop over near Poughkeepsie, and then discover the same table later in another shop and see how much the markup was."

Carrell soon realized that he would have to find a larger market than the ladies from the Ragamont Inn. He began exhibiting in antiques fairs along the Eastern Seaboard. A man named Cliff Nuttle ran most of them. Soon Carrell worked Nuttle's shows at, among other venues, Wilmington, Delaware; Morristown, New Jersey; and White Plains, New York. Carrell moved from one show to the next. He packed and unpacked his wares so often—frequently once a month—that he learned never to throw old newspapers out. One way a showman like Nuttle controlled the action was to insist that his dealers not exhibit with anyone but him. Early in his career, Carrell decided to do a show that was not run by Nuttle, and the result of this imprudent move—Carrell's banishment from all of Nuttle's shows for a period of time that amounted to eternity—taught the young dealer an important lesson.

Fortunately for Russell Carrell, he was a very good dealer with a very good eye, and he was able to succeed without the aid or comfort of Cliff Nuttle. There was so much demand for antiques in the 1950s that other people had begun to move in on Nuttle's fiefdom, and soon enough this group of renegade show managers came to include Russell Carrell himself. He got his first job as the manager of a fair in Greenwich, Connecticut, and proved so adept at organization that ladies in historical societies around the country, eager to raise money, offered him jobs running their own shows.

One day in 1956, at an outdoor antiques auction, Carrell had a brainstorm. While promoters often ran auctions under tents on a farmer's field, they operated antiques shows exclusively indoors. Carrell wondered why someone couldn't run a show just like an auction, and began to conceive the idea for such a fair in his hometown of Salisbury. The state of Connecticut did not cooperate. A circus fire in Hartford had led to exorbitant insurance rates for anyone who wanted to make a profit underneath a tent, and so, in a flash of genius, Carrell did away with the tents. He lined up his friends in the antiques business, set up booths in the open air, and started what he believes to have been the first flea market in the country.

Soon enough, Carrell's reputation led him to organize more prestigious shows. For a time he managed twenty-three shows each year, a schedule that required him to pack and unpack twice each month. He brought the notion of high-quality indoor shows—a concept popular in the East, where the country's leading dealers sold the best merchandise—to places such as Chicago, Cincinnati, and Cleveland. "I brought a different type of standard to the Midwest," Carrell says. "Most of the dealers were eastern, I'll say that, and I got the best of the locals, too." Carrell brought a new feeling to these fairs. Unlike Nuttle, who loved the show above all else, Carrell had entered the antiques business because he loved old things. He liked buying antiques, selling them, and talking about them with his friends. Frequently he set up his own booth at the shows he ran. A happy, festive mood characterized a Russell Carrell show. As one good friend said, "This was just a way for everybody to come together and have a ball." People said things like, "All his shows had style." Or they said, "His shows had a Russell Carrell look." Or they said, "Other people would start new shows, and when you walked in, your first reaction was it was a Russell Carrell show or it was non-Russell. There was a way his shows flowed together. People were happy."

One day in 1958, while Carrell operated a booth at a show in Madison Square Garden—a show he had not himself organized, a decidedly non-Russell show, a show he remembers as "dreadful"—he happened to occupy a space beside a booth run by ladies from the East Side Settlement House. That was Carrell's first encounter with the New York Winter Antiques Show. The ladies of the Settlement House had started their fair in 1955—Mrs. Douglas MacArthur had secured the use of the armory on Park Avenue—and while the turnout for their new fundraiser had thrilled them, the succession of managers had not. Mrs. Edward M. Pflueger, who helped to start the show, explained why: "I had to get one of the managers out of there," she said, "just to sober him up." Looking for a man who understood the proper ratio at which alcohol and antiques should mix, they could not have stumbled on a better man than Russell Carrell.

After he took the job, Carrell did not so much change

the look of the Winter Antiques Show as change its mood. He kept the dealers happy. Though the country's leading dealers had shown there before, Carrell brought in the best of those in the second tier. His decorations leant an elegant tone to the affair. In 1959, the year when he first organized this affair, *The New York Times* called his show "the most important of its kind in this country" and said, "This show is a landmark in the history of antiques collecting." The *Times* used other exalted adjectives to describe the lowboys, silver sauce tureens, and Chelsea porcelain owls that filled the large room.

Russell Carrell never forgot what he had learned from displeasing Cliff Nuttle. As a show manager in the 1960s and 1970s, Carrell employed Nuttle's technique to ensure a steady supply of dealers. Anyone who had the audacity to exhibit at another man's show, as Carrell had with Nuttle, met the same eternal banishment. Carrell organized his fairs on the same principle that works for Major League Baseball. He operated shows at all levels of the trade—from the flea market near his house to the grand affair on Park Avenue. Like baseball players in the minor leagues who want to play in the majors, each of Carrell's dealers aspired one day to exhibit in New York. Though simple mathematics ensured that most would never succeed, Carrell disdained to dash their hopes. He told each man and woman who asked that one day they would make it. The dealers always believed him. When other aspiring managers asked these dealers to leave one of Carrell's lesser shows, they'd say, "We're up for East Side this year," or "We've been nominated for the Winter Show," perhaps in the hope that saying would make it so. It almost never did. Some dealers waited fifteen years to exhibit at the great antiques palace in New York, where Carrell maintained firm control until the day he retired, in November of 1987.

As a young dealer, Fred Giampietro knew little about hierarchies like the one Russell Carrell controlled. He remembers that he approached the baron of antiques one day and said, "Gee, I'd really love to do the Winter Antiques Show." Carrell politely explained that for this to happen, a dealer currently exhibiting there would first have to die. Giampietro laughs about that now. He didn't yet understand the politics required to secure an invitation to the fair. He hadn't yet grasped who mattered and who did not, whom to flatter, and what to say. In the antiques world, a hierarchy of goods exists along with the hierarchy of dealers. Only the best antiques got to come to the Winter Antiques Show, and only the most knowledgeable dealers firmly grasped which antiques were best. Fred Giampietro did not understand this yet. He was still selling crummy candlestands. He did not yet know that the things he owned were not good enough to be there. "It was naiveté on my part," Fred says now, "thinking I was ready for it."

It took Giampietro fifteen years of steady application to understand the beauties of the blue blanket chest. When he first saw this object on the back cover of the *Painted Furniture* book, he felt what he would later call a "connection" to it—a gut feeling that is crucial to the business. But it took more than a "connection" to succeed. It took years of training and looking and sorting to fill his gut with cold and hard and sometimes unpleasant facts. It took years for Fred Giampietro to understand much of the beauty of the blanket chest. As soon as he had it, he was ready for the Winter Antiques Show.

Giampietro incurred considerable costs in showing his things at the Park Avenue armory. A booth went for $50 a square foot, and even a small one like Fred's ran to $10,000. He chose to spend $3,500 on a new lighting system, $1,500 for an ad in the show's catalog, and another $1,500 to buy opening night tickets for his best clients. Like the dealers and the things they sell, clients also fit into hierarchies. Giampietro spent some of his money on tickets to the Patrons' Party, which began at five o'clock on opening night. These tickets cost him $500 each. Other clients—those who stood somewhat farther down the pyramid, or who couldn't make it any earlier—received the $250 tickets that allowed them to arrive at six. In addition to these expenses, Fred had to figure the salary of one full-time employee to run errands and to staff the booth when he and Kathy took a break. He had a $90 charge for the installation of a telephone, and a hotel bill that he expected to exceed $4,500. He and Kathy had to eat, of course, and they wanted to eat well. The place they chose to dine each evening was a French restaurant around the corner called Sel & Poivre, a restaurant Giampietro always refers to as "Salt and Pepper." In all, Fred Giampietro calculated that the Winter Antiques Show cost him about $30,000.

Giampietro had no trouble justifying the expense of tickets when a client like John Heinz paid $100,000 for a couple of weathervanes. "That was a good $250 investment," Fred explains. "Some dealers don't know you have to spend money." Calculating profits from the Winter Antiques Show is a task most dealers find impossible. A man might spend $30,000 to hang up his old things, and sell very little all week long, and still he will return eagerly the next year. It is difficult to estimate the value of such exposure. One doesn't know, when one sells something several months later, whether the Winter Show had anything to do with it.

By Tuesday afternoon, Giampietro had not yet sold the blue blanket chest. For five days it had endured handling by amateur collectors who thought they knew the prices of great folk art. One couple in particular came back again and again to open its drawers and to rub their hands across its top. They had paid $10 to enter the show, every day since opening night, and with only one purpose in mind. They began to imagine the blue blanket chest sitting in their living room, around the other antique folk art objects they loved. People who express such interest generally have the capital to back up their desires. People do not usually return again and again to look at something they cannot possibly afford to have. These were the people who placed a semihold on the chest Friday night. The couple studied the chest, pulled out its drawers, admired it from different angles. They looked over their shoulders at it. They turned quickly to see it, as if for the first time. They walked away to look at other things, and when they returned, they peeked around a corner at it. They asked endless questions of Fred Giampietro, about its history and its construction, and about why it was worth $250,000.

Fred told them what he could. He explained when it had been made, and where, and told them the history of Queen Anne design. Fred had never seen so much interest as that expressed by these patrons over his blue blanket chest.

Nineteen

RICHARD ROSEN STOOD IN THE MAIN AUCTION ROOM AT SOTHE-
by's. As a few employees wandered in and out, Rosen
spoke to Bill Stahl about the sale that would begin that
Friday morning. A few of Rosen's larger things lined the
carpeted walls on either side of the room. The sofa table
lay with most of Rosen's possessions behind the folded
curtains on the stage. The room seemed peculiarly quiet
that morning. Rosen's wife, Marguerite, sat alone amid a
sea of empty folding chairs. Their two children, Annie
and Andrew, moved about in the excited, nervous way
that children have at events of great moment to their
lives. Two men in Sotheby's uniforms added chairs to
those already in place, to make room for some two hundred bidders.

Sotheby's large saleroom suggested the possibility that
beautiful things sell best when set in ugly places. A taste for
carpet prevailed there. Carpet ran over the huge expanse of
floor, spread across the high partition walls, and covered a

dozen small lecterns where employees would take bids by telephone.

To the right of the stage stood the mahogany podium from which Sotheby's chief auctioneer, John Marion, would conduct the sale. This piece of furniture, massive and imposing, with a wooden hood partially covering it, gave the feeling more of a tribunal than a marketplace. Perhaps its designer had patterned it after the benches of an English courtroom, or perhaps after the pulpits of an English church. One would not have been surprised to see a man in a powdered wig mount it. Sales of great import occurred from this spot. Standing there the previous May, Marion had sold a single painting, Renoir's *At the Moulin de la Galette,* for $78.1 million. Sotheby's had estimated all of Rosen's things combined—the George Washington chair, the wrought-iron whirling toaster, the hanging wall boxes, and one sofa table—to bring less than $2 million. But the podium blessed all things equally. It offered consignors the further comfort of knowing that once blessed, each thing had earned the reward of a fair hearing.

Two weeks previously, Rosen had gazed into the fading glass of his own mirrors, hefted his weight onto the sturdy legs of his chairs, and placed his socks inside the drawers of his chests. He knew the histories of these things. He had arranged them with an eye for beauty, but lived among them as if they were members of the family. Bags of bagels and boxes of Tide had stood on his painted country kitchen table. Books whose titles ranged from *The Takeover Barons of Wall Street* to *The Last of the Mohicans* had piled atop a child's chest. Rosen hadn't wanted to create a museum, but a home, and now the things that made the home had left it. Now they waited for their own blessings and their own impartial hearings.

Rosen held in his hands the catalog with his name printed in gold on the cover. As he told one person after another how rare and important his things were, it became apparent that Rosen himself wanted to be rare and important. But you couldn't tell how much Rosen's things meant to him. He employed the clichés of the trade to talk about them, as if the words in the catalogs provided a refuge from his passions. Only the language of selling could express Rosen's deepest yearnings.

One knew that Rosen loved his things because he spent much of his waking life thinking about them. He frequently spent six hours studying the catalog of an upcoming sale and another eight hours inspecting the merchandise in person, and then sat for the better part of a day among the auction-room crowd. Hearing a description of Rosen's life as a collector, one thought of his "caring for precious vases," as Henry James once wrote, "only less than for precious daughters."

Under Rosen's close inspection, the uniqueness of each object grew paramount. One believed when Rosen said, "I could show you things that you'll never see anyplace ever again." Under the weight of Rosen's descriptions, his things seemed almost to awaken. His house filled with the sounds of objects telling stories of their lives, much like the things that filled the house in D. H. Lawrence's short story "The Rocking-Horse Winner." "The whisper," Lawrence wrote, "was everywhere." Each object spoke to Rosen, and through this medium to anyone who cared to listen. The things in Rosen's house whispered their singularities.

Annie Rosen, aged nine, could hear them. Annie had decked herself out for the sale that morning. She wore a low-waisted party dress, white shoes like those favored by Minnie Mouse, and an elastic hair tie covered in yellow fabric, of the sort known to many who wear them as a "scrunchy." While the men from Sotheby's unfolded chairs, Annie flitted between her mother and her father. She understood what was happening that day. She had heard the whispers for years. As the things began to leave her house, she had heard the murmurs that sounded like roots being torn from the earth.

A bedroom on the second floor of Annie's house held Annie's deepest thoughts. Annie had placed her stuffed animals behind an antique fire screen, as if in a pound. A beautiful Hudson Valley painted chest stood against one wall. Annie regarded this chest more highly than any other possession and would not consider parting with it. One knew that Annie's father saw her connection to this thing because of the way he said, "She wouldn't let it be moved for anything." In fact, her father saw her connections to all the things inside their house, now displayed against the walls or hidden behind the curtains on Sotheby's saleroom floor. "Annie doesn't want the things to sell," he said.

As Rosen stood in Sotheby's that Friday morning, amid the things he had so recently found "wonderful," one knew that he did not want to part with them. In the winter of 1991, many sellers felt this way. It was a time when collectors talked nostalgically of the expansive 1980s. Reflecting on the Garbisch sale—at the estate in Maryland where he'd bought so much with John Walton—Rosen once said, "That was a very happy time in our lives. We had more money then. You can't be a serious collector without money."

Now came the not-so-happy times. Now came the weeks when worry over business prospects brought knots to people's stomachs. One awoke one morning to find that one's possessions no longer whispered "I am singular." Now, like the things in Lawrence's story, they whispered, "There *must* be more money." In such times as these, people detach themselves from the things they love. People try to remove, one feeling at a time, each emotion they've placed inside their things. In circumstances of financial pinch, people try to objectify their objects. They no longer look for beauty, or history, or singularity, but for profit. In the hard times, they sometimes try to profit too much.

Of the two hundred chairs ready to accommodate guests, only sixty had filled as the hour of the sale approached. Most who came were dealers. They thought the estimates in Rosen's sale catalog to be very high. The reserve prices, or the figures below which items would not sell, were as always not made public. With only one bidder, an auctioneer like John Marion can use these reserves to create the illusion of a second bidder—to pretend to have some competition. Though the dealers never know for sure that Marion doesn't have a real bidder somewhere, they often have a good idea of what Marion is up to. Amateurs have a more difficult time, since Marion can also take bids from the telephone, or from a book where buyers have left their bids in advance. In the case of Rosen's sale, the dealers suspected that these reserves would be unusually high, just as the estimates were. Psychology often makes the prices at an auction house. Dealers resent collectors who wish to profit too quickly from the things they have acquired. These dealers felt that Rosen was trying to squeeze too much out of his things. Their distaste for this, and their lack of enthusiasm for the merchandise itself, gave the room an air of lethargy. One sensed that many had turned up out of unpleasant obligation, as if for a funeral. "It's depressing when the reserves are consistently at the low estimates," one dealer observed that morning. "Richard paid high retail prices for these things, and they have not appreciated much."

John Marion strode into the saleroom at a quarter after ten. He wore a finely tailored suit and tasseled loafers, and when he strolled down the center aisle, sixty heads turned in his direction. Everyone stopped talking. In these situations, Marion has the bearing of a game show host. His value to Sotheby's owes to his charisma, to his social connections, and to his ability to bring in business. In 1990 these assets made him worth $460,000 annually to the firm. Marion has capitalized these assets through his skills on the podium, which can sometimes make the difference of hundreds of thousands of dollars to a sale. Many people consider him the best auctioneer in the world.

Bill Stahl is himself a quite good auctioneer. He conducts most of the Americana sales, while Marion saves his voice for the paintings of Van Gogh. But some clients have at their disposal the leverage of choice merchandise, and so can command Marion's services even in hard times. Rosen was one of these people. Having great faith in the auctioneer's abilities, he had obtained Sotheby's assurance that John Marion would conduct this sale.

Marion moved briskly down the center aisle. He stopped only once, at the exact location where he always stopped whenever he conducted a sale of American furniture, beside the chairs of Albert and Harold Sack. Most dealers prefer a particular area of the saleroom during the auctions they attend so regularly. These areas become something like homes, so that each time they return they feel as though they belong. Wayne Pratt almost always stands at the back of the room, as does Leslie Keno's twin brother, Leigh. The Sacks' home at Sotheby's is on a plot of carpet three rows from the front. Marion bent over to Albert and Harold with a kind, pleasant word, and then moved to the podium.

He began the sale with a small antique dish. In short order, he sold a wall cupboard, a watercolor of a lady and gentleman, and another dish with a picture of a carp painted on it. For a time, things seemed to do well. Sotheby's had issued a number to every bidder. Each time Marion offered a lot of merchandise, blue paddles with these numbers on them leaped into the air. Someone paid $24,000 for a pair of wall sconces. Harold Sack bought a mirror for $110,000. While the bidding moved briskly along, Rosen sat with a copy of the sale catalog propped on his midsection and wore a satisfied smile.

Marion took the bids in practiced cadences. He'd give a brief description of the object for sale—"the maple inlaid table"—and then look for a bid. "I have eight thousand dollars now, say five hundred," he'd announce. Like many great auctioneers, Marion knew far more about the people who were bidding than about the things for which they bid. The same qualities that gave Peter Cecil Wilson such a presence on the podium existed in Marion as well. He knew who was likely to bid, on what things, and for how much. He knew where each dealer generally sat. When offering an object of interest to a particular dealer, he'd look that dealer in the eye. He knew so much about the dealers' habits that when one grew distracted, and Marion knew he should be bidding, the auctioneer could wake the man up with his voice. Marion believes that conducting an auction requires a sixth sense. "I've been doing it a long time and I very often can feel that people are going to bid again," he says. "Usually I'm right about that. I've convinced myself that if they don't bid again they've just changed their mind. It may just be body language. But very often I can feel a bid coming from one part of the room, and I look over there, and sure enough, there comes a bid. Nobody had bid there before. I can't explain all that. It's just feeling akin to your audience."

Among the dealers Marion knew well was a man named Clarence Prickett. He operates a large shop outside of Philadelphia, and his customers include many substantial collectors of American furniture. Prickett often wears blue blazers, plaid ties, and khaki slacks pressed to please a drill sergeant—an ensemble that might occasionally involve a pair of green socks and a pair of wing tips. He is a brown furniture man's brown furniture man. He has a creased, leathery face, a head of short white hair, and extremely long ears. Not an ounce of fat shows anywhere on his body.

"Prickett almost always sits on the left in front," Marion says. "I think he usually has a limit going in. He's a pretty good bidder. He's not a cheap bidder. When he wants something he goes after it. And he might throw one more in at the end just for good measure—just to make sure he didn't miss it by one bid. He's not a bargain hunter. He's made up his mind before. You can tell they've gone one bid over their limit just by looking at them. Especially a dealer. They go up to a limit and they say no more, and then you just give them a little rest. Then you go right back at them and sometimes they bite."

The sofa table for which Richard Rosen had paid $47,300 swung around on the lazy Susan to face the crowd. "Lot number eight hundred and eleven, now," Marion said. "And fifty thousand dollars to start this. At fifty thousand dollars for it, fifty. Fifty thousand dollars." Clarence Prickett held up his bidding paddle with the number 203 printed on it.

Prickett runs his business with his two sons, Todd and Craig. They have a number of clients who buy Federal furniture, and after one of these expressed an interest in the sofa table, the young men traveled to New York to examine it. They turned the table upside down and shone high-wattage lamps into its crevices. With an object that once belonged to Sack's, and around whose feet had dropped the ashes from John Walton's cigar, there could have been little doubt of the table's authenticity. But it is the mark of a reliable dealer to be satisfied for himself. The Pricketts saw that the secondary wood was pine, and this helped them to confirm that the table was indeed American. They looked for evidence of damage or repair. Since Sotheby's had estimated the table to bring $80,000 to $120,000, the Pricketts also discussed how far they would go to acquire it. Neither the Pricketts nor anyone else knew the reserve price.

Fortunately for Sotheby's—fortunately for Richard Rosen—at least one other collector had shown an interest in the table. This was a man whom Bill Stahl would describe only as "an extremely private collector from the South."

"Fifty-five thousand now, at fifty-five," Marion called out.

Someone entered the fray on behalf of the reclusive collector from the South. "I have sixty thousand dollars now, at sixty," Marion said. The bidding seesawed back and forth between Prickett and the agent. Sixty-five thousand. Seventy thousand. The sofa table waited. Rosen wore his usual smile of self-confidence—a self-confidence he might not have felt. At seventy-five thousand dollars, Prickett stuck his paddle in the air once more. "Bid's over here at seventy-five thousand dollars for it, seventy-five," Marion said. "Seventy-five thousand dollars. This side." He waited patiently. "At seventy-five thousand dollars. Down it goes then at seventy-five." Bang. "203 at seventy-five thousand."

The sale of the inlaid table took only thirty seconds. The reclusive bidder from the South had withdrawn, and Prickett found this very gratifying. He'd been prepared to go at least $50,000 higher, but he had not needed to.

Rosen, of course, could not have known that. After the sale was over Rosen pretended that all had gone well. When someone asked how his things had fared, Rosen said, "We didn't get all that much back." But nearly half his things had failed to sell.

Rosen's daughter conferred meanwhile with her mother. What would be coming home again, Annie Rosen wished to know, and what was gone forever? Annie showed particular concern for the chair once owned by George and Martha Washington. She had apparently concluded that Martha Washington would whisper to her once more. "It's coming back," Annie told her mom. Yes, said Marguerite, the chair was coming home again. The mother held her daughter by the hand and stared for a moment into space. "I guess we'll have to reupholster it now," she said. The sofa table was on its way to the home of a collector in the Midwest. It had found a new friend, and Martha Washington's chair had found an old one.

Twenty

ON FRIDAY FRED GIAMPIETRO WAS DOING FINE. HE HAD ALREADY
sold a couple of urns. He'd sold furniture. People had come
by to look at the blue blanket chest, but it had still not sold.
The couple who had expressed the greatest interest in it,
who had placed a semihold on opening night and returned
every day to peek at it from around corners, seemed like the
only ones who might buy it. From the care with which they
had examined the chest's drawers—the way they looked for
hand-cut dovetails and evidence of shrinkage and wear—
Fred could tell that this couple obviously had some experience with antiques.

Many of those who passed through Fred's booth knew
very little about antiques. They came because the decorator
Mario Buatta had found ways to draw them in. Fred gave
Buatta a grudging respect. Though Buatta knew little about
American furniture, he did know how to get people inside
the armory. As chairman of the Winter Antiques Show,
Buatta had organized a series of lectures, parties, and dances

throughout the week. For a $35 ticket, one could hear Martha Stewart present a slide show called "Entertaining with Antiques." Sometimes the people who came to such lectures wandered afterward through the cavernous hall. Sometimes they were turned into collectors.

Descriptions of Buatta generally include the salient facts that he is a charming and gregarious man, and that he stands more than six feet tall "in his Ferragamo shoes." However, these sketches fail to indicate that one remembers Buatta as wide rather than tall, and that he possesses a store of energy that never seems to diminish. At his small, cluttered shop on East Eightieth Street, Buatta wears a headset to talk on the telephone, while simultaneously conducting conversations with people sitting on the other side of his desk, and rummaging through piles of papers that might include correspondence, receipts, grocery lists, and telephone bills. He has a wide following of fans, and they were disappointed to hear him announce, shortly before the opening of the Winter Antiques Show, that this was to be his last year as its chairman. In the course of his seventeen-year tenure, Buatta had changed the notion of the show. He invited celebrities, politicians, and New York socialites to the opening night party, began the programs of lectures, and otherwise through his energies did much to bring fresh money into the dealers' pockets.

Buatta was born on Staten Island in 1935. The seminal moment in his professional career came while he was studying at the Parsons School of Design branch in London, where he met the British decorator John Fowler. "My dear boy," Fowler often told him, "if you're going to copy me, then at least do it well." Buatta made a career of doing just that. Using a chip of Avery Row yellow paint that was Fowler's trademark, he arrived at his own signature color— what he has described as a "lemony shade." In 1969, after decorating his New York apartment, Buatta received some good press notices. He soon landed wealthy clients. He achieved acclaim for his use of bows to hang pictures, for his use of chintz on every sofa, chair, and pillow that could reasonably accommodate it, and for his other efforts to popularize the look of the English country house. Every time he moved, he redecorated, and every time he did, another magazine wanted to photograph the newest home of the man every magazine liked to call "the Prince of Chintz." Buatta's reputation reached its zenith, however, only after he took charge of the Winter Antiques Show.

Buatta secured a commission to decorate the show in 1972. Two years later he became chairman, a move that eased Carrell out of arranging the show's opening night party while leaving him to manage the dealers on the floor. Under Carrell, the party had become a somewhat stuffy affair. Buatta changed that. He saw that if he threw a bash, he could make the show into something important. Along the way, he might also enhance his reputation. Under Buatta, the Winter Antiques Show soon glittered as a real New York society event. He made friends with New York society matrons. He got people such as Jacqueline Onassis's sister Princess Lee Radziwill to organize the parties. *The New York Times* began to send its society reporters along with its antiques reporters. The opening night party became an event that stood high on the A list. People discovered that to have one's name engraved on the invitation as a host of the party was to be one of the right sort of people, and they began to use any means available to get their names put there. Buatta's supreme social achievement probably came in 1979, the year he secured Henry and Nancy Kissinger as honorary cochairmen, and persuaded Françoise de la Renta to help conceive the decorations for the opening night party.

Thereafter, Buatta's name became a household term among those who knew the meaning of the word "chintz." The prominence of the Winter Antiques Show led him to such clients as Henry Ford II, Malcolm Forbes, and Billy Joel, and to lines of carpeting, fabrics, sheets, and china that carried Buatta's name and were sold in both Bloomingdale's and Sears. Buatta had a talent for publicity and a knack for forming close friendships with others who shared his talents. He hung around people who were known in his business to have "good PR"—people such as Dr. Ruth Westheimer and Martha Stewart—and as long as a person had good PR, Buatta stayed in touch. The New York society decorator Sister Parish asked him once, "Mario, are you going to promote yourself or are you going to decorate houses?" Buatta himself recalled this story happily and often. "Why can't I do both?" he replied.

Like most decorators, Buatta found American furniture too plain and too provincial for his expansive tastes. He worked exclusively with English antiques, and took comfort in the fact that people around the world shared his convictions. Though one finds dealers of English antiques in Florence and Sydney and Rio de Janeiro, one rarely finds American antiques anywhere but in America. American things are not only too plain for Buatta's tastes, they are too expensive as well. Rarity allows them to command prices that are very different from their English counterparts. Who but a passionate collector would pay $600,000 for an American chest of drawers that looks, to the untrained eye, to be identical to an English chest that's selling for a tenth as much? Who but someone who wanted to connect to an American past would spend the hours of research involved in making these distinctions?

Despite his disdain for American antiques, Buatta's influence on the Winter Antiques Show has nevertheless done much to enhance their status. A dealer like Fred Giampietro believes that he can show anybody who wants to learn the beauty of his things. A promoter of Mario Buatta's skill knows how to lead these people to him. In 1973, his first year as chairman of the preview party, Buatta managed to get two thousand New York socialites to buy tickets, and the money he raised for the East Side Settlement—more than $50,000—exceeded that of any other party in the show's history. By 1986, fifteen hundred people paid $250 each, and another thousand people paid $150 each, and Buatta had raised more than $500,000. Those who paid to attend his parties also had money to spend on antiques. Lita Solis-Cohen, a reporter for the *Maine Antique Digest,* estimated that in 1986 dealers sold $5 million to $12 million worth of merchandise. Graham Arader, who deals in antique prints, boasted sales one year in excess of $3 million.

Reporters from newspapers around the country now covered the East Side show, and German magazines ran cover stories on it. After things had died down, Buatta's publicity people photocopied every article, bound the clippings into volumes two inches thick, and sent them to the dealers with his compliments. Dealers received free publicity for selling $1 million desks, had their profiles written up in the *Times,* and soon came to see themselves less as parochial tradesmen than as international stars.

Mario Buatta succeeded because he knew the power that antiques hold over people. He didn't care as much about the objects themselves as what the objects looked like together. As a man who reproduces English country homes, Buatta has an unusually fine sense of what makes the original houses so remarkable. These old mansions are filled with objects that people have carried inside over the past seven or eight generations, "with each generation," Buatta once explained, "leaving behind its collections of things, the stories of one's life." These homes possess the sorts of contexts that one cannot re-create. Their associations are powerful, just like those the historian William Hosley encounters when he walks into a Vermont farmhouse that has passed through the same family for seven generations. Such rooms hold centuries of history at a glance. Time, of course, is against a decorator like Buatta. He must achieve the look of layered history not in two hundred years but in a couple. His philosophy is simple: He will not do a house all at once, but as he says, "a few dabs today, a few more tomorrow, and the rest when the spirit moves me."

Objects tell stories, and in combination with the things that have surrounded them for a long time, they tell other, more powerful stories. This is something antiques dealers don't often understand. They concentrate on the single thing, isolated as art against a wall, while decorators share with scholars such as Hosley a love for combinations—for the many things together. Serious collectors come to the Winter Antiques Show to see the one thing, but Fred Giampietro knows many of these people already. He wants to meet the novices. He wants to meet those who have come to see the many things, in the hope he can help them to see the beauties of his own.

One day during the week of the Winter Antiques Show, Buatta moderated his own panel discussion, "Decorating with Antiques." This was exactly the sort of program that brought new people into the armory. The panelists seated beside him included Mary Louise Guertler of the huge interior decorating firm McMillen, as well as Noel Jeffrey and John Saladino. Three hundred women had paid $35 each to hear these famous decorators. The ladies did not share much in common with collectors such as Paul and Alice Eckley. They seemed to care less about what made one antique unique and another not, than about the way such things fit together. They wanted the same thing from antiques that Joseph Hirshhorn had wanted. They wanted their homes to tell stories the same way that real English country homes tell stories. They wanted history right then. They didn't want to wait two hundred years to have it. Mario Buatta was happy to oblige. He knew it was his job not to help others connect to the past, but to invent a past. "A lot of us didn't inherit these things," he explained that day to his admirers. "But we want our houses to look that way. That's what we all want to strive for."

John Saladino was the most interesting panelist. The rooms he showed through a slide projector looked like those in Italian villas, where ancient walls and arrangements of crusty Continental furniture gave one a sense of history. Saladino understood the power of what he called "the hand of man" worn into the objects over the centuries. He understood their power to connect us to the past. In Rome,

Saladino explained, he had learned to love corrosion. He was, he said, "a stickler for the original finish." He pointed out how an old mirror, with its original mercury plating, brought one in touch with "all the people who have gazed in it."

Decorators tend to see objects in the context of a room, while the eyes of a collector always fall on a single object. Most decorators do not understand as Saladino does what makes the one thing so important. They think nothing of stripping off original finishes to suit the fashions of the moment. They will paint columns onto Biedermeier chests because they view objects differently from dealers. They will destroy the one thing to achieve a notable success with the many. In their own way, such decorators are as shortsighted as those who appreciate the one thing, but not the many things together. Encountering the tasteless room full of beautiful objects—no less than encountering the tasteful room full of ordinary things—helps one to appreciate people such as John Saladino and Henry Francis du Pont, who have cared about both.

Twenty-one

AT FIVE MINUTES PAST TWO ON SATURDAY AFTERNOON, THE DAY
Sotheby's has scheduled its sale of the Willing card table,
John Marion walks into the saleroom. Marion wears a dark
suit and white shirt with French cuffs, and his entrance once
again captures the crowd's attention. Two hundred fifty
people fill this room. All of them lower their voices. They
watch Marion walk down the center aisle, stop to whisper
something to Harold Sack, and mount the great, hooded,
Chippendale mahogany podium.

Standing at one of the six small lecterns before the
stage, Leslie Keno holds a telephone to his ear. Beside him,
Bill Stahl watches the crowd. Because the card table appears
on the cover of the catalog, and because the commission on
this one object might exceed $100,000, its fate will do much
to determine the success or failure of all Sotheby's sales this
week.

Of the ten Americans who might pay $1 million for a
piece of furniture, not one would do so without first know-

ing its provenance in great detail and without also hearing the good opinion of respected experts. Upon acquiring the table, the auctioneers set Wendell Garrett to the task of researching its history—a task he performed with such energy that the table's description and provenance occupy two full pages of the sale catalog. Those in the audience with catalogs can read about Alan Miller's research on the Garvan carver, see how the Willing table relates to similar card tables, and skim a history of Willing's descendants.

The auctioneers mailed photographs to every potential customer and then followed up their letters with phone calls. They budgeted large sums to entertain the consignors and advertised the table with full-page spreads in *Antiques* and other magazines. Altogether the expenses of marketing this table ran to $30,000—or about $3,000 for each potential buyer. Stahl and Keno also invited important dealers such as Harold and Albert Sack to examine the table in person. They contacted museums, put Garrett to the task of writing an article for the firm's own magazine, *Preview,* and in other ways tried, as Stahl will say, "to get the word out."

Now on Saturday afternoon, the auctioneer John Marion has to sell a lot of items. The Willing card table is only the most important among them. He begins this sale with a recitation of its conditions. The first lot, No. 1400, is a map of Virginia drawn in 1775. Stahl and Keno have estimated this object at $5,000 to $7,000, far below what they feel sure it will bring, to ensure a high selling price and to set a spirited tone. "And start off now with lot fourteen hundred," Marion says. He speaks quickly, taking bids from the paddles darting up across the roomful of faces. "And I have a good deal of interest in this lot at thirty-five hundred for it, four thousand, five hundred, five thousand, five hundred, six thousand," and so on until the map sells for $12,000. It is always smart, Marion believes, to start an auction with a winner.

John Marion's rich, deep voice, his head for numbers, and his practiced and rhythmical cadences reassure those who are about to part with colossal sums of money. The dealer Wayne Pratt says of him, "In a city environment, John Marion is about as fine an auctioneer as you'll find. He has a way of making people feel relaxed. He can make a really good joke. He can be subtle."

Through the course of his career, Marion has trained dozens of people to conduct a sale. He has never ceased to be astonished at who succeeded and who did not. A great auctioneer must have a commanding presence, a voice that carries, and a head for the quickly moving action. "Some people are good at it and some people are horrible, and it's impossible to tell until they try it," Marion will say. "I've seen people who were marvelous public speakers who don't have the facility with numbers and don't think quick enough to be able to translate that presence before an audience to an auction; and I've seen people who are really good with numbers, but who have a voice like a metronome that would put anybody asleep." Marion has supplied countless prospective auctioneers with tapes of those, like himself, who have mastered the art. The students carry the tapes home, study them, and practice. Marion has observed that all begin by imitating someone else, but that those who succeed eventually develop their own styles.

All auctioneers must be able to move quickly among bidders, but a great auctioneer will eke out bids beyond the limits that buyers have set for themselves. "I really feel that I can look in somebody's eye and I can tell often whether they're going to bid or not," Marion will say. "Or whether they're interested or not, or if I should keep holding the lot open a while longer."

Marion moves the sale briskly along, selling such objects as a brass telescope, circa 1860, for which he gets $4,750. Within a few minutes, he has sold a pair of paper-and-foil wall sconces, a pewter porringer, and a number of tall-case clocks. "Lot number fourteen hundred and forty," he calls out, indicating a Massachusetts blockfront chest of drawers. "And for the chest I have three thousand dollars to start."

Peering down from the boardroom windows on the third floor, the Hughes family waits for Marion to call out lot No. 1459, the Willing card table. These windows offer a good view of the second-floor saleroom. Large regency tables, George III mahogany side chairs, and plush green carpet give the room its character. Old Master paintings from an upcoming sale decorate its walls. Standing at the windows, the Hugheses hold drinks in their hands and listen to Marion's words, which reach them through loudspeakers.

Stahl and Keno wait before the stage just below Marion. They are as anxious as the Hugheses because their best customers have shown little interest in the table.

Many in the antiques business speculated that Eddy Nicholson might want this object. In 1986, Nicholson sold out his interest in Congoleum Corporation for tens of millions of dollars and began to fill his New Hampshire home with what he once described as "the best in Pilgrim, William and Mary, Queen Anne, and Chippendale." He bought a tea table that was the first piece of American furniture sold in public for more than $1 million. He paid $1.1 million for a wing chair, $250,000 for a silver tankard, $198,000 for a wristwatch, and $110,000 for a quilt. He had also underbid the $12.1 million the Sacks paid to buy the Newport secretary-bookcase for Robert Bass.

Most collectors of Americana are very private people, but Nicholson loves attention. During the 1980s, he was always being quoted in the trade papers. He is brash and loud in a way sometimes associated with self-made men. While Stahl believes that this sort of collector "is an exception, in terms of being public," he feels the publicity is good because, he says, "it gives some confidence to the marketplace." Nicholson has by now, however, filled his house with antiques, and he does not have the kind of money a man might find useful to buy antiques for a museum.

Collectors of Nicholson's generation have acquired certain tendencies that Stahl regrets. Like Nicholson, Bill Cosby concluded his collecting days after furnishing his house. Others did the same. "I look at the collections that have been formed over the last ten or fifteen years, and they're by and large very sterile," Stahl says. "Forms are represented. 'I must have a hairy-paw foot chair. I must have a turret-top card table. I must have a Philadelphia lowboy dressing table with a provenance as long as my arm.' If you look at the history of this business, that's not the way things were collected when du Pont was doing it, when people were collecting in the thirties and forties. Now granted, there was a lot more material available then. But there was a lot more sharing knowledge, camaraderie, less competition." Though Stahl's firm might profit from the competition, he holds sharing a love for objects above such petty rivalries, and wishes for a world that has ceased to exist.

Despite the disconcerting absence of buyers at the $1 million level, Stahl and Keno have not entirely despaired. Both men spent a lot of time on their telephones. They contacted clients who had never before paid $1 million for a piece of furniture but who might be induced to. Months later, Leslie Keno will remember these trying weeks as a time when "I thought of a very private collector who maybe could be moved up to that level, who maybe has not bought those kind of pieces in the past. But once he was convinced of the importance of this and he liked it, I think he could afford it." Stahl, too, knows of "a couple of others coming along that are happily collecting at the six-figure level," and thinks "if the right thing comes up they could have been here."

In Sotheby's saleroom, Marion brings his gavel down on a Queen Anne Newport highboy, which goes for $32,000. The Willing card table is next.

"Lot number fourteen hundred and fifty-nine," Marion says.

On the stage, a man stands beside the table. He wears a blue Sotheby's blazer and has the attitude of a carnival barker. He points to the card table just as he has pointed out other objects in the room. "Showing here!" he shouts.

"Showing on the stage," Marion says. "And what do we say for the card table?"

Marion has decided to begin the bidding on this card table at a level that Bill Stahl will later describe as "fairly high—to give the room the sense that it's not going to be given away." Sotheby's has started American furniture at proportionally higher prices. Bidding for one famous wing chair, which the firm auctioned off in 1987, started at $500,000 even though the low estimate was only $700,000. This chair once belonged to a friend of Thomas Willing named John Cadwalader. It was so coveted by Americana collectors, and reached the market in such a strong economy, that the auctioneers believed it would do very well. The bidding moved so quickly between the first two bidders that at least two collectors who wanted to bid did not even manage to get their hands in the air. "The underbidder in that was somebody we didn't suspect," Stahl recalls. "And we knew who was gonna buy it." The Cadwalader wing chair sold to Leigh Keno for $2.75 million.

"Five hundred thousand dollars to start it now," Marion says. "At five hundred thousand dollars they'll have for it. At five hundred thousand dollars for it, five hundred."

Marion understands that bidders will be scarce on this day. He holds a great advantage over those auctioneers who operate without reserve prices, because he can pretend to have bidders even when he has none. Knowing an object has a $10,000 reserve, for example, Marion can call out that figure even when no one has actually bid. Marion can be patient. The absence of bids at this point does not daunt him. No paddles rise, no nods come from the four Sotheby's employees like Keno who staff the white telephones, and Marion quickly resorts to the reserve. "At five hundred and fifty thousand," he says. Many of the dealers in the room who are as attuned as Marion to the nuances of the play can guess that no one has actually bid.

Long before today, Stahl and Keno have established the reserve price for the card table at $1 million. This means that should only one bidder contend for it, that person will have to spend at least $1 million to buy it. The auctioneers know that the seven-figure barrier scares people. Over the past decade, in fact, Stahl has spent a great deal of energy with what he calls "the process of getting people to feel comfortable with a million dollars—to feel it's okay."

If one does not believe that a few thousand dollars can make a difference to someone prepared to spend close to $1 million, one need only suggest this possibility to John Marion. "Well, you spend it like your own, my friend," Marion will say. "If you're sitting in the other seat spending the money, let me promise you that there are intellectual price barriers. That barrier could be ten thousand, it could be a hundred thousand, it could be a million." Marion believes that "just saying that figure" is enough to scare people. "I've seen it time and time again. Once they say a million, then they'll keep going on. But to get them over that hurdle is hard."

Stahl had been so worried about the prospects for selling the card table that he approached John Marion yesterday afternoon with a proposal regarding the table's reserve. The estimated selling price of the table was $1 million to $1.5 million. Nothing could change this estimate, since Sotheby's had already printed it in the catalog. But something could be done about the table's reserve. Sotheby's has not guaranteed a sale of the table, but will use the reserve to ensure that if the bidding doesn't reach a high enough price, the Hugheses can have it back. Though the reserve can be no higher than the low estimate, it may fall anywhere below that figure. That was what Stahl wanted to talk to Marion about. Having first placed the reserve at $1 million, Stahl now wondered if Marion shouldn't have the power, at his discretion on the podium, to lower it to $950,000.

Sotheby's entertained the Hughes family at a dinner party on Friday night. Stahl found the dinner a convenient opportunity to suggest this option to Elizabeth and her brothers. The Hugheses' contract had called for a lavish meal to be served by Sotheby's chef Bernard, in the same way that the contract spelled out a suite of four rooms at the Carlyle Hotel, and catalogs to be mailed free to Elizabeth for the rest of her life. The Hughes siblings all but knocked each other over to offer as a toast this shared sentiment: that no matter what happened at their sale the next day, they believed Sotheby's had done a terrific job. Once the toasts were finished, everyone felt happy. Stahl calmly explained that after consultation with Marion, he advised allowing Marion to stop the bidding at $950,000.

"Very often you'll talk to people in a difficult market about putting the reserve just below these tidewater marks," says John Marion, who was himself quite happy that the family had agreed. "I think in that case it was probably a good idea." A reserve price of $950,000 holds the advantage for the buyer of falling short of the $1 million barrier and thus making the table seem obtainable. The seller will benefit by unloading it. And along with the 10 percent commission that the auction house draws from everything it sells, Sotheby's might get the publicity that often follows $1 million sales.

In the saleroom on Saturday, Marion scans the faces before him. He has long known that Keno will be handling a significant telephone bidder, and yet Keno has failed to indicate the slightest interest. It puzzles Marion that he has no real bid as yet. He must resort once again to the reserve. "Six hundred thousand, now, at six hundred," he says. "I have six hundred thousand dollars for it, six hundred. At six hundred, say fifty."

Standing at one of the Greek columns, Keno holds the white telephone receiver to his ear. He is connected by this apparatus to Alan Miller, who is sitting at his home in Pennsylvania. Stahl will later reflect that none of his marketing mattered so much as getting Alan Miller involved with the table. Sotheby's own restoration department could have performed the necessary repairs to the leg, but Stahl believes that "somebody—if not two or three people—would be interested in having him a part of it, given all he's done on Philadelphia furniture." These people will not buy the table without Miller's own blessing. Stahl will also say, "We had a feeling that Alan Miller would find the ultimate purchaser for this."

Stahl and Marion scan the room for any sign of a bidder. "I have six hundred thousand dollars now, at six hundred," Marion says. "At six hundred thousand dollars for it, six hundred. At six hundred thousand dollars now. I have six hundred." Still no paddle in the room is raised. None of the employees standing at the telephones so much as arches an eyebrow. The three auctioneers have begun to worry. Marion's hopes rest with the silent disembodied person of Alan Miller. He scans the room, but returns often to Keno's face. Finally, Keno nods. Alan Miller has entered the bidding at $650,000.

The auctioneers all know that Miller is bidding for Luke Beckerdite. They know that Beckerdite has only recently taken a job as director of Chipstone, the collection

Stanley Stone put together with John Walton. On the death of Stone's widow, Polly, Chipstone will become a museum, and Beckerdite has already begun to think of filling gaps in the collection. Beckerdite has a background as a scholar of American furniture, and also happens to be a good friend of Alan Miller. He has worked closely with Miller for many years researching arcane points of Philadelphia furniture. Wanting to get Beckerdite involved with the table, Stahl struck on the idea of having him write a scholarly article about the table for the firm's *Preview* magazine. "The reaction was, he'd love to do it, but there were two problems," Stahl remembers. "One, he was new in his job and that was pretty time-consuming. And the second thing was he said, 'We may have an interest in that table, and I think I would prefer not to get involved.' " This news did not assure Stahl that Beckerdite would actually bid on the table. The auctioneer had watched too many customers back out at the last moment to count on anything as certain. But among all the news in those weeks, none gave Stahl any more hope than this. "It's a clue," Stahl thinks as he waits for Marion to continue.

"Six-fifty," Marion says. No one in the room responds. Marion must use the reserve again. "Seven hundred," he says quickly. "I have seven hundred thousand dollars now, at seven hundred."

Marion and Keno and Stahl are disappointed. In their belief, the reserve is a second-rate bidder largely because an experienced buyer knows very soon if he is competing alone. Many objects that fail to reach their reserves are available after the auction at reduced rates. Knowledgeable dealers will sometimes stop short of a successful bid in the hopes that they can acquire an object more cheaply by other means. Telephone bidders have a more difficult time. Though Alan Miller can hear Marion's voice through the receiver, he cannot tell much about his competition.

Most auctioneers greeted the introduction of telephones reluctantly. These auctioneers preferred to see the faces of those who were bidding. They knew that they could eke out another bid or two with the right sort of eye contact at the right moment. But John Marion loves the telephone. "The phones have added a tremendous amount to this business," he says. "Everybody can't always be here. People can think of more reasons not to buy something than to buy it. So it makes it easier for them to take part in the process. You can be on your plane, your boat, your train; you can be in the country, in China, anywhere; and you can bid at that auction, live. That's really a terrific thing. It didn't happen when I began in the business. What it's done is greatly enlarge the audience and the participation of the ultimate consumer, which is really important."

The audience did not know who was on the telephone, or from what sort of vessel he or she might be bidding, or even from which continent. The telephone added a sense of mystery to the affair.

"At seven hundred thousand dollars for it, seven hundred," Marion repeats. "At seven hundred thousand dollars now."

Again, no one in the room raises a paddle. Again, Marion must wait. Miller finally agrees to the new price. Keno nods. "I have seven hundred—seven-fifty, on the phone here," Marion says. "At seven hundred and fifty thousand dollars now. I have seven hundred and fifty."

The most important thing on Marion's mind is to sell the table. So long as Miller bids up to the reserve—$950,000—Marion will be content if no other bidder enters the fray. When Marion says, "The bid is up front at seven-fifty, say eight," he is looking for someone else, some real person, to bid against the man on the telephone. Marion cannot pretend to have bidders once bidding reaches the reserve price. Without a second person bidding, the table must sell at its reserve. To drive this price to astronomical levels, the auctioneers need two equally eager bidders. In this hope, they have not given up. New bidders often emerge after the bidding has begun.

Marion looks around the room and finally gives up. A second bidder will not be coming in at $800,000, so he must use the reserve. "At eight hundred thousand dollars now," Marion finally says. "At eight hundred thousand dollars for it, eight hundred."

Again, Keno looks at Marion and nods.

"Eight-*fifty*," Marion says. "Eight hundred and fifty, on the phone. At eight hundred and fifty thousand dollars now, at eight-fifty. Say *nine*."

The table has nearly reached the reserve. Now the auctioneers all know it's unlikely another bidder will enter the fray. Now they only want the table to sell. They hope that Alan Miller will utter the words, which Keno will communicate with a nod, that will prevent this sale from becoming a disaster. The expenses of $30,000 to market this table, the hopes of the Hughes family, the prestige of the auction house and its ability to sell $1 million objects successfully, and the perception of a healthy Americana market—all rest on the next few moments. "Nine hundred thousand now," Marion says, resorting to the reserve again. "At nine hundred and—*fifty* thousand dollars in front here," Marion says, motioning toward Keno, who is standing just below him and to his right. Alan Miller has uttered the words that many have waited to hear.

Everyone is relieved. Now at least the table has sold.

"At nine-fifty. I have nine hundred and fifty thousand dollars. The bid is on the phone now, at nine hundred and fifty thousand dollars for it, nine-fifty." The official reserve remains at $1 million, and Marion can if he chooses use this figure to bid the table to one last level. The choice to employ the figure of $950,000—to stop now—is entirely his. If he uses the $1 million reserve, Miller will have to commit one last time. He will have to bid at least $1.05 million. Since the firm receives a 10 percent commission on all sales, the auctioneer's decision could mean a difference of $10,000.

But if Miller chooses not to bid, the table goes unsold and Marion has failed. Marion must weigh such factors as the weak economy, the absence of competition, and Miller's bidding habits against the additional $10,000 profit to be made if Miller hangs in for one more bid. He must decide whether to risk losing the commission of $95,000 to gain $10,000 more, and he must make this decision in the next few seconds.

"At nine hundred and fifty thousand now," he says. "I have nine hundred and fifty thousand dollars for it. Nine-fifty." No paddles leap suddenly into the air. No employees twitch their noses by the telephones. "At nine hundred and fifty. I have nine hundred and fifty thousand dollars for it." Marion is patient. "Nine-fifty now, say a million. I have nine hundred and fifty thousand dollars. The bid is up front on the phone. At nine hundred and fifty thousand dollars."

The choice seems clear to the best auctioneer in the world. He will not take the risk of losing the only bidder he has heard from. "I have nine hundred and fifty thousand dollars for it, nine-fifty." Marion scans the room one last time. "And down it goes then at nine hundred and fifty thousand dollars," he says. "The bid is right here." Marion pounds his gavel on the podium. *"Sold* for nine hundred and fifty thousand."

Twenty-two

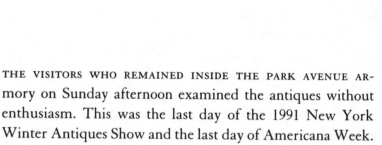

THE VISITORS WHO REMAINED INSIDE THE PARK AVENUE AR-
mory on Sunday afternoon examined the antiques without
enthusiasm. This was the last day of the 1991 New York
Winter Antiques Show and the last day of Americana Week.
Across town at Sotheby's, European paintings had replaced
the American quilts and watercolors. Most of the collectors
and decorators who once flooded into New York City had
long since departed for their homes in Boston, or Cleveland,
or Atlanta. The armory seemed lifeless that Sunday afternoon. Its flowers hung limply in their pretty vases.

Over the course of the past week and a half, Fred
Giampietro had stood in the same spot each day for ten or
twelve hours at a stretch. Although he later described the
East Side show as "grueling," Giampietro would have preferred to be nowhere else. Twenty-five thousand people had
walked past his booth since opening night. People with
serious money—people with names like Lauder and Astor,
not to mention Harrison Ford—had inspected his wares.

For a dealer of American folk art, no marketplace in the world held such possibilities for success. Fred liked to sell his things, but he also enjoyed teaching people about them, and the Park Avenue armory had provided an opportunity to do both. "When I find people who are genuinely excited, it's great," he says. "I respect the person who really understands. Then I respect the person who doesn't understand but wants guidance."

Educating the public is one of Giampietro's most important jobs. He's learned to make the work interesting. If he is selling a chair once owned by a famous person such as George Washington, Giampietro uses this piece of information. If a thing is rare or its condition is of consequence, he will explain how and why. But the aspect Giampietro most likes to talk about is the one he refers to as "as-tetics."

The beauty of a thing is its most subjective quality, and the one that requires the lengthiest initiation. It's also the aspect that a man such as Giampietro can use to command the largest profits. Who is to say what makes one thing more beautiful than the next? Who knows what beauty is? What is art? One person who asked these questions and tried to answer them was Leo Tolstoy. In the end, the novelist decided that something was beautiful only if it changed his mood. Art, he said, was that which "infected me."

It's an apt metaphor. Giampietro himself feels infected by a love for the objects. He succeeds in his field because he has learned to buy only those that make his heart beat fast—objects that reveal their secrets slowly over time. "I'm excited about the material," he says. "I believe in it. Being around objects is like being around the right sorts of people."

No object in Giampietro's experience excited him more

than the blue blanket chest. Day after day as Giampietro stood at his booth, he watched as young couples returned to examine it. People approached it cautiously, cocked their heads, and appeared to search their brains for something to relate it to. Some people knelt before it on the carpeted floor and touched their fingers lightly to it. Some tried to pull a top drawer open, and then seemed perplexed when the drawer in question wouldn't budge. It looked like a chest of drawers. They could not understand what Giampietro has described as "the concept of the top opening up like a lid." They could not understand why it had no hardware. They'd never seen anything like it. "They weren't even sure what it was," he said.

To those who asked about the chest, Fred tried to explain. He told them that at its best, Queen Anne furniture employed no carving or other form of decoration. He explained that the form itself—the pure form of the graceful lines and nice proportions and the curving cabriole legs— was its decoration. In Giampietro's experience, most objects of Queen Anne country furniture possessed extraneous ornamentation. Chairs often employed the turned rails of an earlier period, while some tables used the inlays of a later one. Most had hardware. But the blue blanket chest held no such imperfections. Fred told people, "Of all formal furniture, that's the purest form." He pointed out how it hadn't been "embellished," or it hadn't been "screwed with," and he told them, "This piece is at the bull's-eye." Fred believed the chest to be "the epitome of Queen Anne design." He tried to explain why he thought it was a piece of sculpture—a work of art. For those who took the time to listen, Fred Giampietro placed beauty inside the chest.

Giampietro tends to put all people into two categories. Either they have what he calls a "high level of as-tetic judgment," or they have a "low level of as-tetic judgment," and what amazed him most about the Winter Antiques Show was that it brought together "so many affluent people with a low level of as-tetic judgment." Some people told Giampietro that the blue blanket chest would look better with hand-pulls on the drawers. Some wanted it bigger. Those visitors who most appalled Fred insisted that its maker should have cut hearts out of the apron that ran around its base. Such people followed a fashion for hearts popularized by the decorator Mary Emmerling. Fred tried to teach these people, but even after he took the trouble to explain the chest's aesthetics, some of them still wanted hearts. Fred could only shake his head. "You'd destroy it with cutout hearts in the apron," he says. "What they don't like about it is the whole point of it. That's the kind of people I can't address. They can't learn."

Americans are known for many commendable qualities, but a high level of aesthetic judgment is not one of them. When the fashion writer Holly Brubach searched for a culture that values taste, she had to look someplace else. She settled not surprisingly on the French, a people who can make studying taste seem fun. The French insist on not merely eating, but eating well. They generally care more about their architecture than we do. As Brubach pointed out, they possess a more highly developed sense of fashion. A French luxury-goods catalog once explained the curios it advertised by noting that "They contain our souls." Americans are not a people who dwell on the present locations of their souls. Americans are a practical people. Except for rare old objects, Americans buy things to give good use, and then discard them when they've worn out. America is a nation of materialists because its people don't value the material.

Fred Giampietro has the un-American virtue of valuing the things he sells. He has chosen each one because it speaks to him, and he has staked his reputation on its beauty. Men such as Israel Sack helped to make the taste for formal American furniture many years ago, but Fred Giampietro is making the taste for folk art today. He shares a conviction about what is beautiful with Bill Samaha and David Schorsch and ten or fifteen others. Walking their separate ways through affairs like the Winter Antiques Show, these people will independently—and habitually—pick out the one object among thousands that they agree to be the best. In large part they possess the code of beauty because they are creating the code. Each time Giampietro sells an object, someone has approved his taste. The market has validated his judgment. The words "Provenance: Fred Giampietro" will one day fill the catalogs of collections he has put together. His name will add value to the things inside because his vision has helped to make them valuable.

People cannot understand Giampietro's things without first responding to them. After an object has moved a person—even if only to puzzle over—the person can sometimes benefit from an explanation of what he or she is seeing. People who see Fred's things need words. Fred has words to give them. His long and patient explanations, his little lectures, his studied and remarkable descriptions can all help to heighten one's sensibilities. Fred Giampietro's language can create a container for one's feelings. His words provide a place to put emotions.

Objects like the blue blanket chest survive because people through the centuries have responded to them. There's something about the integrity of the thing that makes its owners want to preserve it. The same impulse that makes someone stop before Thomas Willing's card table, and to stare for a time at the leaves full of rainwater, has led Alan Miller to spend his life understanding the man who made the leaves. The pursuits of men such as Alan Miller and Fred Giampietro, the concerns of heirs, and even the intuitions of the most ignorant passersby help these things survive.

Like all beautiful things, the blue blanket chest affected people. The chest held their desires, so that days later, when they had left it behind and thought they'd forgotten it, this beautiful thing would hold their memories as well. Things possess the possibility of immortality. They are pieces of human industry frozen in time. They connect their makers to everyone who ever owns them and everyone who ever touches them and even to those who only stop to look at them. When a mother hands down her silver service, she is connecting her child to a past full of rich texture and meaning to her. She is connecting the child to her past, but she is also connecting herself to her child's future. She is passing a piece of herself to the hands of her great-grandchild. She wants to survive.

Even those things people don't inherit—things that hold no ancestors inside—can affect their owners through their histories. The objects tell stories. They hold the dents from broom handles and the oils from a thousand hands and the unconscious thoughts of everyone who has dusted them. Antiques dealers don't usually care about the past lives of the things they own. Unless George Washington once sat in the chair, its history seldom serves a dealer's purpose. Sometimes the stories are better left untold. Trying to unload the blue blanket chest, for example, Giampietro did not frequently feel called to discuss its history of rejection. To those without a material interest, the story of the blanket chest can bring this thing to life. But to those who might consider spending a quarter of a million dollars for a thing, its past can be a problem.

The blue blanket chest had a history of wild swings in its price, of people needing to unload it at reduced rates and people who couldn't unload it at any rate, of passage into and out of the homes of those who didn't want it. Such stories are forgotten because they are not useful or because they are uninteresting or because we ourselves have never learned their value. Although people may forget them, these stories are not lost. They stir inside the thing itself. As the blue blanket chest makes its way through history, it will connect each new owner with its past and its future. Its story lives, waiting to be found.

Standing in the armory on Sunday afternoon, Fred Giampietro knew that he would not sell the blanket chest that day. It had appeared from nowhere thirty years earlier, at a time when people thought it worth a few hundred dollars. Fred had bought the chest to make a profit. He paid $150,000, and now he hoped to get nearly $250,000. Selling it for the sum he had set would validate his aesthetic judgment. But Giampietro loved this object as much as any he had ever owned, and he would enjoy living with it for a while longer. If the stories didn't matter much to him, the grace of its proportions did. He knew he'd carry it home with him to New Haven, set it in his bedroom, and once more fill it full of clothes. As long as he had owned the chest, it revealed new characteristics to him. The longer he had it, the more he came to understand its purity and its subtleties. Its beauty took his breath away.

Giampietro had found that the meanings of great objects sometimes changed depending on what sat around them. For example, having once hung an abstract painting above the blue blanket chest, the result startled him. "I saw the abstraction to the piece for the first time," he says. Something from his picture revealed a quality he'd never seen in Queen Anne furniture. Its proximity had turned the chest into a piece of modern sculpture.

The longer Fred lived with the chest, the more it showed him. He had come to appreciate the man who made it. Like many great works of art, the chest held a spontaneity that made it nearly perfect. Fred often ran across something which might show a fluid vision on its top but whose feet had been overworked. Such objects lacked a perfect balance and they failed as art and Giampietro had decided not to buy or sell them. The blue blanket chest had balance throughout. It was fluid and spontaneous. Giampietro could tell that its maker had probably started and finished it within a single day. He thought a great deal about this man. It astonished him to think that an eighteenth-century mind could create a thing whose beauty had survived for two hundred years. Fred would say, "It's amazing people thought this way," and he would say, "It transcends all art of all categories." That's why Fred Giampietro loves his things. "What's so great about what I deal in, is it transcends art and transcends time."

Just as the joiner placed a piece of himself inside the chest, so has Fred Giampietro. As it has held Fred's clothes, so the chest now holds his vision of beauty. It will hold his memories, his tastes, his deep, unarticulated desires. Standing inside the Park Avenue armory on Sunday morning, Fred discussed the future disposition of this object with his wife, Kathy. Upon consideration, they decided not to place advertisements for the chest in trade journals, to make a single telephone call on its behalf, or in any other way to try to market it. This was, perhaps, a practical response. But it seemed to suit the nature of the piece. Anyone who bought the chest would have to see it casually, on a tour of his house, where it would sit among his other objects. As Fred explained later, "We said if it's gonna sell, we'd let it sell itself."

Acknowledgments

I WANT TO EXPRESS MY APPRECIATION TO ALL THE DEALERS, collectors, furniture makers and furniture restorers, show managers, decorators, art historians, sociologists, museum curators, and experts at the auction houses, whose guidance and experience was essential.

Many people also helped to shape the writing of the book. Most especially, I want to thank my editor, Linda Healey, without whom this project would not have been possible. I would also like to thank Liz Darhansoff, Jonathan Harr, John Hassan, Meredith Kahn, Ralph King, Dan Okrent, Dick Todd, Jennifer Trone, and Laura Underkuffler. Finally, I'd like to express my gratitude to my parents, Karen and Warren Freund, for their patient and enduring confidence.

About the Author

Thatcher Freund was born in Austin, Texas. He received a degree in history from Stanford University and a masters degree in journalism from Columbia University. He lives with his wife, Laura, in Chapel Hill, North Carolina.